G000127753

SOCIAL JUSTICE, EQUALITY AND EMPOWERMENT

SOCIAL INDICATORS: STATISTICS, TRENDS AND POLICY DEVELOPMENT

SOCIAL JUSTICE, EQUALITY AND EMPOWERMENT

Additional books in this series can be found on Nova's website under the Series tab.

Additional E-books in this series can be found on Nova's website under the E-books tab.

SOCIAL JUSTICE, EQUALITY AND EMPOWERMENT

SOCIAL INDICATORS: STATISTICS, TRENDS AND POLICY DEVELOPMENT

CANDACE M. BAIRD
EDITOR

Nova Science Publishers, Inc.
New York

For permission to use material from this book please contact us:
Telephone 631-231-7269; Fax 631-231-8175
Web Site: http://www.novapublishers.com

LIBRARY OF CONGRESS CATALOGING-IN-PUBLICATION DATA

Social indicators : statistics, trends and policy development / editor,
Candace M. Baird.
p. cm.
Includes index.
ISBN 978-1-61122-841-0 (hbk.)
1. Social indicators. I. Baird, Candace M.
HN25.S643 2010
301.01'5118--dc22
2010042625

Published by Nova Science Publishers, Inc. † New York

CONTENTS

PREFACE

Social indicators measure the quality of life and encompass the whole spectrum of society, including the individual, public and private organizations, municipal, country, regional, national and international systems. This book presents topical research in the study of social indicators from across the globe. Some topics discussed in this compilation include social scientific metrology as the mediator between sociology and socionomy; discretionary time and freely disposable time as social indicators of welfare, poverty and freedoms; socioeconomic status and the incidence of illness and social capital.

Chapter 1 - Without doubt, there is a growing interest within the political community and society in general in both the development and application of social indicators. However, the scientific basis that is required to construct valid social indicators is weak. Firstly, there is a sharp divide between interpretativist and neopositivist ontological worldviews which cannot be expected to be resolved in the near future. Secondly, the social sciences lack a general theory of measurements, a theory of measurement error, principles for providing unified measurements, etc.: in short, there is lack of a social scientific metrology. The latter problem pertains to a plurality of methodological approaches (both quantitative and qualitative). An important step towards maturizing the social sciences is for researchers to make a more concentrated effort to explicate rigorously the various choices they made in conducting their research. The authors therefore identify the various phases in the research process where choices are being made, and discuss the impact of these choices on the validity of the resulting research. Increased explication of the research choices made facilitates the identification of differences of opinion within the social scientific community, and ultimately, makes the developing of precise and unambiguous definitions regarding the measurement of specific social scientific constructs possible.

Chapter 2 - The economics of life are ruled by time, money, their exchange rate and how much of it is needed to satisfy the basic needs of the household. Discretionary Time (DT) and Freely Disposable Time (FDT) are two newly developed conceptually equivalent but methodologically different social indicators that integrate these time and money elements into a single metric. Both indicators express how much time the productive members of a household have left after fulfilling the basic needs (of food, shelter, care, sleep, consumables etc.) of themselves and their dependents. This chapter discusses (1) the principles of DT and FDT assessment and some outcomes in various countries, (2) the linkages of DT and FDT with freedoms, potential income, development, poverty and happiness, (3) the caveats that may be identified in these linkages and (4) indicator choice in relation to mono-dimensional, pure time and money indicators of welfare and poverty.

Chapter 3 - This chapter introduces the concept of functional time use (FTU). To this end, the first part is devoted to a review of time use studies with special consideration to labour time, followed by introducing the theoretical, conceptual and methodological framework within which functional time use is embedded. The third part of this chapter presents the empirical case study results in time use from Campo Bello, an indigenous Tsimane' community in the Bolivian Amazon. The research findings are presented along the following lines: first, the socially disposable time at the system level is discussed for different age/sex groups along their life-cycle. The second research interest entails a more holistic approach and scrutinises the number of person-hours invested in the reproduction of the four different social subsystems: the person system, the household system, the community system and the economic system. The third subsection looks into locally implemented strategies to increase the productivity of time. Finally, this chapter also argues for the FTU approach to serve a useful purpose in planning and monitoring the impact of development projects.

Chapter 4 - The existence of an inverse association between socioeconomic status and the incidence of most diseases is well-established in literature: higher rates of morbidity and mortality have been reported among lower socioeconomic groups in many European countries.

The relation between socioeconomic factors and health inequality may be proved at the individual level, or at the geographical area level. In this paper we follow the second stream of literature, i.e studies on deprivation relating the state of disadvantage suffered by an individual, with the living conditions of the area where the individual resides. Deprivation underlines the characteristics of a group (that is, the population living in a defined geographical area) by measuring similarities and dissimilarities of the individuals forming that group.

Knowledge of deprivation indexes is, therefore, very important for resource allocation: according to equity's considerations, more deprived areas should be assigned a larger amount of resources.

The first part of the proposed chapter examines, in a historical perspective the more commonly used deprivation indexes, i.e. the ones proposed by Jarman, Carstairs, Townsend, MATDEP and SOCDEP the Index of Multiple Deprivation (IMD 2000) developed by the U.K. Department of the Environment, Transport and the Regions. The second part presents an index of material deprivation which has been applied to "small areas" of the city of Genoa (GDI).

Chapter 5 - Social capital is an important factor influencing several issues both in individual and collective level. Various indicators have been presented in the relevant literature for its measurement. The most commonly known are: social trust, institutional trust, social networks and social norms. The aim of the chapter is to analyze social capital indicators and to underline their connection with the development of environmental policies. Specifically the influence of social capital indicators on different environmental policy instruments will be presented. Through this analysis the importance of exploring social capital during the formation of environmental policies and the need to develop measurement techniques for this purpose is highlighted. The above issues will also be explored taking as an example environmental policies for the protection of areas with high biodiversity value.

Chapter 6 - Many developing countries have formulated their poverty reduction strategies taking into account their development priorities, resource base and aid from the international community. Ghana's poverty reduction strategy, for example, has it to assist rural farmers to add value to their food crops so that they can benefit from relatively better returns. With the assistance of the government, farmers are increasingly processing raw cassava locally into gari (i.e., cassava grains) making it a less perishable food. While agro-processing is becoming a popular strategy to reduce poverty, an understanding of how its impact on households is important in tweaking development initiatives for better results on poverty reduction. Thus, we examined how the government–assisted gari processing is changing social conditions of rural women and their households involved within the Eastern Region of Ghana. Findings from the case study of *Milenovisi* gari processing Association demonstrated that, not only did the women's incomes improve; they were also able to afford food and health costs, and contributed to funerals and religious activities, although they faced difficulties with transportation and credit facilities. Their local political leader and families significantly influenced women's decision to be involved in this initiative. Consequently, we propose increased use of families as medium for recruiting and passing along skills to potential beneficiaries. Also, we argue that agro-processing initiatives need to be accompanied with credit facilities, and that tackling transportation barriers which create additional workload and health problems for the women on top of the already labor intensive task of processing gari, is critical for achieving greater impacts.

Chapter 7 - The modern study of the social determinants of health were said to have begun with Rudolph Virchow and Friedrich Engels whom not only made the explicit link between living conditions and health but also explored the political and economic structures that create inequalities in the living conditions which lead to health inequalities. (Rather 1985; Engels 1987). Recently, international interest in the social determinants of health has led to the World Health Organization's creating a Commission on the Social Determinants of Health. (WHO 2008) In its final report *Closing the Gap in a Generation: Health Equity through Action on the Social Determinants of Health* the commission succinctly summarises the current state of knowledge:

"Social justice is a matter of life and death...These inequities in health, avoidable health inequalities, arise because of the circumstances in which people grow, live, work, and age, and the systems put in place to deal with illness. The conditions in which people live and die are, in turn, shaped by political, social, and economic forces."

Chapter 8 - This chapter uses an amenity-productivity theoretical framework to classify European Union sub-group of countries (EU-27, Eurozone-16, EU-15) according to the extent to which they are influenced by supply-side (producer) and demand-side (consumer) responses to their specific bundle of economic and environmental attributes. The assessment of the environmental quality in each state is based on the development of environmental indices. This kind of classification is useful because it provides information about the relative attractiveness to producers and consumers of the combination of economic and environmental attributes indigenous to each region. It therefore has implications for the design and focus of the regional and environmental policies of the European Union and the Eurozone.

Chapter 9 - Several studies have used generalized trust as an indicator of social capital. However, its validity in Japan due to cultural differences is questioned. Here, the authors emphasize the need for more sophisticated discussions underlying trust measurement for social capital, specifically generalized and particularized trust. The aim of this study is to investigate which questions are appropriate as a indicator of social capital of small area analysis in Japan.

The authors conducted a nationally representative survey based on the geodemographic segmentation system, which classifies households by allocating them to one of 212 segments. Each neighborhood was randomly selected from within each segment. A postal questionnaire was sent out in 2008 to household heads and their spouses in these neighborhoods. A total of 8,221 individuals responded to the survey. Generalized and particularized trust was measured by a single item. These questions were rated on a 10-point scale. The authors finally conducted a multilevel analysis on 6,863 individuals nested within 202 neighborhoods.

The null model with no predictors revealed a significant variation in the generalized trust between neighborhoods. However, this variation was insignificant after adjusting for potential confounders. The second multilevel analysis showed variance in the neighborhood trust between neighborhoods. The null model revealed a significant variation in this trust. This variation remained after adjusting for potential confounders. Neighborhood trust could be seen as a truly contextual factor; generalized trust might be confounded by compositional factors. This indicates that neighborhood differences in generalized trust may arise from differences in personal characteristics. We need more nuanced attentions toward measuring social capital in different cultural contexts.

In: Social Indicators: Statistics, Trends...
Editor: Candace M. Baird

ISBN 978-1-61122-841-0

Chapter 1

SOCIAL SCIENTIFIC METROLOGY AS THE MEDIATOR BETWEEN SOCIOLOGY AND SOCIONOMY: A CRI DE COEUR FOR THE SYSTEMIZING OF SOCIAL INDICATORS

Jarl K. Kampen[1] and Hilde Tobi
Wageningen University and Research centre, Research Methodology Group, Hollandseweg, Wageningen, The Netherlands

Without doubt, there is a growing interest within the political community and society in general in both the development and application of social indicators. However, the scientific basis that is required to construct valid social indicators is weak. Firstly, there is a sharp divide between interpretativist and neopositivist ontological worldviews which cannot be expected to be resolved in the near future. Secondly, the social sciences lack a general theory of measurements, a theory of measurement error, principles for providing unified measurements, etc.: in short, there is lack of a social scientific metrology. The latter problem pertains to a plurality of methodological approaches (both quantitative and qualitative). An important step towards maturizing the social sciences is for researchers to make a more concentrated effort to explicate rigorously the various choices they made in conducting their research. We therefore identify the various phases in the research process where choices are being made, and discuss the impact of these choices on the validity of the resulting research. Increased explication of the research choices made facilitates the identification of differences of opinion within the social scientific community, and ultimately, makes the developing of precise and unambiguous definitions regarding the measurement of specific social scientific constructs possible.

ALREADY IN THE HELLENISTIC AGE, the faculties of astrology and astronomy where distinguished from each other. Astronomy dealt with the prediction of celestial phenomena, and Plato (in the book Timaeus) advocated that these had to be described by a geometrical, that is, quantitative model. Astrology dealt with the interpretation of celestial phenomena, and

1 Email: jarl.kampen@wur.nl.

was of a qualitative interpretativist nature. Astronomy became successful as a scientific discipline in the Age of Enlightenment, when quantitative science matured, and simultaneously astrology slipped into oblivion. A similar evolution may also be crucial for the social sciences to move forwards. The social sciences are in a crisis, because generally valid scientific explanations of observable social phenomena are still hardly available (Faber and Scheper, 2003). Kagan (2009) gives four reasons for the current malaise among social scientists. Firstly, Kagan points out that as an independent scientific discipline, the social sciences are only about one and a quarter century old. Secondly, and contrary to natural scientists, social scientists start investigation with the defining of a concept and then look for evidence in empirical settings, that is, they presuppose validity of an a priori idea. Thirdly, social scientists make unjustified generalizations of specific events to broad sets of events. And fourthly, despite many efforts social scientists have failed to measure human psychological states. In sum, the crisis in sociology springs from the fact that social scientists are much too reluctant to acknowledge that no conclusion is independent from its source of evidence, and as a result, says Kagan (2009: 130), "the proportion of government funds supporting social science research has been reduced over the past twenty-five years and talented youths who chose one of the social sciences two generations earlier are now attracted to one of the natural sciences."

Because social science is a human endeavor, like any other human endeavor it merits being subjected to rigorous social analysis (Bricmont and Sokal, 2001). Paul Feyerabend (1987: v) observes that like all institutions in a free society, the sciences should be subjected to democratic control: it is up to the taxpayers to decide what is to be taught in public schools and how public moneys are to be spent. For instance, if taxpayers want schoolteachers to teach their children Intelligent Design rather than Darwin's evolutionary theory, then in democracies they can have their wish realized – by gaining electoral majority. Of course, such electoral decisions cannot change physical conditions. That is to say, even when there is a universal consensus amongst all inhabitants of the planet Earth to the contrary, such consensus will not change the condition that the inhabitants live on a planet, that they are attracted to its centre because of gravity, etc. It is the essence of natural laws that they exist independently from the observer: e.g., gravity will exist long after mankind has become extinct. Precisely because mankind is transient, laws about society, or sociological laws, cannot be constructed with equal rigidity as natural laws.

Besides the transience of its subject, social science is further characterized by the fact that it influences its own subject area. Such a science is what Alroe and Kristensen (2002) have called a systematic science. The human, social and cultural sciences are systematic, because persons and social systems have some ability to react to what science says. The crisis in social science, according to some, may in fact be acute because most Westerners are postmodernists, and postmodernism undermines the claim that problems in this world can be solved by reason because reason itself collapses under the weight of self-scrutiny (Legg and Stagaki, 2002). Postmodernists frontally attack the modernist "meta-narrative" that human reasoning can potentially produce fundamental truths (see e.g., Prus, 1990). That is, there are only world-versions, and no method to determine which one scientific world version is correct (Hacking, 1996: 45). And the critics are right, since it is a broadly accepted philosophical observation that radical skepticism – the idea that no reliable knowledge of the world can ever be obtained – is irrefutable (e.g., Bricmond and Sokal, 2001). Nevertheless, even when social science has produced no laws that are real or recognized as such (Lopreato and Crippen, 1999), and even when Feyerabend and others are correct in stating that such laws should or could not exist, straightforward scientific reasoning will produce at least one social scientific law, namely, that none can be formulated. That single law will hold so long as it has not been falsified; and should it be falsified, then we will have witnessed the birth of Social Science!

Less postmodern or hypercritical social scientists believe that the scientific basis for social science can be found in evolutionary theory (e.g., Lopreato and Crippen, 1999; Massey, 2000). Based on ideas initially laid out by neodarwinists such as Jacques Monod and of course, Richard Dawkins, surviving civilizations must adapt to changing physical circumstances. This adaptation ultimately implies that the associated culture must evolve in harmony with these changing conditions. Biological life and human culture can be explained in terms of copies, where the copied matter is called "genes" in biology and "memes" in culture. For instance, Dawkins (1976, 2007) regards religion as a virus of the mind, meaning that the "God-complex" replicates itself in human brains at the cost of mental space and capacity that could be used for different (scientific? artistic? philanthropic?) purposes. Distin (2005) shows however, that Dawkins introduces a subjective element in his socio-cultural analysis when he distinguishes between good (e.g., evolutionary theory) and bad (e.g., creationism) memes. Another weak point, as pointed out by Gould (2002) amongst others, is that evolution is misconceived as a process that inherently progresses to better, more advanced individuals and/or societies. Evolution has no known goal and any claim that there is a purpose of the universe and of life is void of scientific evidence.

Establishing a goal of evolution (of societies) requires the study of empirical data. All phenomena open to scientific investigation must have features that are open to empirical evaluation. This is why other social scientists plea for the development of standardized measurement in social sciences (e.g., Bain, 1942; Noll, 2002; Wright, Manigault and Black, 2004; Kampen, 2007; Kagan, 2009). Leydesdorff (2002) goes even further, and argues that in order to solve the crisis in the social sciences, the developing of a "socionomy" besides a sociology needs to take place:

> "Sociologists have hitherto interpreted the world in terms of metaphors. Socionomy can make a difference by testing sociology's knowledge-based distinctions and by thus extending the knowledge base of the self-organizing system under study. The knowledge-based society which results, can be considered as the subject of an emerging socionomy."

Socionomy would relate to sociology in the same way as astronomy relates to astrology. That is, socionomy would deal with the description of social scientific phenomena by means of quantitative models, and sociology would continue to deal with the interpretation of social phenomena. The link between sociology and a socionomy is to be established by developing the discipline of social scientific metrology, that is a scientific discipline that occupies itself exclusively with measurement in society. This chapter will elaborate on precisely that strategy.

The Need for a Social Scientific Metrology

We could extend the above discussion on metaphysics to the extent of a complete chapter. However, in order to show the relevance of a discipline that occupies itself exclusively with measurement in society, that is, a social scientific metrology, it is not necessary to go to much philosophical depth. Already, this relevance is self-evident as reflected by an increasing interest in reliable indicators which quantify the level of social wellbeing in society, both in the political community and in the social sciences. An important reason is the growing consensus that the gross national product does not suffice as an indicator of well-being (see e.g., Grasso and Canova, 2008; Wiseman and Brasher, 2008). This economic indicator does not reflect any of the aspects of social capital, social exclusion, poverty or feelings of safety and security of the citizens.

Accordingly, a growing number of initiatives have been taken to provide better measures of social well-being than the macro-economic situation in the country (Fahey and Smith, 2004). For instance, the Dutch Social-cultural Planning Bureau (SCP) has published results for a Living Conditions Index (see e.g., Boelhouwer and Stoops, 1999). Other countries have issued measures of poverty, human capital, public health, and so on. Recently, efforts have been made to systemize such measures into a framework that can be used to quantify social well-being at the European level, that is, to provide a European System of Social Indicators (see e.g., Noll, 2002). The aim of the ESSI is to cover a variety of different topics that affect social well-being, on the levels of population, households and families; housing; transport; leisure, media and culture; social and political participation and integration; education and vocational training; labour market and working conditions; income, standard of living, and consumption patterns; health; environment; social security; public safety and crime; and total life situation.

The drawing up of meaningful indices poses formidable challenges for the agencies which are responsible for their production, e.g., national statistical offices and planning bureaus, because the composition of social indices is subject to large controversy, both concerning the selection of indicators and dimensions (operationalization), and concerning the statistical methodology by which the indices are to be constructed and analyzed. The field of “social indicating” says Frønes (2007), is fragmented and lacks a unifying theory. Typical criticism is that meaningful social indices cannot be constructed because the underlying concepts are too abstract, too multi-faceted, cover a too wide range of issues and lack a common unit of measurement (see e.g., Yale Center for Environmental Law and Policy, 2005: 19). Thus, the construction of meaningful social indices presents many challenges. First, the operationalization of (aspects of) concepts in terms of indices is subject to much controversy. The second challenge is presented by the methods by which the indices are to be constructed. A third challenge is the development and assessment of sociometric quality criteria of such social indices. These challenges and criticism are relevant to most if not all social indices.

The basic aspects of metrology as a science (Shirokov, 1972; see Isaev, 1993) include a general theory of measurements, a theory of measurement error, principles for providing unified measurements, establishment of systems of units of measurement and the creation of corresponding standards, and the development of methods and means of measurement. Whereas in the natural sciences metrology has been developed for both scientific and industrial purposes, in the social sciences both theoretical and applied metrology is lagging behind. Of course, in the natural sciences too concepts are used that lack clear and adequate definitions (Meinrath, 2007). However, measures of length, area, volume, mass, temperature, time, speed, force and pressure, energy and power have been systemized to a large degree in natural sciences (see e.g., Whitelaw, 2007). A good scientific concept says Bain (1942), “is simple, precise, denotative, widely accepted, and clearly understood by those who use it." Although the *Système International* or metric system, first introduced under Napoleon in 1801, gained international acceptance only slowly, presently the metric system is firmly in place and remains unchallenged. The metric system led to consensus amongst scientists even when they spoke different languages, adhered to different ideologies (e.g., during the Cold War era), and had conflicting interests (Meinrath, 2007). This guaranteeing of the robustness of scientific claims to subjective properties of researchers and scientists is the main purpose of metrology.

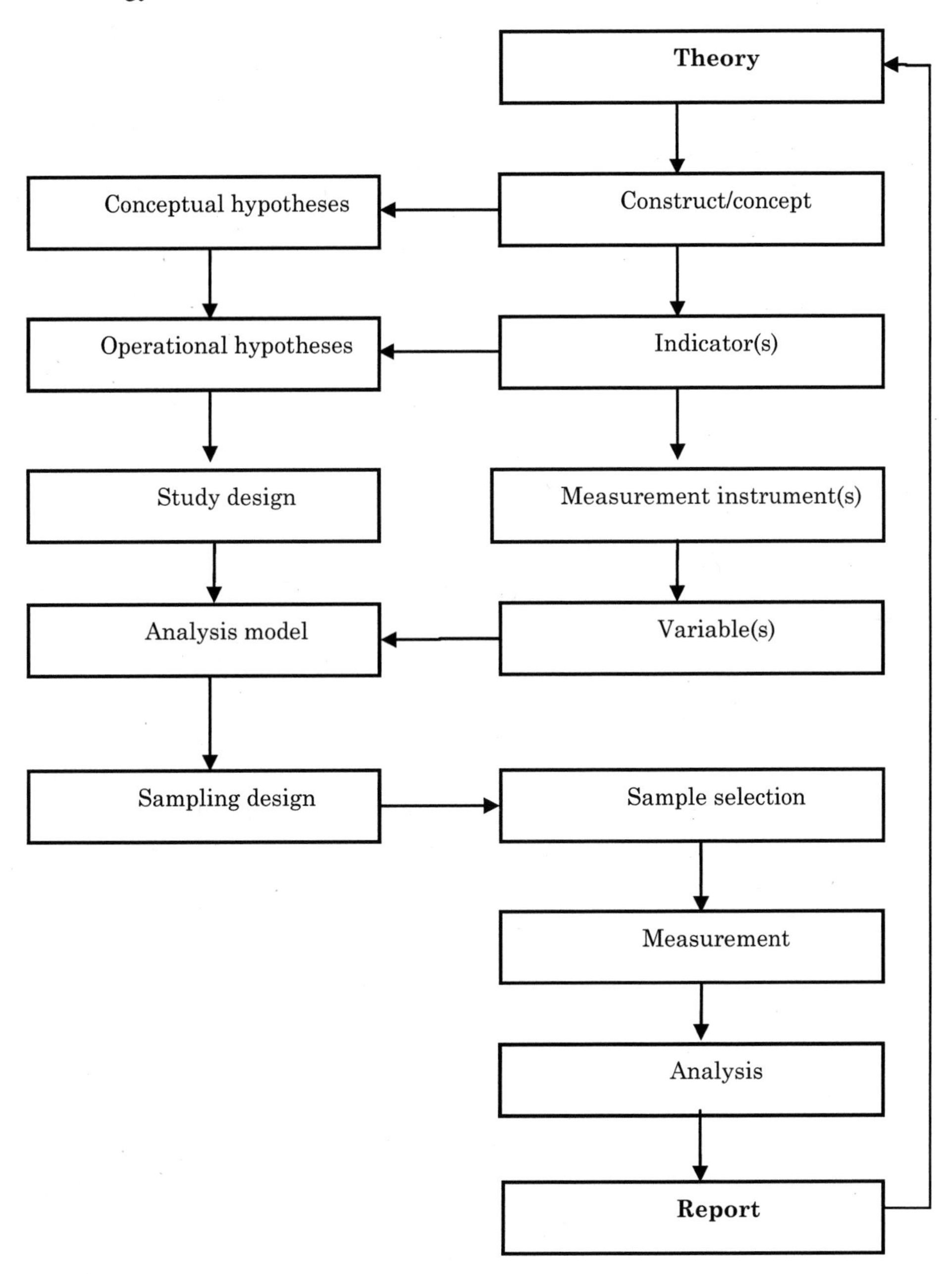

Figure 1. The empirical social science research cycle.

It is worth noting that a social scientific metrology is not only useful for neopositivist social scientists believing in "one single world where objects and their properties exist independently of the subject perceiving the effects of the objects and/or their properties" (e.g., Meinrath, 2007). Proof of correctness of the interpretativist ontological position asserting that truth is a construction, can be gathered by showing that equal instruments and methods consistently produce different conceptual results in comparable empirical settings. Needless to say that the use of different instruments cannot supply evidence for different world views. In order to construct standardized instruments however, the most practical approach is to pretend at least for the duration of the research cycle, that the neopositivist single world "Book of Nature" ontology is correct. This pretence can then be shown to be wrong after running through the empirical research cycle again.

Figure 1 displays the empirical social science research cycle. The cycle starts with a theory (which may of course, have varying levels of sophistication) and ends with an assessment of its validity and possible adjustments to be denoted in a report open to the public (typically an article in a social scientific journal). Most steps in between have direct or indirect links with metrology. The whole empirical social science cycle with associated problems and some suggested solutions relating to (the lack of) social scientific metrology is discussed in the next sections. The chapter ends with an array of conclusions and recommendations.

FROM THEORY TO INDICATOR

The Construction of a Theory

Empirical social science begins with a theory. Even in data-driven research leading to "grounded theory" or "thick descriptions", researchers either implicitly or explicitly set out with a theory, because they chose to look at certain collections of data and not others. And any research in the social sciences starts with a "literature overview". The methodology for carrying out a *systematic* review is, however, an underdeveloped field in the social sciences. Contrary to medical science, for example, where the publication of tens of thousands of scientific articles each year has led to the development of a detailed methodology for carrying out systematic reviews for over half a century (see e.g., the Cochrane Collaboration), in social science methodological publications on systematic reviews are scarce. Of course, the social sciences are not entirely void of literature on systematic reviews (see e.g., Petticrew and Roberts, 2006; Gomm, 2004; and the work of the Campbell Collaboration), but the approaches that are proposed for such reviews in the social sciences without exception draw on methodologies designed for medical sciences where hypotheses deal primarily with causality and the predominant study design is the experiment.

A methodology for systematic reviews of social scientific articles would recognize that different types of research questions require different types of reviews (see e.g., Newman *et al.*, 2003, for a typology of research purposes). Research questions may deal with for instance, operationalization, cause-and-effect, effect size, association etc., and each different type of question requires different search criteria, different selection and exception criteria, and consequently a different protocol in order to meet the required quality standards. But these quality standards are a gap in existing social scientific research methodology (*mea culpa*). The simple rule, for instance, that "theories that explain much with very economic means are to be preferred over theories that assume much in relation to what they explain" (Creath, 1996) cannot be applied in social sciences because there, the explanation and the explained can rarely be separated. The main purpose of a protocol for systematic review is the prevention of cherry-picking only those pieces of evidence that fit in the narrative of the researcher. Conscious and unconscious biases are a constant threat to the internal validity of social scientific research. A common source of such biases is the adhering to mainstream thinking and to dominant ideologies (see e.g., Diefenbach, 2009), when it is the aim of fundamental scientific research to invalidate *common sense*, Right Reason, the Norm, and General Opinion (e.g., Schaffer, 1996: 219).

Operationalization of Concepts

Any research (including a systematic review) sets out with the selection of one or more topics. These topics consist usually of one or more constructs or concepts. The literature is not consistent on the definition of the phrases construct and concept, and we shall use the terms interchangeably. As defined by Kumar (2005), concepts (constructs) are "... mental images or perceptions and therefore their meanings differ from individual to individual." Social scientific theory expresses links (e.g., causality, correlation, etc.) between various concepts in terms of conceptual hypotheses. For example, "variation in social capital can be explained by citizens' psychological involvement with their communities, cognitive abilities, economic resources, and general life satisfaction" (from: Brehm and Rhan, 2007). However, concepts in the social sciences are usually of an abstract and multi-faceted nature and therefore they cannot be measured directly but must be broken down into one or more indicators that are more amenable for direct measurement.

The challenge in empirical social scientific research is the translation of the conceptual hypotheses into operational hypotheses using indicators as proxies for the theoretical concepts. An indicator is an observable variable that is assumed to point to, or estimate, some other (usually unobservable) variable (Bunge, 1975). Take as an example, the concept "social capital" which was broken down by Putnam (2000) into four different dimensions: community organizational life, engagement in public affairs, measures of informal sociability, and social trust. Often, a second round of operationalization will further break down the indicators, such that we obtain indicators of indicators. For instance, the social capital indicator "engagement in public affairs" is further broken down into turnout in presidential elections, attendance of public meeting on town or school affairs in the last year (percent), measures of community volunteerism, number of nonprofit organizations per 1,000 population, mean number of times worked on community project in the last year, and mean number of times doing volunteer work in the last year. In the latter list, the indicator's indicator "community volunteerism" needs further breaking down, leading to indicators of indicators of indicators of a concept. Needless to say, that the level of abstractness of concepts used in the social sciences leads to obfuscation and unnecessary controversy among scientists.

FROM INDICATOR TO VARIABLE

Data Collection Tools in the Social Sciences

Once the set of indicators in a study is defined, the next step is to design measurement instruments that measure the value of the indicator, that is, that produce the actual variables under study. Data collection tools in social sciences include observed behaviors, verbal statements, and to a far lesser degree, biological measures (Kagan, 2009: 131). Observation invariably requires people as measurement instruments. The impact of subjective properties of the observers can be minimized by subjecting them to training with the aim of increasing inter-rater reliability. The impact of subjective properties of the observers can also be maximized, as in participatory observation or in so-called action research. Verbal statements in the broadest sense include both data collected by questioning people, and existing documents. Questioning people can be done in a standardised closed form (the questionnaire) or by an open interview (which one can think of as "participatory questioning"). As for the analysis of documents, the obtained data depend very much on subjective choices of the researcher who makes various decisions in the process of selecting, labelling and coding fragments of text

In those instances where the researcher serves as the measurement instrument (observation, open interview, and to a varying degree content analysis), measurements are subjective by definition. The least subjective data collection tool within social science is usually considered to be the standardised questionnaire, but also for this instrument a whole array of problems affect measurement validity. Obviously, measurement error in surveys can result from bad phrasing of questions. In the case of a categorical variable, omission of one or more categories provides an example. Another example is when two questions are contained in a single item, as in "Do you agree with the statement that England should become a republic with Margaret Thatcher as its president?" But survey errors include more complicated forms than just bad questions. The fact that even a simple variable such as income, when collected with a single question in a survey produces biased measurements (see Micklewright and Schnepf, 2010) is not promising for the reliability and validity of concepts operationalized by indicators. As the standardized questionnaire is the least subjective and perhaps most promising measurement tool in social science (although some authors state that the sample survey's glory days are in the past; see Savage and Burrows, 2007), we will discuss the major sources of survey error in the next sections.

Questionnaire Mode

Much research has addressed the question whether the mode of data collection changes measures of central tendency of items (see e.g., Fowler, Roman and Di, 1998; Van Tilburg and De Leeuw, 1991; Kryson et al., 1994; Aquilino, 1994; De Leeuw and Collins, 1997: 205; Hox and De Leeuw, 1994; Kampen, 2007). In Fowler, Roman and Di (1998), we find a comparison of 1) mail and telephone (conducted in the US) and 2) face-to-face and mail (conducted in Massachusets). One of their conclusions is that questions that ask respondents about a current description of themselves are more likely to yield a socially acceptable answer by interview then by mail. This is a "mode" effect in its purest form, where a direction of bias can be predicted.

Krysan *et al.* (1994) study differences between mail and face-to-face surveys, carried out on identical area probability sampling frames, with stratified samples. They also find that mail surveys elicit less socially acceptable answers, and the difference can with reasonable certainty be attributed to the intervention of an interviewer in the measuring process. The same is true for the research conducted by Aquilino (1994), where method effects are detected in surveys of drug and alcohol abuse in a study controlled for sampling procedures. He reports that respondents are less reluctant to report socially undesirable behavior (drug use) in mail surveys.

The clearest explanation for differences between self- and interviewer-administered questions, according to Fowler, Roman and Di (1998: 30), is that respondents are less willing to articulate socially undesirable answers to an interviewer than to write them down: any question that asks respondents for a current description of themselves is likely to yield a more positive result by (telephone) interview than by mail. One might therefore expect that data quality is highest using the latter mode of survey, a conclusion reached by de Leeuw and Collins (1997). However, in the case of sensitive data, self-administered questionnaires sometimes appear to fare less well than face-to-face interviewing (Mangione, Hingson and Barrett, 1982). Determining which items are sensitive is in itself problematic, because consistent theories about what makes answers sensitive or strongly undesirable are lacking (Fowler et al., 1998).

Questionnaire Satisficing

Many theories on (non)response behavior in survey research apply cognitive psychology in their explanations (see e.g., Jobe and Mingay, 1991, for a historical overview). Answering a survey question, in this approach, involves the solving by respondents of a series of tasks: Interpreting the question and the issue involved, retrieving relevant information and/or previously formed judgments on the issue, rendering the appropriate (final) judgment, and selecting an appropriate response (Tourangeau and Rasinski, 1988).

According to Krosnick (1991), a potential source of bias of data quality in survey research is caused by unwillingness of respondents to make the cognitive effort of producing an optimal answer, that is, of solving these tasks in the best possible way. This is because respondents, although initially motivated to participate in a survey, become increasingly fatigued, disinterested, impatient and distracted. As a result, the steps necessary to produce a high-quality answer are executed in decreasingly diligently and comprehensive ways, leading to the selection of the first satisfactory answer (Krosnick, 1991: 215). This process is called survey satisficing, and it can have three basic causes: respondent ability, respondent motivation and task difficulty (Holbrook, Green and Krosnick, 2003).

Among the effects of satisficing are not only the above mentioned selection of the first acceptable response alternative, but also the tendency to agree with any assertion, and lack of differentiation in the use of rating scales (Krosnick, 1991: 225-229). Respondents that give equal answers to items produce a positive contribution to association measures of the items such as the Pearson correlation coefficient (see Kampen, 2007). This means that associations between items become overestimated, and may lead, for instance, to factor models that produce measures of fatigue rather than "real" underlying variables that the researcher might have expected.

Survey Context and Cross-Cultural Issues

Context effects in surveys include changes in response distributions as a result of differences in question order and overall questionnaire contents (Moore, 2002). These differences may result in changes of the subject matter that is being judged, changes in the information that is retrieved from long-term memory in order to formulate the judgment, changes in the norms and standards that are applied in making the judgment, and changes in the way that the judgment is reported (Taurangeau and Rasinski, 1988: 311). In short, context effects originate from the fact that respondents use the information that is contained within a survey (Billiet, 1993). This information may also include characteristics of the purpose and commissioner of the survey (Kampen, 2007).

In international comparative studies, issues on cross-national and cross-cultural comparability of the data collected come on top of these concerns (Lynn, 2003; Frønes, 2007; Lynn, Japec and Lyberg, 2006). Examples include cross-cultural differences in response style of respondents, for example in providing extreme responses of socially acceptible responses (see Johnson et al., 2005; Smith and Fisher, 2008; Beukelaer, Kampen and Van Trijp, 2011). At the level of the operationalization of concepts, linguistic problems occur. For example, consider an item probing for "trust in government". In English, the term government is used both for the individual members of the government (i.e. ministers) and for "the system by which a state or community is governed" (Concise Oxford Dictionary, 1999). In Dutch, three basic concepts are used to differentiate between parts of government: 1) "regering", which refers to the political authorities with executive power (the cabinet of the PM and ministers); "administratie" which refers to the public administration (civil service, bureaucracy); and "overheid", refers to the total of political institutions (including e.g., parliament), public services and administrations collectively. Similar (but not equal) differences regarding the word government exist between the English and German, and English and French language.

As another example of issues relating to comparability and equivalence, Canache, Mondak and Seligson (2001) give a discussion of a widely applied measure of "satisfaction with democracy". The authors state that this measure suffers from fatal flows because it may relate to support for authorities, system support, or "democracy as a form of government". In an effort to support this thesis empirically, they conduct a cross-cultural study (Romania, El Salvador and Latin America) examining the association of satisfaction with democracy with several political indicators. Canache and colleagues conclude that because magnitudes of associations differ substantially across countries, there are cultural differences in the interpretation of the satisfaction-with-democracy item. Of course, besides the fact that the countries under study would not strike anybody as textbook examples of democracies, the reasoning can be turned around, in that there are no differences regarding interpretation of the word democracy but rather, the underlying reality regarding democracy is different across countries. Such ontological discussions are not easily resolved, even when sophisticated techniques of analysis reveal cross-cultural inequivalence at the item level (see e.g., Welkenhuysen-Gybels and Billiet, 2002).

Validity, Reliability and Discriminating Power

Validity, reliability and discriminating power are key quality attributes of indices and tests (Kirshner and Guatt, 1985). Validity deals with the question whether the test score "really" measures the concept it is supposed to measure (e.g., Anastasi, 1950; Gomm, 2004; Kumar, 2005). The polemic on validity has resulted in a pile of literature being too large to even begin to quote. Issues of measurement validity were addressed above. Concerning the validity of the operationalization, so-called construct validity, it is clear that if the operationalization is not solidly founded in the theory, consensus about issues of validity will never be reached. In other words, the validity of social indicators can only be established after ensuring that all components of the concept from the theory are represented within the indicator(s).

Any kind of scientific evidence either comes with an estimate of uncertainty or is irrelevant (Meinrath, 2007). This touches upon the topics of reliability and discriminating power. Reliability of a test refers to the amount of error variance present in an obtained test score variance (e.g, Lord and Novick, 1968; Ebel, 1972; Laenen et al., 2009). Reliability of social indicators concerns the issue whether repeated measurements yield the same results in identical cases. This implies that reliability can not be assessed in cross-sectional study designs where only a single measurement per individual is available for analysis.

For application of social indicators in comparative research, however, reliability is a necessary though insufficient condition. Another defining feature of useful social indicators is the so-called discriminating power. Discriminating power addresses the issue that differences between cases are meaningful and can be detected as such when present (e.g., Loevinger, Gleser and DuBois, 1953; Hankins, 2007). Of course this characteristic is crucial for the fruitful use of social indicators in policy research and other social scientific disciplines. In comparison to validity and reliability however, hardly any attention has been paid to the power of the indicator score to make meaningful differentiations between subjects.

From Study Design to Analysis

Model Choice and Operational Hypotheses

The type of operational hypothesis determines the choice of the study design that is to be selected in order to test it. For instance, causal hypotheses require experimental study designs for testing. Correlational hypotheses are tested in cross sectional designs or, when a time component is involved, in longitudinal study designs (e.g., trend, cohort, panel studies) and in special cases, a case-control design. Study of a phenomenon in its natural context requires a case study design. And so on. The study design together with the properties of the involved variables (such as measurement scale and distribution) in turn, determine the choice of the adequate analysis model, for instance, a statistical model. This is why a social scientific metrology must also deal with the issue of model choice.

During the last decades, the arsenal of statistical models for social scientific datasets has grown enormously. The time when relationships among variables were illustrated by presenting a number of one-parameter association measures (Pearson correlation, Kendall's tau-b, crude odds-ratios, etc.) is far behind us. The contemporary social researcher chooses among a variety of models, for instance log-linear models, multivariate (logistic) regression, covariance structure models, latent class models, multilevel models, and so on. The improvement of the interface of computers along with their growing arithmetic capacity allows for fitting increasingly complex models to increasingly large datasets.

The scientific climate of this day invites social scientists to use these increasingly complex models, and seems to indicate that any (exploratory) analysis leading to the formulation of a set of significant parameters will yield scientifically more acceptable results than a simple description of the data in relation to the social scientific theory that one intends to corroborate or falsify. However, many social scientists don't fully comprehend the models that they are fitting. They are ignorant of the mathematics necessary to estimate the model parameters, and as a direct effect have only a shallow understanding of the effects of violations of assumptions underlying the model. The consequences for the quality of social scientific research are discussed below.

Model Misspecification

The goal of a statistical analysis is to make statements about a population which we can study only indirectly by means of a random sample. A random sample only allows for limited conclusions. However, the conclusions at which we *do* arrive should be robust in the sense that if we take another random sample from the population, we arrive at exactly the same set of conclusions. One hundred percent certainty can never be achieved; the level of certainty in any test is 1 minus the probability of making a Type I error. However, levels of significance in statistical tests are estimated, and the accuracy of that estimate depends on the accuracy of the chosen model. If we are wrong in our assumptions and we misspecify the statistical model, then standard errors and overall model fit statistics are biased.

When we make up a list of models for which the effects of misspecifications have been studied, we find that misspecification leads almost always to unreliable significance tests or biased parameter estimates; in short, to wrong conclusions. For instance, in multiple linear regression the omission of one of several explanatory variables leads to conservative testing or an increased type II error (Kmenta, 1971); polychoric correlations are biased when the underlying variables are not normally distributed (Ethington, 1987; Coenders et al., 1997); estimates of (standard errors of) fixed effects are biased in underspecified multilevel models (Lange and Laird, 1989; Bryk and Raudenbush, 1992; Berkhof and Kampen, 2004); goodness-of-fit statistics in covariance structure models are biased when researchers violate sample size or distributional assumptions (Hu et al., 1992); and so on.

The bias that results from misspecification often results in underestimated standard errors and overestimated model fit statistics, so that the probability that in the end, we make a Type I error (rejecting the null hypothesis "no differences",when there are no differences in the population, assuming significance of correlations, regression coefficients, etc., when they are not) is much higher than the estimate returned by the model estimation procedure. Thus, for example, you may have thought that you tested at 5% significance level when in fact, you tested at 20%. The result is that models are published that contain too many parameters that have falsely been assumed to differ from zero in the population.

Correctly specifying models becomes more difficult with increasing numbers of variables to be analyzed. This is why Achen (2002: 446) proposed a Rule of Three (ART), stating that any statistical specification with more than three explanatory variables is meaningless, because with more than three independent variables the task of carrying out the careful data analysis to ensure that the model specification is correct cannot be handled by any researcher. As such, the recommendation to keep the complexity of models in social sciences low is valuable if the purpose of statistical analysis is to produce replicable results.

Model Choice and Measurement Scale

Path models, like the ones in the LISREL i.e. structural equation modeling approach, require metric variables in the analysis. In social sciences, usually the best we can do is measurements on an ordinal scale. Often, for practical reasons, the paradigm is adopted that ordinal variables are realizations of normally distributed underlying variables. This assumption leads to the formulation of so-called polychoric correlation coefficients that represent the correlation of the underlying variables. Many studies point out that the polychoric correlation coefficient is the best estimator of the correlation of the underlying variables (e.g., Jöreskog and Sörbom, 1988; Holgado–Tello et al., 2010) provided that the underlying variables are multivariate normally distributed. Bias occurs when the underlying variables are non-normal (i.e. skewed and/or with significant kurtosis; see Ethington, 1987; Quiroga, 1992; Coenders *et al.*, 1997). The importance of the latter findings however, is open for dispute; in practice researchers are unable to verify the assumptions about underlying variables (e.g., Kampen and Swyngedouw, 2000: 94). Overall fit statistics of path models are ill-defined because the uncertainty in estimating the polychoric correlations is not accounted for in computation of the model. Therefore, ordinal variables in LISREL may lead to underestimated standard errors and overestimated overall fit statistics. The ultimate result is the publication of path coefficients and associations that are wrongly assumed to differ from zero in the population.

Model Choice and Sampling Method

Of all types of error, sampling error has received the major share of attention by statisticians because it can often be expressed in mathematical formulas, basically expressions of standard errors of estimated parameters (means, correlations, regression coefficients, etc.). In principle, sampling error is inversely related to sample size: the higher *N* is, the lower the standard error. However, the size of the standard error depends on the method of sampling. In the classic statistical paradigm, standard errors are based on random (or "simple probability") samples with replacement. Sampling designs in social scientific practice are rarely of that kind. Often, they involve stratified, clustered, or multi stage sampling frameworks. Each of these methods affect the standard error in different ways.

In stratified samples, the population is divided into strata (e.g., categories of age, education, cities, etc.) and within each stratum, a random sample of predefined magnitude is taken. The underlying idea is to prevent the realization of a "bad" random sample, e.g., one where no-one of over fifty years old is included. Stratification can substantially decrease standard errors of estimated parameters, for instance those of estimated means within strata when these means are estimated by Horvitz-Thomson estimators (e.g., Levy and Lemeshow, 1999). However, standard software packages by default will simply overestimate the involved standard errors. In fact, in order to compute accurate standard errors for e.g., Horvitz-Thomson estimators, special software scripts are required.

Another important type of sampling framework is the cluster or multistage sample. In many cases, the population of interest can be clustered in groups of units. Examples are pupils in classes, clients in banks, citizens in municipalities, etc. A clustered sampling framework first takes a random sample of groups (e.g., classes, cities), and then includes all units within the selected groups or clusters in the sample. The random sample of groups can be done proportional to its size (in which case equal prior probability of unit selection can be guaranteed) or not. If a random sample of units within groups is analyzed, we are dealing with nested data. Nesting of data must be accounted for in statistical analyses (e.g., Goldstein, 1997: 1; Snijders and Bosker, 1999: 7). Firstly, because respondents in the same group tend to be more similar than respondents from different groups, causing observations to be correlated within groups. Secondly, the information contained in the nesting levels can contribute to the substantive interpretation of the behavior of respondents (this is in fact the purpose of panel studies). A family of models that have been developed to account for the nesting of data is the hierarchical linear or random effects model (e.g., Bryk and Raudenbush, 1992; Goldstein, 1992; Longford, 1993; Snijders, 1996; Kreft and De Leeuw, 1998; Snijders and Bosker, 1999; Berkhof and Kampen, 2004). These models account for the dependencies of measures within groups, for instance by allowing variability of intercepts and/or slopes of covariates across groups. Not accounting for the nesting of data in linear models leads to underestimated standard errors, causing parameter tests to become liberal, and models to become overfitted. As a result researchers will report "significant" findings that have no prospect of replicability.

Issues in Analysis

Statistical Hypothesis Testing

The testing of the significance of more than one regression coefficient, correlation measure etc. by either the Student-t, Wald or score test necessitates that adjustments are made to control for capitalization on chance (e.g., Aitkin, 1977; Stevens, 1992). That is, the reported significance level of a coefficient should be evaluated while taking into account the fact that several parameters are tested for significance. This is because, if you try enough models, you will always find a model that has a good fit in terms of statistical significance of its parameters (fishing). A well-known procedure to adjust for multiple hypotheses testing is the Bonferroni-Holms correction (e.g., Shaffer, 1994). However, popular statistical packages used in the social sciences do not automatically apply these procedures. As a rule the computations must be done manually, are rather time consuming, and will be omitted in total in practice. Not correcting for capitalization on chance leads to publication of models that contain parameters that are in fact zero (over fitting).

Another instance where the use of statistical "hard evidence" leads to wrong conclusions is in the assessment of absolute and relative model fit statistics. For instance, the usual measure of overall fit of linear regression models is the so-called explained variance R^2. The absolute fit of a model increases of course, with an increasing R^2. In small samples R^2 is positively biased (i.e. overestimated) and should be controlled for the number of predictors in the model (see e.g., Stevens, 1992: 99). This measure, the so-called adjusted R^2, is always lower than its raw counterpart, and social scientists are often tempted to report the unadjusted explained variance in order to make their models look better than they really are. Needless to say, that this practice brings great damage to the reliability of quantitative social scientific research. Not correcting explained variance measures for the number of parameters used in the model leads to the reporting of overestimated model fit.

A third example concerns structural equation models and path models. In no other scientific discipline have these models enjoyed so much popularity as in social science. Statistical inference of model fit is problematic especially in small samples and when the model is misspecified (Hu *et al.*, 1992). Hoogland and Boomsma (1998) have performed a meta-analysis of robustness studies of the structural equation model. Their main conclusions are that regardless of the estimation method, parameter estimates are biased when sample size is lower than 500, and that the overall model fit statistic is biased when $N < 5df$ where df denotes the degrees of freedom of the model under study. Failure to use samples that are large enough leads to overfitted models.

As a final example, in both regression analysis and path models, researchers often report models that do not have significant overall fit. Usually, the best they can do is report a relative fit statistic that reveals that the model is better than nothing (typically, R^2 or "explained variance" measures in factor analysis with magnitudes in the order of 10–30% rendering measurement errors of 70% or more). In the discussion of the results however, the misfit of the model is often neglected and instead, the relative fit statistic is treated as an overall fit statistic. Failure to recognize that such a model-is-better-than-nothing fit statistic is not an overall model fit statistic leads to overrated models and of course, the impossibility of replication of the results in new research. Particularly in the discussion of predictive or confirmative validity of the indicators, overly optimistic conclusions about the value of the applied indicators will be drawn.

Nonresponse and Errors in Statistical Generalization

Last but not least, the ignoring of total nonresponse in a sample leads to unjustified generalization of sample results to a population (generalization error). Coverage error occurs when the analyzed sample is drawn from a subsample of the population of interest, for instance, when results of a telephone questionnaire are being generalized to the population. Knowing that not all citizens have telephone and that many people cannot be reached by phone because their phone number is not listed, we know beforehand that there is coverage error. Generalizing internet questionnaires to a population is another example. In statistical analysis, coverage error can never be repaired. The risk of making a coverage error can be reduced a priori by using appropriate listings of the respondents in the target population (Dillman 2000: 198). A posteriori however, coverage error is caused by the selective drop-out of respondents refusing to fill in the questionnaire (total nonresponse) or refusing to answer specific questions (item nonresponse). Here, the mode of surveying also plays a role: interviewers may induce item nonresponse, for instance, when they skip questions to save time (De Leeuw, 2001: 156). Sensitive questions in some instances, have a larger probability of getting answered using the (anonymous) mail method than probing by interviewer (e.g., Dillman, 2000: 226). Unfortunately, these well-documented sources of statistical generalization errors are often ignored in applied social scientific research.

FROM ANALYSIS TO REPORT AND BACK TO THEORY

Matters of Presentation

The scientific report should allow for an assessment by the reader of both the process and the results of the research. A first requirement is that the report respects the different phases of the research cycle. That is, the section on theory and societal relevance (the "what" and "why" of the research, the conceptual and operational hypotheses, operationalization of the concepts in terms of indicators) should be separate from the section on methodology (the "how", "when" and "where" of the research, including instrument design, study design, sampling design). The section on results should include results only and no discussion of the results. The discussion of the results should be in terms of the operational hypotheses and should not introduce new theory other than a section suggesting directions for further research.

A second requirement is that all choices made by the researcher should be made explicit. In the previous sections, it was shown that at numerous places in the empirical research cycle, choices are being made by the researchers. The most important of these choices refer to the operationalization of the involved concepts, the design of measurement instruments, the selection of the study design, the analysis model, and the sampling design. In exploratory research the researcher may have gone through the steps of the empirical research cycle (in Figure 1) more than one time: in "grounded theory" approaches, as many times as required to reach "saturation". In the report the various choices and motivation thereof must be made explicit. This includes a discussion of external validity, that is, a motivation to what extent the results from the sample can be generalized to the target population, and the extent to which the operational hypotheses can be generalized to the conceptual hypotheses. The latter issue will be discussed in the next section.

Theoretical Generalization

The indicators we started out with will lead to the translation of conceptual hypotheses into operational hypotheses. Too often empirical verification of the operational hypothesis is taken as empirical evidence of the conceptual hypothesis without any critical account. Consider for instance, the conceptual hypothesis that "social capital leads to good governance". The concepts social capital and good governance may be operationalized with selected indicators "group membership" and "trust in government institutions" respectively The result of the choice of indicators is that the operational hypothesis becomes something like "communities with relatively high numbers of inhabitants that are member of an association have relatively more trust in local government institutions." Ignore for a moment how "trust in local government institutions" is measured, and suppose that a researcher finds statistical evidence in data that the operational hypothesis is true. In such instances the researcher is tempted to conclude that the conceptual hypothesis is also true, in a reasoning process known as "theoretical generalization". What if the researcher chose to operationalize social capital by "turnout in presidential elections" and good governance by the municipality budget deficit (a reasonable choice, according to e.g., Coffé and Geys, 2005), finds no association in real data, and rejects the operational hypothesis? Would that imply that the conceptual hypothesis is untrue? Or can the conceptual hypothesis be true and untrue, depending on the way a researcher chooses to operationalize the involved concepts? In the literature, no criteria for the kinds of (empirical) evidence that would justify the generalization of operational hypotheses to conceptual hypotheses can be found.

The issue of deciding what kinds of evidence of validity of operational hypotheses provide actual proof of validity of conceptual hypotheses is not easily resolved. This decision involves the reaching of consensus among social scientists, and only in totalitarian states (fake) consensus can be forced upon people which is of course undesirable from any perspective. Moreover, when reaching consensus within the scientific community over research results becomes the main aim of social scientists (a "regulative idea" put forward by e.g., Swanborn 1996), we are in grave danger of replacing knowledge with "common sense". A feasible first step towards a more mature social science, however, is for researchers to make a more concentrated effort to explicate rigorously the choices they made in conducting their research, This challenge to the social scientific research community pertains to a plurality of methodological approaches (both quantitative and qualitative). Increased explication of the research choices made facilitates the identification of differences of opinion. Social scientific metrology concerns both the process of conducting research and the product of research in terms of measurements. If more information is dissipated about the process of research, it becomes possible to begin to think about the developing of strict and specific definitions regarding the measurement of specific social scientific constructs.

TOWARDS A SOCIONOMY

Aspects of a Social Scientific Metrology

In the assessment of the empirical social science process carried out in the previous sections, a large number of potential mishaps in social scientific reasoning have been identified. Important problems relate to measurements and operations on measurements, including analyses. The first major problem relates to the relationship between concept and indicators, and the lack of formal means to justify the generalization of operational hypotheses to conceptual hypotheses. Elsewhere it has been argued that this issue could be settled if the economy principle is applied, meaning for instance, that when we use "membership of associations" as an indicator of "social exclusion", we must continue to speak of the (alleged) impact of "membership of associations" and not of "social exclusion" (Kampen, 2010). In any case, lack of consensus on how to *define* and *operationalize* a concept makes it impossible to *measure* the concept. Increased clarity of choices made on operationalization would help direct the discussion.

A second important problem concerns the difficulties in the designing of adequate measurement instruments. Much measurement in the social sciences relies on the answers people give on multiple choice questions in surveys. Survey errors include mode effects, survey satisficing, and context effects. Only a rigorous standardizing of questionnaires can solve this problem. That is to say, the measuring of social scientific constructs is possible only when the mode and context of the surveys is kept constant, and furthermore, when the (virtual) length of the questionnaires is kept constant (Kampen, 2007). Calibration and standardization of questionnaires must become priorities if a survey is to serve as a reliable instrument capable of monitoring effects of changes in public opinion. Of course, the lack of standardization in measurement instruments other than questionnaire should be an important concern as well.

The third problem that was discussed concerned the consequences of making wrong model choices, the wrongly interpreting (or reporting) of the results of a statistical analysis, or both. Wrong choices of a model include model misspecification, and not respecting the sampling methodology used (simple random, cluster, nested). The wrong interpreting of models concerns capitalization on chance, reporting relative fit statistics as absolute fit statistics, not respecting measurement scale, and ignoring the sources of nonresponse. In practice, social scientific research in some instances does not fall short of combining all possible sources of bias and obscurity. It is in other words, wrong to assume that a quantitative approach towards social science by itself leads to more reliable results than qualitative approaches. In both approaches, social scientific research depends on a series of choices that are made by researchers: choice of operationalization, choice of analysis models, choices in the data analysis phase, and so on. The only way of making empirical research less susceptible to subjective choices of researchers is by reducing the number of choices.

A social scientific metrology should establish amongst other things, quantity systems and measurement standards, including regulatory requirements of measurements and measuring instruments for the protection of ethical standards, health, public safety, the environment, etc. In order to become fully operational as a science, the next steps need to be undertaken:

1. Developing of quality criteria for systematic reviews of social scientific concepts, so that such concepts can be linked unambiguously with (a single set of) indicators.
2. Developing of scientific criteria that justify the generalization of operational hypotheses to conceptual hypotheses.
3. Developing of quality criteria for the construction of measurement instruments of indicators, respecting known sources of bias (e.g., mode and context in surveys, observer bias in participant observation).
4. Defining of the requirements of the analysis model including the properties of the sample, and respecting the properties of the variables (measurement scale, distribution) and the operational hypotheses that are tested.

Only after establishing a social scientific metrology, the development of a socionomy becomes possible. An important step towards the solving of the crisis in sociology and social sciences is in the education of social scientists.

Educating a New Generation of Social Scientists

Amongst the best suited candidates for the cultivating of a social scientific metrology are students in the social sciences, both in their capacity as future users (e.g., in policy making and management) and in their capacity as potential developers of social indicators. As many students appear to choose for social sciences because of their interest in the objects of study and not in science *per se*, here lies the first challenge that requires explicit attention in the education of future social scientists. This attention could take on the form of courses on philosophy of science and logic as mandatory parts of the curriculum (in the Netherlands, these topics have been removed from the mandatory part of most curricula in the 1990's). In addition, any social science curriculum should include a number of research methodology courses with contents along the lines of Figure 1. The logic of the empirical social science cycle can help systemize the teaching of methodology. At least five distinct steps in this cycle can be distinguished and ought to receive separate attention:

1. The *conceptual design*, which includes the formulation of the theory in terms of conceptual hypotheses, and the operationalization of concepts in terms of indicators and operational hypotheses;
2. The *technical design*, which includes selection of the study design in function of the operational hypotheses, the developing of measurement instruments (data collection tools), the selection of the analysis model, and the designing of the sampling framework;
3. The *field work*, including sample selection and measurement;
4. The *analysis* of the data, whether quantitative, qualitative or a combination, and finally,
5. The crafting of the *report*.

Courses in social scientific research methodology will typically cover steps 1 and 2. Statistics courses will focus on step 4, as should courses on qualitative data analysis. Steps 3 and 5 often take the form of practical tutorials resulting in a thesis. All too often however, courses teach bits and pieces of each step and fail to provide students with an integrated picture of the logic of social scientific research. For instance, the experiment is taught together with analysis of variance; the case study design is taught together with open interviewing; etc. In our opinion it is crucial to distinguish courses on data analysis, whether qualitative analysis, quantitative analysis or a mixture, from courses on study design, and these in turn should be separated from courses on data collection tools. If these aspects of scientific research are taught separately, students will no longer produce the Pavlov reaction that for example, case studies are qualitative by definition and experiments are quantitative by definition. Instead, they will make choices consciously and choose a study model in function of operational hypotheses, and choose an analysis model in function of the variables. By making explicit that the technical design follows the conceptual design, the choices made are easier to identify and explain. Of course, regarding the conceptual design, the writing of literature reviews should be taught as a systematic enterprise, instead of a haphazard search for confirmation of preconceptions.

In practical work (e.g., the writing of a master thesis), the whole empirical social science research cycle should be followed. Much notice should be taken of how a theory needs to be reworked to result in indicators that allow for meaningful operational hypotheses. Concretely, in social theory courses, students could be invited to critically discuss examples of different operationalizations, and their impact on operational and conceptual hypotheses. With regard to instrument construction or selection, one could make students experience the necessity of standardized surveys, for example by means of class room experiments with different operationalizations of one concept or different versions of a measurement instrument. In addition, to make students realize the necessity of metrology, an assignment could be on one of the many social indicators as tapped on in open-access data bases containing micro data, for example the World Value Survey.

Finally, in our opinion the scarcity of statistics courses in many social science programs posits an additional serious problem. At least, the mandatory program should cover those statistical techniques that social scientists apply the most, including for instance, structural equation models and logistic regression. Furthermore, these course should include an account of the effects of misspecification of these models. Likewise, qualitative data analysis is something that needs to be taught too, as this kind of data analysis requires a structured systematic approach and should not be left in the hands of intuition either.

Concluding Remark

This chapter advocated a social sciences metrology as a requirement to further social scientific progress in both theoretical and applied areas. Such a metrology is a scientific discipline that occupies itself exclusively with measurement in society. A social sciences metrology is well within reach when there is the willingness across social scientific disciplines to let agreement prevail over disagreement. We hope with this essay to have contributed to a continuation of collaborative efforts, in both social scientific research and education, to the systematic construction and use of social indicators, that is the systemizing of social indicators.

Acknowledgments

We would like to thank doctors Jennifer Barrett (Wagening University, The Netherlands), Alain De Beuckelaer (Nijmegen University, The Netherlands), and Sabine Stiller (Wageningen University, The Netherlands) for their critical comments and their helpful suggestions on an earlier draft of this chapter. Of course, the *cri the coeur* expressed is that of the two authors.

References

Achen, C. H. (2002). Toward a new political methodology: microfoundations and ART, *Annu. Rev. Polit. Sci.* 5: 423-450.

Aitkin, M. (1979). A Simultanuous Test Procedure for Contingency Table Models, *Applied Statistics* 28: 233-242.

Aquilino, W. S. (1994). Interview mode effects in surveys of drug and alcohol use. *Public Opinion Quarterly* 58: 210–240.

Alroe, H. F. and E. S. Kristensen (2002). Towards a systematic research methodology in agriculture: rethinking the role of values in science, *Agriculture and Human Values* 19: 3-23.

Anastasi, A. (1950). The Concept of Validity in the Interpretation of Test Scores, *Educational and Psychological Measurement* 10: 67-78.

Bain, R. (1942). Sociometry and social measurement. Prepared for meeting *American Sociological Society, Dec. 29-31, Cleveland, Ohio.*

Berkhof, J. and Kampen, J. K. (2004). The asymptotic effect of a misspecification in the random part of the multilevel model. *Journal of Educational and Behavioral Statistics* 29(2): 197–214.

Beuckelaer, A. de, Kampen, J.K, and Van Trijp, H.C.M. (2011). An empirical assessment of the cross-national measurement validity of graded paired comparisons. Forthcoming in *Quality and Quantity.*

Brehm, J. and W. Rahn (2007). Individual-Level Evidence for the Causes and Consequences of Social Capital, *American Journal of Political Science* 41(3): 999-1023

Bryk, A. S. and Raudenbush, S. W. (1992). *Hierarchical Linear models.* London: Sage.

Bricmont, J. and A. Sokal (2001). Science and sociology of science: beyond war and peace. In: Labinger, J. and H. Collins (eds.), *The one culture: a conversation about science.* Chicago: Chicago University Press.

Bunge, M. (1975). What is a quality of life indicator? *Social Indicators Research Series* 2(1): 65-79.

Canache, D., Mondak, J. J. and Seligson, M. A. (2001). Meaning and measurement in crossnational research on satisfaction with democracy. *Public Opinion Quarterly* 65: 506–528.

Cetina, K. K. (1996). The care of the self and blind varietion: The disunity of two leading sciences. In: Galison, P. and D. J. Stump, *The disunity of science. Boundaries, contexts and power.* Stanford, CA.: Standford University Press.

Coenders, G., A. Satorra and W. E. Saris (1997). Alternative approaches to structural modeling of ordinal data: A Monte Carlo study. *Structural Equation Modeling: A Multidisciplinary Journal* 3: 261-282.

Coffé, H. B. Geys (2005). Institutional performance and social capital: an application to the local government level, *Journal of Urban Affairs* 27(5): 485-501.

Creath, R. (1996). The unity of science. In: Galison, P. and D. J. Stump (Eds.). *The disunity of science. Boundaries, contexts, and power.* Stanford, CA: University Press.

Dawkins, R. (1976). *The selfish gene.* Oxford University Press.

Dawkins, R. (2007). *The God delusion.* Bantam Books.

De Leeuw, E. (2001). Reducing missing data in surveys: An overview of methods. *Quality and Quantity* 35: 147–160.

De Leeuw, E. and Collins, M. (1997). Data collection methods and survey quality: An overview. In: Lyberg, L. et al. (eds.), *Survey Measurement and Process Quality.* New York: Wiley.

De Leeuw, E. D., Mellenbergh, G. J. and Hox, J. J. (1996). The influence of data collection method on structural models. *Sociological Methods and Research* 24: 443–472.

Dilman, D. A. (2000). *Mail and Internet Surveys: The Tailored Design Method.* New York: Wiley.

Diefenbach, T. (2009). Are case studies more than sophisticated story telling? methodological problems of case studies mainly based on semi-structured interviews, *Quality and Quantity* 43: 875–894.

Distin, K. (2005). *The Selvish meme.* Cambridge, UK: Cambridge University Press.

Ebel, R. L. (1972). *Essentials of educational measurement.* Englewood Cliffs: Prentive Hall.

Ethington, C. A. (1987). The robustness of LISREL estimates in structural equation models with categorical variables. *Journal of Experimental Education* 55: 80-88.

Faber, J., and W. J. Scheper (2003). Social scientific explanations? *Quality and Quantity* 37: 135-150.

Fahey, T. and E. Smyth (2004). Do subjective indicators measure welfare? Evidence from 33 European countries, *European Societies* 6(1): 5-27.

Fowler, F. J., Roman, A. M., and Di, Z. X., (1998). Mode effects in a survey of medicare prostate surgery patients. *Public Opinion Quarterly* 62: 29–46.

Feyerabend, P. (1987). *Farewell to reason.* London: Biddles Ltd.

Frønes, I. (2007). Theorizing indicators. On indicators, signs and trends. *Social Indicators Research* 83: 5-23.

Goldstein, H. (1995). *Multilevel Statistical Models.* New York: Wiley.

Gomm, R. (2008). *Social research methodology. A critical introduction.* New York: Palgrave-Macmillan.

Gould, S. J. (2002). *The structure of evolutionary theory.* Harvard University Press.

Grasso, M. and L. Canova (2008). An Assessment of the Quality of Life in the European Union Based on the Social Indicators Approach, *Social Indicators Research* 87(1): 1-25.

Hacking, I. (1996). The disunities of the sciences. In: Galison, P. and D. J. Stump (Eds.). *The disunity of science. Boundaries, contexts, and power.* Stanford, CA: University Press.

Hankins, M. (2007). Questionnaire discrimination: (re-)introducing coefficient delta, *BMC Medical Research Methodology* 7: 19-23.

Holbrook, A. L., Green, M. C. and Krosnick, J. A. (2003). Telephone versus face-to-face interviewing of national probability samples with long questionnaires: comparisons of respondent satisficing and social desirability response bias. *Public Opinion Quarterly* 67: 79–125.

Holgado–Tello, F. P., S. Chacón–Moscoso, I. Barbero–García and E. Vila–Abad (2010). Polychoric versus Pearson correlations in exploratory and confirmatory factor analysis of ordinal variables, *Quality and Quantity* 44(1): 153-166.

Hoogland, J. and Boomsma, A. (1998). Robustness studies in covariance structure models: An overview and a meta-analysis. *Sociological Methods and Research* 26: 329–309.

Hox, J. J. and De Leeuw, E. D. (1994). A comparison of nonresponse in mail, telephone and face-to-face interviews. *Quality and Quality* 28: 329–344.

Hu, L., P. M. Bentler and Y. Kano (1992). Can test statistics in covariance structure models be trusted? *Psychological Bulletin* 112: 351-362.

Isaef, L. K. (1993). The place of metrology in the science system: On postulates. Translated from *Izmeritel'naya Tekhnika* 8: 10-11.

Jobe J. B., and Mingay, D. J. (1991). Cognition and survey measurement: History and overview. *Applied Cognitive Psychology* 5: 175–92.

Johnson, T.P., Kulesa, P., Cho, Y.I., Shavitt, S. (2005). The relation between culture and response styles. Evidence from 19 countries. *Journal of Cross-Cultural Psychology* 36, 264-277.

Jöreskog, K. G. and D. Sörbom (1988). *Prelis 2 User's Reference Guide*. Uppsala: Scientific Software.

Kagan, J. (2009). *The three cultures. Natural sciences, social sciences, and the humanities in the 21st century.* Cambridge University Press.

Kampen, J. K. (2010). On the (in)consistency of citizen and municipal level indicators of social capital and local government performance, *Social Indicators Research* 97: 213-228.

Kampen, J. K. (2007). The impact of survey methodology and context on central tendency, nonresponse and associations of subjective indicators of government performance, *Quality and Quantity* 41(6): 793-813.

Kampen, J. K. and Swyngedouw, M. (2000). The ordinal controversy revisited. *Quality and Quantity* 34: 87–102.

Kirshner, B. and G. Guyatt (1985). A methodological framework for assessing health indices, *Journal of Chronic Diseases* 38(1): 27-36.

Kmenta, J. (1971). *Elements of econometrics*. NY: Macmillan.

Kreft, I. and J. De Leeuw (1998). *Introducing multilevel modeling*. London: SAGE.

Krosnick, J. A. (1991). Response strategies for coping with the cognitive demands of attitude measures in surveys. *Applied Cognitive Psychology* 5: 213–236.

Krosnick, J. A., and Alwin, D. F. (1987). An evaluation of a cognitive theory of response order effects in survey measurement. *Public Opinion Quarterly* 51: 201–219.

Krysan, M., Schuman, H., Scott, L. J. and Beatty, P. (1994). Response rates and response content in mail versus face-to-face surveys. *Public Opinion Quarterly* 58: 381–399.

Kuder, G. F. and M. W. Richardson (1937). The theory of the estimation of test reliability, *Psychometrika* 2(3): 151-160.

Kumar, R. (2005). *Research methodology*. London: Sage.

Laenen, A., A. Alonso, G. Molenberghs and T. Vangeneugden (2009). A family of measures to evaluate scale reliability in a longitudinal setting, *J. R. Statist. Soc. A* 172(1): 237-253.

Lange, N. and N. M. Laird (1989). The effect of covariance structure on variance estimation in balanced growth-curve models with random parameters, *Journal of the American Statistical Association* 84: 241-247.

Lanskov, A. B. (1974). Economic questions of metrology: Aspects of effects of metrological scientific research and experimental design. Translated from *Izmeritel'naya Tekhnika* 10: 87-88.

Legg, C. and P. Stagaki (2002). How to be a postmodernist: a user's guide to postmodern rhetorical practices, *Journal of Family Therapy* 24: 385-401.

Lopreato, J. and T. Crippen (1999). *Crisis in sociology: the need for Darwin*. New Brunswick, NJ: Transaction Publishers.

Levy, P. S. and S. Lemeshow (1999). *Sampling of populations. Methods and applications.* New York: Wiley.

Leydesdorff, L. (2002). May there be a “socionomy” beyond “sociology”? *The Journal of Science and Health Policy* 2(1).

Loevinger, J., G. C. Gleser and P. H. DuBois (1953). Maximizing discriminating power of a multiple-score test, *Psychometrika* 18(4): 309-317.

Longford, N. (1999). Standard errors in multilevel analysis, *Multilevel Modelling Newsletter* 1: 10-13.

Lord, F. M. and M. R. Novick (1968). *Statistical theories of mental test scores*. Reading: Addison Wesley.

Lyberg, L., Biemer, P. Collins, M. De Leeuw, E. Dippo, C. Schwarz N. and Trewin D. (1997). *Survey Measurement and Process Quality*. New York: Wiley.

Lynn, P. (2003). Developing quality standards for cross-national survey research: five approaches. *International Journal of Social Research Methodology* 6: 323–337.

Lynn, P., L. Japec and L. Lyberg (2006). What's so special about cross-national surveys ? In: Harkness, J. A. (Ed.) *Conducting cross-national and cross-cultural surveys. Papers from the 2005 meeting of the International Workshop on Comparative Survey Design and Implementation (CSDI).* Mannheim: ZUMA.

Mangione, T. W., R. Hingson and J. Barrett (1982), Collecting sensitive data: A comparison of three survey strategies, *Sociological Methods and Research* 10: 337-346.

Massey, D. S. (2000). What I don't know about my field but wish I did, *Annual Review of Sociology* 26: 699-701

Moore, D. W. (2002). Measuring new types of question-order effects. *Public Opinion Quarterly* 66: 80–91.

Meinrath, G. (2007). The intention of truth, objectivity and metrology, *Accred. Qual. Assur.* 12: 515-523.

Micklewright, J. and S. V. Schnepf (2010). How reliable are income data collected with a single question? *J. R. Statist. Soc. A* 173(2): 409-429.

Newman, I., C. S. Ridenour, C. Newman, and G. M. DeMarco Jr. (2003). A typology of research purposes and its relationship to mixed methods. In: A. Tashakkori and C. Teddlie (Eds.), *Handbook of mixed methods in social and behavioral research* (pp. 167–188). Thousand Oaks, CA: SAGE.

Noll, H. H. (2002). Towards a European system of social indicators: theoretical framework and system architecture, *Social Indicators Research* 58: 47-87.

Petticrew, M. and H. Roberts (2006). *Systematic reviews in the social sciences. A practical guide.* Oxford: Blackwell Publishing.

Prus, R. (1990). The interpretative challenge: the impending crisis in sociology, *The Canadian Journal of Sociology* 15(3): 355-363.

Quiroga, A. M. (1992). *Studies of the polychoric correlation and other correlation measures for ordinal variables.* Stockholm: Almqwist and Wiksel International.

Savage, M. and R. Burrows (2007). The coming crisis of empirical sociology, *Sociology* 41(5): 885-889.

Shaffer, J. P. (1994). *Multiple hypothesis testing: a review.* Berkely: Technical Report of The National Institute of Statistical Sciences, Univ. of California.

Schaffer, S. (1996). Contextualizing the Canon. In: Galison, P. and D. J. Stump (Eds.). *The disunity of science. Boundaries, contexts, and power.* Stanford, CA: University Press.

Smith, P.B., and R. Fischer, R. (2008). Acquiescence, extreme response bias and culture: a multilevel analysis. In Van De Vijver, F.J.R., Van Hemert, D.A., Poortinga, Y. (Eds.) *Individuals and Cultures in Multilevel Analysis*. Mahwah, NJ: Lawrence Erlbaum Associates.

Snijders, T.A.B. en R. Bosker (1999). *Multilevel analysis*. London: SAGE.

Stevens, J. (1992). *Applied multivariate statistics for the social sciences.* New Jersey: Lawrence Erlbaum.

Stoop, I. and J. Boelhouwer (1999). Measuring well-being in the Netherlands: The SCP index from 1974 to 1997, *Social Indicators Research* 48(1): 51-75.

Tourangeau, R., Rips, L. J. and Rasinski, K. (2000). *The Psychology of Survey Response.* Cambridge, UK: University Press.

Tourangeau, R. (2003). Cognitive aspects of survey measurement and mismeasurement. *International Journal of Public Opinion Research* 15: 3–7.

Tourangeau, R., and Rasinski, K. (1988). Cognitive processes underlying context effects in attitude measurement. *Psychological Bulletin* 103: 229–314.

Van Tilburg, T. and De Leeuw, E. (1991). Stability of scale quality under various data collection procedures: a mode comparison on the 'De Jong-Gierveld Loneliness Scale'. *International Journal of Public Opinion Research* 3: 69–85.

Welkenhuysen-Gybels, J. and J. Billiet (2002). A comparison of techniques for detecting cross-cultural inequivalence at the item level, *Quality and Quantity* 36(3): 197-218.

Whitelaw, I. (2007). *A measure of all things. The story of measurement through the ages.* Hove: Quid Publishing.

Wiseman, J. and K. Brasher (2008). Community Wellbeing in an Unwell World: Trends, Challenges, and Possibilities, *Journal of Public Health Policy* 29: 353-366.

Wright, B. E., L. J. Manigault and T. R. Black (2004). Quantitative research measurement in public administration: An assessment of journal publications, *Administration and Society* 35(6): 747-764.

Yale Center for Environmental Law and Policy (2005). *Environmental Sustainability Index: Benchmarking National Environmental Stewardship.* Retrieved from internet (30.03.2009) at sedac.ciesin.columbia.edu/es/esi/ESI2005_Main_Report.pdf.

In: Social Indicators: Statistics, Trends...
Editor: Candace M. Baird
ISBN 978-1-61122-841-0

Chapter 2

DISCRETIONARY TIME AND FREELY DISPOSABLE TIME: TWO NEW INTEGRATED INDICATORS OF WELFARE, POVERTY AND FREEDOMS

Marieke Hobbes and Wouter T. de Groot
Leiden University, the Netherlands

ABSTRACT

The economics of life are ruled by time, money, their exchange rate and how much of it is needed to satisfy the basic needs of the household. Discretionary Time (DT) and Freely Disposable Time (FDT) are two newly developed conceptually equivalent but methodologically different social indicators that integrate these time and money elements into a single metric. Both indicators express how much time the productive members of a household have left after fulfilling the basic needs (of food, shelter, care, sleep, consumables etc.) of themselves and their dependents. This chapter discusses (1) the principles of DT and FDT assessment and some outcomes in various countries, (2) the linkages of DT and FDT with freedoms, potential income, development, poverty and happiness, (3) the caveats that may be identified in these linkages and (4) indicator choice in relation to mono-dimensional, pure time and money indicators of welfare and poverty.

1. INTRODUCTION

Poverty is often said to be a multi-dimensional phenomenon. Indicators of poverty then usually take the form of some addition of all 'life satisfactions'. Equating poverty with lack of 'total' well-being robs the term poverty of its primary, economic meaning, however, and does not add anything to the well-being or happiness concepts. In this chapter, we keep the concepts of poverty and welfare in their original, primarily economic domain. We may then find that empirically, poverty and welfare correlate with objective and subjective well-being and happiness in many cases, but not in others.

This does not imply that poverty and welfare are purely mono-dimensional concepts, as if they only depend on monetary factors such as income or expenditure. Our point of departure is that a household with a low income per capita with all its able members needing 10 hours per day to earn that income is much worse off, also in economic terms, than a household with the same low income per capita but needing only 5 hours per day of work by its able members. The latter household has not only much more time to raise the children, acquire knowledge or build social capital, but usually also to raise its income if needed, e.g. by working some hours per day more.

This insight has been the source of inspiration for a family of combined time/money indicators that we will present in the next section. Within that group, we will focus on two indicators that may be called TIMs (Time Integrated with Money), defined as indicators that express the time and money aspects of livelihoods into a single time metric. The basic idea that underlies both TIMs is that:

- The productive household members have to supply their own basic needs plus those of their dependents (e.g. food, care and a roof for the children).
- These basic needs can be written in time or money terms.
- The average wage rate determines how much time per day the productive household members have to spend on the monetary basic needs. For instance, if five hours of work deliver 100 dollars, a need of 100 dollars is equivalent to a need of five hours of work.
- This determines the total time per day needed to supply the basic needs.
- 24 hours minus that amount can be called 'Surplus Time' (ST).

'Freely Disposable Time' (FDT) and 'Discretionary Time' (DT) are two methodologies to make ST operational. As we will show later, the DT and FDT methodologies differ sufficiently to retain the separate terms here besides the general ST.

ST is the time not dictated by the necessities of life. ST is not spare time, free time or leisure time. Leisure is only one of the things you can do with surplus time. In fact, most people prefer to work part of their surplus time, e.g. in order to acquire luxury goods or send a child to college. This illustrates what is in fact the great and direct relevance of ST: surplus time is the time you can have preferences about. ST is freedoms. Though differently in any local context, it can be used to acquire luxuries but also for investments in the farm or the community, for education, for braiding your hair.

As will be discussed in later sections, it is likely that ST will correlate with well-being to some degree. This does not imply that people will always feel what their ST in fact is. Many people in Western societies have much ST but feel time-pressured nevertheless; see Goodin et al. (2008) on the 'time pressure illusion' and Gershuny (2005) on being busy as a status symbol.

The ST concept is applicable to the rich and the poor alike, and may therefore be used to set a poverty line. The fundamental poverty line is when ST = 0, meaning that people need all they can do, i.e. all the time they have and all the cash they can generate with it, to satisfy their basic needs. At this level, people are trapped in poverty, with neither time nor cash left to invest in the future. Reardon and Vosti (1995) have proposed the term 'investment poor' for households that avail of only a little more than bare basic needs satisfaction, assuming that they will spend this little surplus on expanded consumption rather than investment (in knowledge, soil and water conservation, social capital etc.) In ST terms, an ST of, say, 2 h/day may be set as the 'investment poverty line'.

Having a very high income, on the other hand, implies that the acquisition of basic needs requires only very little time spent on income generation. Yet, everybody has only 24 hours per day and needs some 10 of those for basic sleep, self-care and leisure. All very high incomes will therefore congregate in a range between, say, 13 and 14 h/day of surplus time, while the relatively poor will be assessed in a broad area between ST = 0 and, say, 6 h/day. As Goodin et al. (2008: 3) put it, the time metric is egalitarian, and expresses the decreasing marginal utility of income.

Against this background, the objective of this chapter is to document, illustrate, test and discuss the meaning of a metric of Surplus Time. The chapter is structured as follows. Section 2 gives a brief overview of the history and members of the family of combined time/money indicators. Sections 3 and 4 then present the FDT and DT methodologies to assess the ST indicator. In Section 5, we study ST properties through the outcomes of various behaviors of a simplified example household, and Section 6 compares these to what a number of monetary indicators say about the same behaviors. Section 7 then moves to empirical outcomes of DT and FDT applications, comparing the rich and the poor, in the West and the developing world. On that basis, Section 8 supplies an analysis of the meaning surplus time, discussing its connotation of freedoms and development capacity and its linkages with potential income and well-being, taking special care to unearth the caveats present in these relationships. Section 9 broadens this discussion to also include monetary indicators of poverty and welfare. Section 10 is the general conclusion.

2. The Family of Combined Time/Money Metrics

The 'Freely Disposable Time' (FDT) or 'Discretionary Time' (DT) concepts and methodologies belong to a recently sprouted family of social indicators that combine time and money flows. This section supplies a brief overview.

Origins: Becker (1965) and Vickery (1977)

Becker (1965) proposed that a household's resources could be measured by its 'full income', defined as what it could earn by devoting all its time to income-generation activities and activities directly necessary to sustain these activities, such as a minimum of sleep. Becker's method has been criticized for failing to take into account that paid work to fill all these hours may be locally unavailable (Folbre, 2004). Vickery (1977) followed subtler course, calculating a combined money/time poverty spectrum. People with little spare time have a higher income poverty line than people who have more time available to compensate low income by searching for bargains, cook food from fresh ingredients, etc.; see Douthitt (2000) for an update.

Land-Time Budget Analysis

From within the rural development and farming systems tradition, Giampietro (2004) developed 'land-time budget analysis' to assess the performance of the time and land budgets that people have available. Starting point of the analysis is the total number of hours per year available in the studied group (society, village, household). Various categories resembling basic needs are then subtracted, such as the time needed for sleep, leisure, education and chores, the total time of the non-productive household members, and the time needed to farm for auto-consumption, pay taxes and buy agricultural inputs. The time left can be used to produce cash, either on or off farm. How much 'net disposable cash' this can be depends on a parallel system for the availability of land.

Land-time budget analysis does not offer a coherent system of data categories and calculation rules, which hampers application in empirical cases (Pastore et al., 1999; Gomiero and Giampietro, 2001; Grünbühel and Schandl, 2005; Hobbes, 2005). For instance, food needs are either not (Giampietro, 2004: 396) or fully (Pastore et al., 1999) subtracted from net disposable cash. Yet, Giampietro's principles have been a major source of inspiration for developing FDT (Hobbes et al., in press).

Paired Money/Time Indicators

Vickery's (1977) idea has recently been carried forward in the form of paired money/time indicators, exemplified by Bardasi and Wodon (2009) on Guinea and Burchardt (2008) on the UK. Bardasi and Wodon (2009) focus their analysis on people who are time as well as consumption poor, i.e. those who work long hours out of necessity to make basic ends meet. Burchardt (2008) defines 'free time' as 24 hours/day minus time spent on sleep, personal care, paid work and unpaid work. The analysis of households then takes place on the two-dimensional plane defined by the axes of disposable income and free time, e.g. distinguishing between people with low pay and few obligations of unpaid work, people with low pay but many obligations, and so on.

Integrated Time/Money Indicators: TIMs

All methods described above use a wage rate to convert money and time. Burchardt (2008), for instance, applies the income per hour to set the slope of the various income/free time combinations that households have available. Bardasi and Wodon (2009) apply the income per hour to assess if households would hit the income poverty line if they would work a decent number of hours per day. Both paired indicator approaches refrain, however, from using the income per hour to calculate a single metric in which time is integrated with money. This reluctance has reasons. Paired indicators maintain more detail on time and money separately, enabling for instance to distinguish income-poverty caused by a low wage rate from income-poverty caused by working only few hours. On the other hand, the two-dimensional character of paired indicators makes them cumbersome in comparative work. It is noteworthy that both Burchardt (2008) and Bardasi and Wodon (2009) discuss single-country cases, contrary to the cross-country comparisons made with the integrated indicators DT and FDT.

Welfare indicators that have Time Integrated with Money (TIMs) may be designed in many variants, e.g. with or without basic needs and with either time or money as the outcome variable. Becker's (1965) 'potential income' that includes basic needs and takes money as its outcome variable is probably the earliest TIM. We will re-encounter potential income in the Discussion but focus here on DT, designed by Goodin et al. (2008), and FDT, designed by Hobbes et al. (in press).

As said in the Introduction, DT and FDT are conceptually equivalent, both referring to the time not used for basic needs (surplus time; ST). They were developed independently from each other, originating from time and welfare studies and from rural development studies, respectively. As a result, many differences between DT and FDT show up on the lower, methodological level. First, DT has been constructed for industrialized countries and FDT for the developing world. With that, the DT assessment method gives more attention to tax and welfare regimes, less attention to multiple livelihoods including subsistence, and less attention to non-child dependents (e.g. elderly or HIV/AIDS patients). Second, DT was developed as a system to interpret national statistics while the FDT framework was constructed through and for field-level work, paying more attention to mastering livelihood complexities and less to handling dataset complexities. Third, contrary to the DT methodology, the FDT framework keeps temporary or chronic deficiencies on separate categories (food, sleep, care, goods etc.) explicit until the very last moment before everything is collapsed into the single FDT indicator. Fourth, the DT approach ignores non-wage income components and consequently leaves people with only such income (e.g. people on welfare) out of the sample Goodin et al., 2008: 137). Finally, the DT and FDT methodologies differ in their approach to basic needs. In the DT system, they are largely relative, e.g. setting the income poverty line as 50 percent of the median income in a country. In the FDT system, basic needs are largely absolute, e.g. the FAO food calories standard. This requires more empirical work but makes FDT independent from national statistics and more open to explore scenarios such as the impact of changing prices, the addition of a child or sick to a household or the acquisition of a solar heater that frees female time from firewood gathering. The two methodologies will be described in the next sections.

3. The Freely Disposable Time (FDT) System

FDT assessment uses primary data on incomes, time use and expenditures, gathered through the FDT framework. The full framework can be found in Hobbes et al. (in press). It can handle different basic needs per household member, subsistence production, temporary or chronic deficits in basic needs, and all income elements such as wages, farm profits, remittances and 'time gifts' such as help from neighbors.

The composition of a household is important for FDT. A young child or sick person, for instance, adds to the household's basic needs but its freely disposable time does not make a relevant difference for the household. Therefore, the FDT assessment focuses on the productive adults (PAs), with the other members of the household present in the analysis in the form of adding to the basic needs that these PAs have to provide. Non-PA members may sometimes help out, e.g. doing chores; this is added as gifts or aid to the PAs' account. Hobbes et al. (in press) differentiate between male and female household members in terms of basic needs but the calculations then take the household as a whole, averaging over its PAs, hence (as yet) non-gendered.

As said, basic needs are largely absolute in the FDT system. For their field study in India, Hobbes et al. (in press) used a list based on literature and field observations, displayed in Table 1. Note that income-generation activities have no basic need; the necessary net income of the household can be calculated by adding all basic needs that require money inputs.

Table 1. Categories of activities and basic needs to be provided by the productive adults (PAs) of the households in the India case study of Hobbes et al. (in press). Basic needs are mainly guesstimates based on local informants and secondary sources. Cash is expressed in US$ per day (1 US$ = 40 INR = 0.7 euro). Care basic needs exclude care that can be given simultaneously with cooking, chores etc.

Activities and needs provided by PA	Basic needs in Indian case study
Physical inactivity (h/d)	8 per PA
Leisure (h/d)	2 per PA
Self care (h/d)	0.75 per PA female, 0.4 for PA male
Care (h/d)	1 for non-active elderly, plus 2 if 1 or 2 children, 3 if 3 or 4 children
Chores (h/d)	1 for small, 1.5 for average, 2 for big household
Cooking (h/d)	1.5 for small/average, 2.5 for big household
Food	1200 kcal/d for 0-4years, 1700 kcal/d for 4-8years, 2000 kcal/d for 8-12 years, 1967 kcal/d for PA female, 2540 kcal/d for PA male, etc. (FAO)
Water consumption	15 liter/d for small, 24 for average, 36 for big household
Fuel for cooking	10 GJ/cap/y
Shopping (h/d)	0.3 per household
School for PAs (h/d)	0
School for dependents ($/y)	10 per child of primary school age
Non-caloric consumption ($/d)	between 0.05 and 0.16 per household, depending on composition
Durable goods renewal /depreciation ($/y)	18 for small, 19 for average, 20 for big household (guesstimate)
Saving and investment	0
Income generation	0
Interest/rents/gifts paid ($/y)	32 per household (guesstimate)
House taxes, mortgage, rent, renewal ($/d)	0.03 per household (no taxes, only building materials)
Community work (h/d)	0.2 per household
Religious activities (h/d)	0.1 per PA

The FDT framework is organized by categories of 'things' that people spend time and/or money on (e.g. Table 1). Many of those have a basic need component. This classification can be adapted to fit local situations and research aims, as long as the whole remains consistent and exhaustive. Then, based on household-level time use, cash flow and basic needs data, a *time for the basic need* and a *time deficit or (more often) a time surplus* are generated for each category. The basic formula is that the time equivalent of any activity is calculated as the time spent on it plus the cash spent on it divided by the income per hour.

Keeping the time deficits and surpluses separate helps to identify chronic problems (deficits) of households. It also gives insight into how households may use temporary deficits to create more working time in periods of harvest, exams, disaster or sickness. Basic needs would not be basic needs if deficits could continue for a long time, however. In the longer run and in a principled outlook, therefore, ST is the aggregate of all surpluses minus all deficits. Hobbes et al. (in press) also provide a shortcut method of ST assessment that jumps over the separate calculations of deficits and surpluses. This comes close to the DT methodology described below.

4. THE DISCRETIONARY TIME (DT) SYSTEM

The DT system is designed to work with secondary data, such as national time use surveys, income distribution surveys and tax records. The full system is found in Goodin et al. (2008: 271-325). The great budgetary advantage of using available statistics comes at a certain cost. Many countries, especially in the developing world, lack the necessary statistics. Furthermore, DT system parameters can only be those that happen to be included in the statistics, hence excluding all sorts of phenomena that would appear to be relevant for people's real surplus time, such as informal, non-wage and subsistence incomes, mutual aid and time gifts. Another example concerns people's health status. Chronically ill adults constitute a burden rather than an asset for a household's surplus time, but the DT system can only distinguish between age brackets and not whether adults are productive or not. On the other hand, the DT system includes algorithms that allocate household-level burdens such as childcare cost to the individual household members, so that DT outcomes can be specified by type of adult, e.g. women in dual-earning households.

The DT system distinguishes only four time/money categories: personal care (including sleep), unpaid household labor (chores, childcare, cooking etc.), paid work/income, supplemented by spare time (see below). Within the paid work/income category, many further specifications are made, however, e.g. travel time, alimony and pension incomes, and contributions of spouses to child care cost. Basic needs in the categories are relative, extracted from the same time and money survey datasets as used for the DT assessment as a whole. For personal care, the basic need is set as 80 percent of the median in the sample. For unpaid household labor, the basic need is set as 50 percent of the median, corrected for the number of children. The necessary net income (income poverty line) is 50 percent of the median net income.

Like the FDT system, the DT assessment is organized by the categories. The first step is to establish the basic needs ('necessary times') for personal care and unpaid household labor. The next step is by far the most detailed one. It concerns the calculation of the necessary time of men and women in paid labor, which depends on travel times, childcare cost, contributions of spouses to this cost, household type, taxes and transfers, non-labor income components such as alimonies, the necessary net income and, in order to convert money into time, the hourly wage rate. Discretionary time (DT) per day is 24 minus the three necessary times. The DT system also looks at the actual times spent in the categories. This however is needed only in order to establish 'spare time' defined as 24 minus the actual times in the other three categories. Goodin et al. (2008) then define the difference between DT and spare time as the 'time pressure illusion' mentioned in the Introduction.

5. Surplus Time (ST) Properties Illustrated by a Hypothetical Household

This section gives a numerical example to illustrate the principles and properties of the ST concept, by means of the ST outcomes of various behavioral alternatives of a hypothetical single-actor household living a life of only six categories on which the actor spends time and/or money. These outcomes are then compared to those of some monetary welfare indicators. We have chosen for the FDT method to operationalize ST because of its adequacy in scenarios such as these. In order to illustrate principles as clearly as possible, all complexities have been avoided (hence, basic needs in purely time or money, income as a constant net wage rate, no subsistence production etc.).

Table 2 shows the FDT assessment. Each overarching column focuses on a different profile ('strategy') of how this actor spends his/her time and income. Within each profile, four columns summarize the FDT assessment. The first shows the basic needs (BN) on all categories. The second and third columns depict the time (EXh) and money (EX$) expenditures of the actor on these categories. These three together with the wage rate determine the equivalent time needed to satisfy the basic needs, calculated as the time needed plus the money needed divided by the wage rate. TSUR then is the surplus time, i.e. the equivalent time left after the basic needs have been fulfilled. The total of the time surpluses equals FDT for each profile.

The category of personal care (including sleep, self-care and leisure) has a basic need of 10 h/day. In the initial profile (first overarching column), the actor spends 14 h/day on this category, meaning that this category contains 4 h/day of surplus time. The basic need to keep the household in order is 2 h/day and the actor's time expenditure on chores and care is indeed 2 h/day. Consequently, this category contains no surplus. There is no basic need for labor. Labor time is always cancelled out, irrespective of wage and hours worked, by the cash received for it (= EX$ with a minus sign). Following the basic formula, working 8 hours per day at a wage rate of 1 $/h has a time equivalent of (8 h/day) – (8 $/day) / (1$/h) = 0 h/day. The cash earned is spent on other categories, e.g. to buy food, and then makes FDT visible there if the actor spends more on it than the basic need. In the first profile, the actor spends 5 $/day on food which, at the wage of 1 $/h, is equivalent to 5 hours of work. The basic need of the food category is 4 $/day. Thus, out of the 5 hours time/cash integrated time, 4 h/day is needed to satisfy the basic need and 1 h/day is surplus time (TSUR). Further, we see that the actor spends his/her remaining 3 $/day on other goods, which is equivalent to 3 h/day of time/cash integrated time. With a basic need of other goods of 2 $/day (for lighting, heating, clothes etc.), 1 h/day is FDT. All cash now being spent, nothing goes to the savings category. Adding up all time surpluses, FDT is 6 h/day. What the actor apparently does in this profile is to spend much of this freedom (4 out of the 6 hours) on leisure.

Table 2. Freely disposable time (FDT) profiles of a hypothetical single-person household. Only six cash/time categories are distinguished. The overarching columns denote various behavioral profiles of the actor. For each profile, the columns show the basic needs (BN), the empirical behavior in time and cash expenditures (EXh and EX$) and the resulting time/cash integrated time surpluses (Tsur) per day. FDT equals the sum of the surpluses. For comparison with FDT, the last four rows mention monetary indicators. The poverty line equals the cost of basic needs. The last row is income above the poverty line.

	Initial profile				Savings strategy				Household appliances				Result of investment				Price crisis				Time crisis			
	BN	EXh	EX$	TSUR (h)	BN	EXh	EX$	TSUR (h)	BN	EXh	EX$	TSUR (h)	BN	EXh	EX$	TSUR (h)	BN	EXh	EX$	TSUR (h)	BN	EXh	EX$	TSUR (h)
Personal care	10h	14	0	4	10h	10	0	0	10h	13	0	3	10h	14	0	4	10h	10	0	0	10h	8	0	-2
Chores/care	2h	2	0	0	2h	2	0	0	1h	2	0	1	2h	2	0	0	2h	2	0	0	8h	8	0	0
Paid labor	0	8	-8	0	0	12	-12	0	0	9	-9	0	0	8	-16	0	0	12	-12	0	0	8	-8	0
Food	4$	0	5	1	4$	0	4	0	4$	0	5	1	4$	0	5	0.5	10$	0	10	0	4$	0	5	1
Other goods	2$	0	3	1	2$	0	2	0	2$	0	4	2	2$	0	10	4	2$	0	2	0	2$	0	3	1
Saving/inv.	0	0	0	0	0	0	6	6	0	0	0	0	0	0	1	0.5	0	0	0	0	0	0	0	0
TOTALS		24	0	6		24	0	6		24	0	7		24	0	9		24	0	0		24	0	0
FDT (h/d)			6				6				7				9				0				0	
Unpaid time in FDT			4				0				4				4				0				-2	
Spare time			4				0				3				4				0				-2	
Income ($/d)			8				12				9				16				12				8	
Expend. ($/d)			8				6				9				16				12				8	
Poverty line ($/d)			6				6				6				6				12				6	
Income above PL ($/d)			2				6				3				10				0				2	

What could this actor do alternatively with this FDT? By way of example, the next profile in Table 2 shows the effect of a rigorous savings strategy in which the actor has given up all above-basic sleep, leisure, food and consumables and puts all FDT to work for the savings/investment category. Assuming a sufficient local labor demand to maintain the wage rate of 1 $/h, the actor now works for 12 h/day (24 minus the basic needs for personal care and chores), bringing in 12 $/day. This is the 'full income' as defined by Becker (1965). Out of the 12 $/day, 4 $/day is again needed for the basic needs of food and 2 $/day for other goods. The remaining 6 $/day, equivalent to (6 $/day) / (1 $/h) = 6 h/day of FDT, is in the savings category. Note that all the while, the FDT total has stayed the same 6 h/day. In the FDT method, the actor is not assessed as better off (higher FDT) when working more hours. Neither is the actor assessed as poorer when foregoing luxuries in order to save, invest or leisure. He does get a higher FDT, however, when wages rise compared to basic need prices, or when investments begin to pay off, as the next two profiles show.

The third profile in Table 2 depicts a situation after the actor has decided to buy time-saving household appliances from the savings. The basic need of the chores and care has now dropped to 1 h/day. Consequently, FDT rises to 7 h/day. The actor may decide, as people often do, to maintain the hours worked on chores (EXh), but now to have the house in conspicuously tip-top condition. If the actor then also decides to retain one of the extra working hours, he/she can spend the extra 1 $/day for instance on consumer goods.

Alternatively, the actor may decide to invest the savings in some 'deep', out-of-poverty strategy, e.g. through vocational training or, if he/she is a farmer, hiring labor for building terraces for a higher yield or a new crop. In the fourth profile, we assume that as a result of this investment, the actor's wage rate has risen to 2 $/h. Bringing the sleep, self-care, leisure, chores and labor time back to the initial levels, the actor now earns 16 $/day, out of which he/she spends 1 extra $/day on food, which now costs only 0.5 h/day of FDT due to the doubled wage rate. Of the remaining 11 $/day, the actor spends 10 on other goods, leaving 1 $/day (0.5 h/day) for savings. FDT stands at 9 h/day.

Real poverty, as said, is when FDT = 0. In Table 2 real poverty has been simulated in two ways. One is a price crisis in which the cost of the basic food basket has jumped to 10 $/day. The second is a time crisis in which the chores and care basic need has jumped to 8 hours per day because the actor has been charged with the care of and AIDS patient. The fifth profile illustrates the price crisis. The only option left for the actor is to work maximum hours, 12 per day in this case, for bare survival, spending all time and generated income on basic needs. FDT now is zero, with the actor trapped in poverty without any freedoms left to invest in an escape.

The time crisis is depicted in the last profile. The actor has decided to keep up the little bits of above-basic food and goods and therefore needs to continue working for 8 hours per day. The result is a deficit in the time for sleep, self-care and leisure. This way, the actor is systematically undermining his/her basic health and social functioning. Poverty erodes people's health in many ways, and this is one of them. Other poverty scenarios could be added to Table 2, e.g. showing how declining natural resources (forest, soils) necessitate people to search longer for firewood (creating an increasing basic time need in the chores category) and reduce agricultural yields for the same labor hours, creating a decreasing return to labor (wage rate). The general conclusion may be clear, however, namely that FDT, as any other well-designed ST system, captures the basic features of all livelihood profiles.

6. ST Properties Versus Those of Pure Time and Money Indicators

The outcomes of the FDT assessment may be compared with those of pure time and money indicators in the same profiles. The lower rows of Table 2 are designed for that purpose.

The first two rows below FDT are 'unpaid time in FDT' and 'spare time'. The former is obviously not a pure time measure because it contains FDT. It has been taken up however to support the discussion of the underemployment caveat of ST indicators in Section 8. 'Unpaid time in FDT' is defined as the hours during which people do other things than paid labor in their FDT. Quantitatively in the terms of Table 2, it is 24 hours per day minus basic hours for personal care, minus basic hours for chores and care minus actual hours in paid labor. The next row, 'spare time', is defined in Goodin et al. (2008: 52) as 24 hours per day minus the actual times spent in paid labor, unpaid household labor and personal care. These coincide with the actual time spent on paid labor and chores/care and the basic time needed for personal care in Table 2 because we assume that above basic personal care is leisure time. Spare time is a measure of how busy people are. With spare time at zero, the only things you do are sleep, brush your teeth and be busy with unpaid (household) and/or paid (market) work. The difference between spare time and FDT is what Goodin et al. (2008) call the time pressure illusion.

Incidentally because of the many simplifications implicit in Table 2, spare time and unpaid time in FDT often come out the same. Conceptually however, spare time is the pure time measure and the focus of the discussion here. The salient point in the spare time outcomes in Table 2 is the two ways to have zero spare time. One way is to freely choose for long working hours ('savings strategy' profile). The other is to be forced into working all possible hours in order to supply basic needs (price and time crisis profiles). The one actor is looking with pride at a growing bank account. The other is looking at hopelessness. This phenomenon of having the same indicator outcome while being so different in livelihood terms is caused by that spare time does not take the money aspect into account. Note that FDT does differentiate between the two types of profile.

Income and expenditure, shown in the next rows of Table 2, are the most widely used welfare indicators. The first point to note is that the actor that moves from the initial profile to the savings strategy (profile 2) is assessed as better off than before according to the income indicator but worse off than before according to the expenditure indicator (*cf.* Van Campenhout 2006: 410). It could be argued that this discrepancy, caused as it is by the extreme strategy choice, will be rare in the real world and no fundamental problem. This is different for the last two profiles. In the price crisis and time crisis cases, both monetary indicators assess the actor as equal or even better off than in the initial profile, while the FDT outcomes show that the actor is fully trapped in poverty. The crises force the actor to work all possible hours but the raised basic needs swallow all or nearly all of the increased income.

The anomaly that rising incomes and expenditures can coincide with increasing poverty is largely removed when the cost of basic needs are entered into the picture, e.g. subtracting the cost of basic needs from the actual income. The cost of basic needs in the profiles of Table 2 is 6 $/day, except in the price crisis profile where it is 12 $/day. The bottom line of Table 2 gives the incomes above this cost-of-basic-needs (CBN) poverty line. This indicator stands at zero in the price crisis case, in accordance with FDT. The monetary indicator has picked up the monetary crisis well. It does not pick up the effect the *time* crisis however (last column), where the CBN indicator stands at the same level as in the initial profile even though life of the actor has drastically turned to the worse and FDT stands at zero.

We can conclude that in this analysis,

(1) When changes of income, expenditure and working hours are free choices as in the first two profiles, the pure time and money indicators change with them but not FDT. In FDT terms, these free choices are only different ways of doing with FDT what one prefers to do, without changing FDT itself.
(2) Time-saving acquisitions (profile 3) always improve FDT but are recorded by the pure money and time indicators only insofar the acquisitions lead to more working hours (as in Table 2) or to more leisure hours, respectively.
(3) Financial livelihood progress, e.g. the improved wage rate compared to local prices as in profile 4, is always picked up by FDT and the monetary indicators but not by the time indicators if time use of the household does not change with it. (And if people would increase their working hours because they now like the work better, spare time would even decrease.)
(4) Livelihood crises plunging people into real poverty can be fully misinterpreted by the income and expenditure indicators. This improves if cost of basic needs is subtracted from income or expenditure. Still then however, a 'time crisis' due to chronic sickness, natural resource degradation or any other cause will often be missed by monetary indicators. Time indicators do pick up this type of crisis. FDT duly records both.

Summarizing, it shows that in this analysis, FDT (as any other well-designed ST indicator) tends to ignore changes in household behaviors that are their free choice. It properly reports real progress due to improved time-saving and money-making efficiencies, however. Besides, describes real poverty due to both deteriorating wages compared to prices and heavier time burdens. Pure time and money indicators often pick up changes that are arguably less relevant because they mainly express preferences, and often miss out on relevant changes, e.g. moving into poverty, that are not expressed primarily in their own area of measurement (time or money, respectively).

We may add at this point that ST indicators do have their disadvantages, limitations and caveats too. These will be discussed in Sections 8 and 9.

7. Results of First DT and FDT Applications

This section gives a short overview of the first empirical applications of the ST concept, in order to supply a basic feel of typical outcomes and also to prove that Discretionary time (DT) and Freely disposable time (FDT) are not only applicable on hypothetical households but robust methodologies that can handle real-world complexities. As a primer, we start out with a non-ST study, namely the paired time/money indicator work of Burchardt (2008) on the UK.

Using relative poverty lines of 60 percent of the medians, Burchardt (2008) finds that some 10 percent of the adults is time poor, some 20 percent is income poor and about 2 percent are both. The households of the latter group (which we would denote as having an ST of around zero) contain some 7 percent of the children. Of special interest to the general ST caveat that will be discussed in the next section, Burchardt also studies the paired time-and-money *capabilities* of households. These are defined as all income/free time combinations that households have if they would allocate their free time differently, e.g. by doing less or more paid work. She finds some 2 percent of the households as being in time and money capability poverty, i.e. time poor and money poor *and* unable to improve their situation by more efficient time allocation. In our terms, this would be expressed as that not only their actual but also their potential ST lies around zero. This, we could say, is not only real poverty but the real poverty trap. Burchardt (2008: 78-80) also discusses two examples of actual versus potential time-money positions. One is from a dual earner household that could earn some 10 percent more but more efficient time allocation between the spouses. The second is a lone mother that keeps much more free time than needed in view of her obligations and accepts that her income is only some 40 percent of what she could earn. In fact, she lives below the income poverty line without however being disabled or stating to be looking for work. Burchardt does not provide an explanation; the mother might have some unknown disability or may have been afraid to report non-legal work and income.

Based on time and income surveys, Goodin et al. (2008) report on DT outcomes in Australia, the US, Germany, France, Sweden and Finland. Overall in these countries, it is found that ST is around 11.5 hours per day. Average spare time being found at around 4.7 hours per day, people have some 7 hours per day of 'time pressure illusion', as Goodin et al. put it. The largest differences found in ST are between dual earners without children that command 13.0 hours per day of surplus time (with Sweden highest at ST = 13.6) and lone mothers with children that stand at an average surplus time of 8.4 hours per day (with the US lowest at ST = 6.8). These figures concern averages over the groups, hence with all incomes and child numbers included. Separate households will of course show more extremes.

Hobbes et al. (in press) give fieldwork-based FDT outcomes of separate households with complex livelihoods in peri-urban Kashimpur village, close to Calcutta (India) and three households in the Netherlands. Surplus time in the Indian households varies between ST = 5.4 and ST = 10.8 hours per day. The Dutch outcomes vary between ST = 2.3 for a lone mother with three children and a minimum wage and ST = 10.5 hours per day for a middle-class household with three children and an *au pair* helper.

The DT and FDT outcomes allow for some comparison. First of all it may be noted that the ranges of surplus times in the Western societies overlap with those in India. The lowest ST is found in the Netherlands, the surplus times of the ST-poorest households in Kashimpur lie close to that of the lone mothers in the US and the middle class in the West have much in common with the best-off in Kashimpur. The ST indicator is not only egalitarian between the rich and the poor but also between the West and the South.

In the FDT study, the *au pair* helper makes a difference of 1.7 hours per day of surplus time in the Dutch middle-class household. This resonates with the great attention given to childcare regimes in Goodin et al. (2008). Possibilities for one-to-one DT/FDT comparisons are limited because Goodin et al.'s outcomes represent group averages. The group that should be closest to Hobbes et al.'s (in press) middle-class household with three children is Goodin et al.'s (2008: 89) 'German couples with children', which stands at a mean ST of 11.2 hours per adult per day. The three children in the FDT example being higher than the average number of children in the German group, the best comparison is with the FDT case in which the third child is compensated for by the *au pair* help. This ST is 10.5 hours per adult per day. In other words, even though the two methodologies are different as discussed in Section 2, the results do not seem dissimilar, which may strengthen confidence in both methods.

Goodin et al. (2008: 92) contains group data on lone parents, as remarked already. No comparison is possible with the lone parent example of Hobbes et al. (in press) that has an ST = 2.3 hours per day because that concerns a minimum-wage extreme. Burchardt (2008: 27, 69) shows, however, that figures around ST = 0 for lone parents appear quite possible in Western societies. One of her examples is a lone parent with two children and a moderately low wage rate, who is assessed as below both the time-poverty line and the money-poverty line in the paired indicator graph.

8. Denotation and Connotation: ST Metric Validity and Caveats

What does it mean to have much or little Surplus Time (ST)? It serves at this point to make a difference between a metric's *denotation*, i.e. what it is really meant to 'be' or fully represent, and the metric's *connotations*, i.e. the phenomena it can usually be assumed to correlate with. For the income metric, for instance, its denotation can be something like the net inflow of liquid or liquefiable goods into a household, which is then usually assumed to correlate with its connotations of having enough consumer goods, ability to save, welfare or well-being. Logically however, these connotations depend on more than income only. In order to buy consumer goods, or instance, local markets and social norms come into play. And in order to augment one's well-being with these goods, actors need knowledge and institutions.

The upshot of the distinction between denotation and connotation lies in the degree of severity of caveats. A denotation caveat is true invalidity. For instance, calling 'income' only the net cash flows of households that have substantial subsistence production (e.g. growing all their own rice as many Asian farmers do) disables the whole metric. The same would hold if we would say that ST measures a households' freedoms while in fact households would have substantial freedoms left even of ST = 0, or households with the same ST would enjoy substantially different levels of freedoms.

Connotation caveats on the other hand, are to be looked at differently. We all know that income and well-being correlate to some extent but not in any one-to-one manner, as if the relatively poor cannot live a full life and rich people cannot be unhappy. Stating that over and over as a caveat of the income measure does not make much sense. Connotation caveats are most relevant to identify when common sense tends to leave us unaware of them. One example is the connotation of ST with potential income. The logic of this connotation is strong, because ST denotes the time you are free to act with, hence including going all-out to the labor market and maximize income (see the second profile in Table 2). Contexts of underemployment or legal regulations may preclude this, however, implying substantial mismatches between ST and potential income. This then is a hidden, and therewith relevant, connotation caveat of ST.

Denotation: Surplus Time = Freedoms Time

Surplus time, by definition, is the time you have left after fulfilling the basic needs you have to fulfill. It represents people's freedom to enjoy the present or to invest in the future (*cf.* Alkire, 2006: 246) and indeed appears to operationalize much of Sen's (1999) seminal freedoms concept. "ST = Freedoms" is therefore the shortcut denotation of ST, visible also in the subtitles of the DT and FDT publications. We should continue to bear in mind, however, that ST in fact is freedom *time*, and it depends on the local situation to what degree freedom time can be transformed into actual freedoms. In prison or *purdah*, you have much ST but few freedoms. In general, ST does not denote the full array of freedoms including political participation, full self-realization and so on.

This being said, the denotation of ST as freedoms remains a very strong one. Let us take as a radical example of a household in which the parents, in spite of a relatively low wage rate, have chosen to have five children. It may well be that the parents can make ends meet only by devoting all their time to satisfy the household's basic needs. In other words, they will be assessed with ST = 0. Are they poor? Their income level may not be dramatically low, and in Africa, for instance, they may even be locally considered rich (five children! and all basic needs supplied!). Are they unhappy? Probably they are when having again risen at night to console the baby but on the whole, they may feel quite satisfied with the situation they have chosen for. All the while, it remains true that their freedoms are zero. They have no choice but to continue with what they are doing, no resilience against any disaster or deterioration in their economic context, no capacity to engage in any other livelihood strategy. In other words, FDT = 0 still means freedoms = 0. That is why Hobbes et al. (in press) strongly emphasize that for any household, ST is "the basis for its adaptive capacity, its capacity to invest and the negative of its vulnerability." How this basis works out in any context depends much on that context, but more ST is always more freedoms and more development capacity. Hobbes (2010: 167) extends this idea to an FDT-based community-level indicator of development capacity.

Any caveat in this "ST = freedoms time" denotation, as said, is a basic one. Is there one, especially one that common sense would not readily identify? The answer may be approached by noting that people may display inefficiencies in time use, in the sense that an alternative behavior would give them more free time. An example that may often occur is Burchardt's (2008) household that could have 10 percent more income with a more efficient time allocation. Goodin et al. (2008: 11) mention a hypothetical but probably often occurring example of a corporate lawyer spending one hour per day on cleaning her house instead of hiring a helper at a lower wage rate than her own. Goodin et al. add that this brings no validity problem to their DT measure. They are right if and insofar the inefficient behaviors take place within people's suplus time. In the FDT system, for instance, these choices become visible in people's FDT profile, without affecting the FDT level itself (see Table 2). Inefficient behaviors in the provision of *basic needs* do affect ST, however. In the lawyer example, if this house cleaning is part of basic cleaning, her behavior gives her less ST than she would have had by hiring a helper. Does that undermine ST validity? Not if the behavior is not a free choice, e.g. if she is afraid of helpers. Her actual, reduced ST then exactly represents the reduced freedoms she has due to her inflexibility. If her cleaning is a free choice however, her freedoms are in fact higher than her ST level displays, because she now has some freedoms hidden in her non-ST time for basic needs provision. Many other examples may be given, e.g. a household preferring to supply all basic child care by itself in spite of available cheap daycare, or a farmer desiring to be independent and preferring a low-productive subsistence crop over an available cash crop for which he could have bought more food. In general, people's total 'freedom time' is their FDT as assessed *plus* the time effect of freely chosen inefficiencies in basic needs provision, and the latter component will often differ from zero. This could be called the Preferred Inefficiencies in Basic Needs Provision caveat in ST.

By definition, households may always remove these inefficiencies and create more ST. Also, the ST assessor may try to remove the inefficiencies on paper, e.g. calculating how much ST the corporate lawyer would have if she would hire a helper. This is in fact what Burchardt (2008) does when calculating her time-money capability graph of all possible time-money allocations of a household. A 'corrected' or 'potential' ST with the preferred inefficiencies in basic needs provision removed would theoretically be a superior measure, because of the certainty that actors cannot create more ST than this. As remarked already, a *potential ST* at the zero level is a stronger poverty trap indicator than actual ST at that level. In order to calculate potential ST however, we would need to know what inefficiencies in basic needs provision reduce ST to what extent, and whether these are really free preferences. Going after these questions will probably only pay off when pursuing specific questions such as the effect of subsistence versus cash crops or the happiness that may come with less materialistic lifestyles, or when studying specific groups such as, say, the Amish or lone parents who may feel locked out of the labor market (Burchardt 2008: 80). Our proposal, therefore, is to always stay alert on the fact that households will often have some possibilities to fine-tune choices in their basic needs provision and with that to enlarge their ST, but accept plain, actual ST as a good enough indicator in the majority of cases. This is analogous to accepting plain income or expenditure as good enough monetary indicators, even though we know that people are often not efficient income maximizers (Ellis, 2000) or consumption optimizers (Linssen et al., 2010).

Connotation 1. Connecting ST with Welfare and Potential Income

As said in the Introduction, we here regard poverty and welfare as primarily economic concepts, different from multi-dimensional well-being or happiness. Poverty and welfare are more than income, however, since money and time interplay strongly in the economics of daily life. This has inspired both the DT and FDT variants of the ST concept. Now is the time to look back and ask: does Surplus Time indeed measure poverty and welfare? Can we indeed say that households with more ST are better off than households with less ST, not only in terms of freedoms but also in terms of poverty and welfare? In general, of course, the answer will tend to be affirmative, since ST is the time people may freely choose to do paid work, as they often will. Finding general correlations does not subtract from exceptions, however, as we already saw in the five-children family example.

The real caveat to search here is when exceptions are unexpected and systematic, and this concerns underemployment the 'potential income' interpretation of ST. Potential income is what people could earn by devoting all their ST to paid labor. The step from actual to potential income requires an estimation of the wage rate that people would earn during the hours not worked at present. These hours are usually less than their ST because people usually work at least some of their ST. In other words, the estimation regards the unpaid hours in ST. In Table 2, these are the 3 to 4 hours per day in several profiles. Would people earn the same wage rate as for the hours they currently work? The local context is decisive here. For female part-time workers in the UK, for instance, the wage rate of the extra hours will tend to be higher than of the current ones (Burchard, 2008: 65). In contexts of chronic underemployment, however, as in many of the lagging economies of Sub-Sahara Africa, the reverse may well be true. People may work a few hours per day for a reasonable return (e.g. on the farm) but then continue working for much lower rates, e.g. as laborer. Hobbes et al. (2007) describe a case from Vietnam where people first fully exploit their most profitable land use option and then cascade down to other land use types with ever lower returns. This will create low income rates overall and with that, a low calculated ST. In order to estimate the potential income that people could earn if they would decide to work all these ST hours, the lowest wage rate of the local cascade should of course be taken for the extra hours.

Underemployment can be more severe than this, however. Income-generating options to fill the presently non-worked hours may simply be *absent*. In that case, there is nothing to do with ST that generates income. This underemployment caveat differs much from the preceding one. Preferred inefficiencies in basic needs provision only result in a generally slightly too pessimistic ST figure. Severe underemployment results in a strongly over-optimistic ST interpretation in a specific type of context. In situations of severe underemployment, either the DT or FDT indicator should be joined with a monetary measure or the assessment should follow the paired time/money strategy. Both ways, severely underemployed households can be identified.

Connotation 2. Connecting ST with Well-Being and Happiness

Would ST correlate with subjective well-being and happiness? The general logic is that it should, since surplus time, by definition, allows people to pursue the things they prefer to do or have, e.g. do paid work for luxuries, leisure or bake one's own bread. There are few data available that combine ST with happiness (well-being, life satisfaction). Goodin et al. (2008: 58), report on a study that combined DT with life satisfaction in Germany, and in which DT has a stronger correlation than spare time with life satisfaction and an equal strength as household income. The overall explanation of variance remains relatively low, probably because well-being will always depend on more than time and money, e.g. including health, quality of relationships and relative positions with respect to the neighbors and the past. The first two profiles in Table 2, for instance, have the same ST but differ in income, sleep and self-care, savings and food. What creates more well-being depends on the actor's preferences for these factors. It remains quite likely, however, that all these households with FDT at 6 or 7 have a higher well-being than those with ST = 0 (last two profiles). Note also that spare time is not likely to be a good indicator of well-being in this Table; the second profile has a spare time of zero but since this is free choice, well-being may be unaffected or even higher than in the initial profile with 4 hours of spare time per day.

At this point, it serves to briefly go back to the general 'preferred inefficiencies of basic needs provision' caveat of ST. If people prefer basic needs provision activities that are not fully ST-maximizing, this has different consequences for the interpretation of ST. If they would remove these preferred inefficiencies in order to maximize ST, their ST would rise indeed. Their freedoms would remain the same, because they only shift freedoms from the basic needs provision to the non-basic, ST time compartment. Their potential income would increase. Finally, assuming that their preferences are consistent with their well-being, their well-being would be reduced. In this case, more ST does not mean more well-being.

9. INDICATOR CHOICE

This section explores some issues of indicator choice in research and statistics, structured along a line of ST 'versus' monetary indicators. We first look at the purely scientific merits and then move a broader picture.

GDP per capita is a well-known monetary indicator of wealth. GDP is often criticized from an ecological point of view. What does the GDP of a country mean if the country is at the same time accumulating waste, depleting its resources and overfishing the ocean? Many proposals have been made to establish a corrected, 'sustainable GDP' (e.g. De Groot, 1992: 242). At this point, we may note that exactly the same issue can be raised against the ST or income indicators. What does the ST or income of a farming household mean if that household is at the same time accumulating toxic substances, mining its soil and over-exploiting the village forest? The basic rule appears to be that many validity issues pertaining to monetary indicators also pertain to integrated time/money indicators, and *vice versa*. People may not be ST maximizers but neither income maximizers, and like potential ST, potential income may be the theoretically superior indicator. The income value of ST has its perfect mirror in the time value of freely disposable income. How much time can money buy? Can local contexts also display over-employment, with many people unable to work less for less income (Goodin et al., 2008)?

Therefore, any discussion on the scientific pros and cons of integrated time/money versus purely monetary indicators should focus on where these indicators really differ rather than on what they have in common, and be strongly tied to the research aim. Based on the findings in the present paper, the following general observations may be relevant.

(1) Simply because they are new, time/money integrated indicators can open up new avenues of looking at societies, households and development, e.g. connected with welfare regimes, environmental degradation, class formation, well-being, poverty traps, unpaid work, gender, HIV/AIDS and many other issues.
(2) Probably, all indicators have their own specific interpretation caveats apart from the ones they have in common. As discussed for ST, for instance, this is its interpretation towards potential income in contexts of severe underemployment. Yet the possibility to at least approach potential income is a relative strength of ST (and the paired indicators), because monetary indicators lack this possibility.
(3) Around ST = 0, there are no ST interpretation uncertainties because there is no ST. In that range, therefore, interpretation uncertainties cannot outweigh the intrinsic power of the integrated ST metric compared to one-dimensional time or money indicators. ST = 0 may well be a uniquely valid universal poverty line.
(4) More ST will quite often mean more potential income and well-being, but certainly not always, as discussed. The freedoms and development potential denotation of

FDT appears to be quite straightforward however, also in the sense that within each local context and for each household, more ST always means more freedoms and more development capacity.

Any decision on what will be the focal indicators of research and statistics – ST, monetary indicators, paired indicators or any mix – will involve trade-offs. Data needs of integrated or paired metrics, requiring as they do information on time use as well as cash flows, will be higher than of mono-dimensional indicators such as income. Moreover, needs of comparability should be considered. If these are relatively low, it may serve to maintain more intra-group detail and keep time and money outcomes separate in a paired rather than an integrated indicator.

Indicator choice can also be subject of studies expressly designed for the purpose. Within the ST concept, for instance, FDT and DT have not yet been subject to systematic comparison. One strategy here could be to look how far the FDT framework can come in the interpretation of national surveys compared to DT, and the other way around, looking how the DT framework can come in field research compared to FDT. Within the broader MIT group other concepts than ST may be tried out, and nothing stands in the way of assessing a wide array of indicators (e.g. monetary, ST, paired indicators and subjective well-being) in a single, integrated data gathering effort, and then compare their cost, reliability, cross-correlations, linkages with context, caveats and validity towards broader concepts such as chronic and temporal poverty, subjective potential income, investments and other future-oriented behaviours, happiness and others.

10. CONCLUSION

This chapter has introduced two methods (DT and FDT) to integrate the time and money aspects of livelihoods into a single metric. This indicator, called Surplus Time (ST), is defined as the time that people have left after fulfilling the basic needs that they need to supply for themselves and their dependents. Basic needs comprise physiological needs, food, shelter and care needs, social obligations, basic consumer goods and so on. ST is the freedom that people have to engage, within the range of their agency and options available in the local context, in activities that generate above-basic consumables, in physical or social investments for the future, in above-basic caregiving or leisure. An ST of zero hours per day implies that people need all their time to satisfy their household's basic time and money needs and are trapped in work for bare survival; ST = 0 is the poverty line. A somewhat higher ST (e.g. 2 hours per day) may be necessary for households to invest in out-of-poverty strategies.

In the FDT ('Freely Disposable Time') methodology, the actual income rate of the household is used to convert money into time needs for each category that the household spends time and/or money on. Households can have deficits or surpluses on each category, expressed in hours per day. The total of surpluses minus deficits is ST. Independent from FDT, Goodin et al. (2008) have developed the DT ('Discretionary Time') methodology. Different from FDT, DT takes basic needs as largely relative, does not distinguish between separate time surpluses and deficits and is more geared to work with survey statistics in developed countries.

The FDT framework has been applied to complex livelihoods of peri-urban farming households in India, and some cases from the Netherlands. In India, ST was assessed as between 5.4 and 10.8 hours per day. In the Netherlands, a middle-class household with three small children was found to have ST = 8.8 hours per day, while a minimum-wage lone mother with three small children stood at ST = 2.3 hours per day. The DT framework has been applied on survey datasets from five developed societies and found ST to be 11.5 hours per day on average. The cases in which FDT and DT outcome could be compared (middle-class households with children in Western Europe) showed good similarity with ST at 10.5 and 11.2 hours per day, respectively.

Being a single quantitative measure, ST is suitable for comparative and monitoring purposes, comprising the whole rage of rich and poor, rural and urban. Its methodologies also allows for scenario studies, e.g. on the effects of different livelihood strategies, the effects of macro-level shifts in prices, wages, tax or welfare regimes, and the effects of micro-level changes e.g. children being born, HIV/AIDS spreading, soils degrading, wells drilled close to homes, or solar cookers supplanting firewood gathering. Other ST applications may work the other causal way around, e.g. studying the effect of changes of ST on investments in education, social capital, business initiatives or land quality.

ST expressing as it does people's freedoms to engage in any activity available and allowed in their context, can be expected to correlate well with potential income and well-being. Several caveats should be kept in mind, however. The most basic one is that people may have preferences that lead to inefficiencies in the provision of their basic needs. In these cases, people have some freedoms 'hidden' in their non-ST time, and people may in fact have more freedoms and a higher potential income than suggested by their ST. Apart form this general caveat (which is acceptable in most cases in our view), the interpretation of what the value of ST is to households always requires caution. First of all, the local context (markets, regulations, social norms) determines what people can actually do with their freely disposable time. Contexts of severe underemployment represent a real caveat here, especially when ST is interpreted towards potential income. Adding an income indicator is advisable here.

Several issues of metric validity are shared or mirrored between ST and monetary indicators. For instance, both ST and income may be environmentally unsustainable, and households may not be fully maximizing their ST or income. A number of relative strengths of ST appear to stand out. They are its capacity to shed a new light on persistent problems, its capacity to capture time burdens of households, its openness to assess potential incomes in contexts without severe underemployment, its possible connection with well-being and its straightforward interpretation as a metric of freedoms. Finally, ST = 0 may be a very robust universal poverty line.

Final decisions of indicator choice involved many practical and scientific arguments, as discussed in the preceding section. Major reasons to adopt ST or some likewise integrated time/money metric are its strong validity to gauge what may be called real poverty, its (cautious) connections with potential incomes and actual well-being and its straightforward interpretation as people's freedom of choice. This freedom is a prime value in itself and also a key element in the development capacity of any person, household or community.

AUTHORS' INFORMATION

Marieke Hobbes holds a PhD in rural development studies, based on empirical work in the Philippines, Vietnam and India. She was involved in projects on material flow analysis, sustainable land use, arsenic pollution abatement and the position of smallholders in globalizing markets.

Wouter de Groot is professor in social environmental science at Leiden University and Radboud University, the Netherlands, with current research interests in sustainable land use, water management, environmental ethics and ecosystem services in Europe and Africa.

REFERENCES

Alkire, S. (2006). Needs and capabilities. In S. Reader (Ed.), *The philosophy of need* (pp: 229-251). Cambridge: Cambridge University Press

Bardasi, E. and Wodon, Q. (2009). Working long hours and having no choice; time poverty in Guinea. *Policy Research Working Paper 4961*. Washington, DC: The World Bank.

Becker, G.S. (1965). A theory on the allocation of time. *Economic Journal,* 75, 493-517.

Burchardt, T. (2008). Time and income poverty. *CASEreport 57*. London: London School of Economics.

De Groot, W.T. (1992). *Environmental science theory; Concepts and methods in a one-world, problem-oriented paradigm*. Amsterdam: Elsevier Science Publishers. On the web at https://openaccess.leidenuniv.nl/dspace/bitstream/1887/11548/1/11_511_207.pdf.

Douthitt, R.A. (2000). "Time to do the chores?" Factoring home-production needs into measures of poverty. *Journal of Family and Economic Issues*, 21(1), 7-22.

Ellis, F. (2000). *Rural livelihoods and diversity in developing countries*. Oxford: Oxford University Press.

Folbre,N. (2004). A theory of the misallocation of time. In N. Folbre and M. Bittman (Eds.), *Family time: the social organization of care* (pp.: 7-24). London: Routledge.

Gershuny, J. (2005). Busyness as a badge of honour for the new superordinate working class. *Institute for Social and Economic Research working paper 2005-9*. Colchester: University of Essex.

Giampietro, M. (2004). *Multi-scale integrated analysis of agroecosystems*. Florida: CRC Press.

Gomiero, T. and Giampietro, M. (2001). Multiple-scale integrated analysis of farming systems: The Thuong Lo Commune (Vietnamese uplands) case study. *Population and Environment, 22*(3), 315-352.

Goodin, R. E., Rice, J. M., Parpo, A. and Eriksson, L. (2008). *Discretionary Time: A new measure of freedom*. Cambridge: Cambridge University Press.

Grünbühel,C. M. and Schandl, H. (2005). Using land-time-budgets to analyse farming systems and poverty alleviation policies in the Lao PDR. *International Journal of Global Environmental Issues, 5*(3/4), 142-180.

Hobbes, M. (2005) Material flow accounting of rural communities: Principles and outcomes in South East Asia. *International Journal of Global Environmental Issues, 5*(3/4), 194-224.

Hobbes, M, Stalpers, S. I. P., Kooijman, J., Le Thi Thu Than, Trinh Khanh Chi and Phan Thi Ahn Dao (2007). Material flows in a social context: A Vietnamese case study combining the material flow analysis and action-in-context-frameworks. *Journal of Industrial Ecology,* 11(1), pp. 141-159.

Hobbes, M. (2010). *Figuring rural development: Concepts and cases of land use, sustainability and integrative indicators*. Leiden: Leiden University Press. On the web at https://openaccess.leidenuniv.nl/dspace/handle/1887/15036.

Hobbes, M., De Groot, W.T., Van der Voet, E. and S. Sarkhel (in press). *Freely Disposable Time: A Time and Money Integrated Measure of Poverty and Freedom.* In re-review with an international journal.

Linssen, R., Van Kempen, L. and Kraaykamp, G. (2010). Subjective well-being in rural India: the curse of conspicuous consumption. *Social Indicator Research*, online, DOI 10.1007/s11205-010-9635-2.

Pastore, G., Giampietro M., and Ji Li. (1999). Conventional and land-time budget analysis of rural villages in Hubei province, China. *Critical Reviews in Plant Sciences, 18*(3), 331-357.

Reardon, T. and Vosti, S. A. (1995). Links between rural poverty and the environment in developing countries: Asset categories and investment poverty. *World Development*, 23(1), 1495-1506.

Sen, A.K. (1999). *Development as freedom.* New York: Knopf Press.

Van Campenhout, B. F. H. (2006). Locally adapted poverty indicators derived from participatory wealth rankings: A case of four villages in rural Tanzania. *Journal of African Economies,* 16(3), 406-438.

Vickery, C. (1977). The time-poor, a new look at poverty. *The Journal of Human Resources*, 12(1), 27-48.

In: Social Indicators: Statistics, Trends…
Editor: Candace M. Baird

ISBN 978-1-61122-841-0

Chapter 3

INTRODUCING THE CONCEPT OF FUNCTIONAL TIME USE (FTU) AS A TOOL FOR MEASURING THE "LABOUR BURDEN": A CASE STUDY FROM THE BOLIVIAN AMAZON

Lisa Ringhofer
Institute of Social Ecology, University of Klagenfurt, Austria

ABSTRACT

This chapter introduces the concept of functional time use (FTU). To this end, the first part is devoted to a review of time use studies with special consideration to labour time, followed by introducing the theoretical, conceptual and methodological framework within which functional time use is embedded. The third part of this chapter presents the empirical case study results in time use from Campo Bello, an indigenous Tsimane' community in the Bolivian Amazon. The research findings are presented along the following lines: first, the socially disposable time at the system level is discussed for different age/sex groups along their life-cycle. The second research interest entails a more holistic approach and scrutinises the number of person-hours invested in the reproduction of the four different social subsystems: the person system, the household system, the community system and the economic system. The third subsection looks into locally implemented strategies to increase the productivity of time. Finally, this chapter also argues for the FTU approach to serve a useful purpose in planning and monitoring the impact of development projects.

1. INTRODUCTION

Functional time use (FTU) is a concept embedded within the sociometabolic transition studies paradigm which describes patterns of society-nature interactions. Transition studies look at common historic and contemporary development trajectories (so-called sociometabolic "regimes") from a biophysical perspective and establish socio-economic and environmental pressure indicators. Each regime displays a certain metabolic profile—in its use of material, energy, land and time—and each of these resource use patterns causes certain environmental and social impacts. This chapter deals with the social impacts caused by the life time/labour time ratio of a social system. This will be done through the application of functional time use. This approach provides a functional perspective on daily time use at the social system level that aims to give insights into the specific opportunities, challenges and the "labour burden" a society, or certain subgroups, are facing.

The chapter consists of four parts. The first section is devoted to a review of time use studies with special consideration to labour time. Consequently, the theoretical, conceptual and methodological framework of functional time use is presented and discussed. The third part of this chapter presents the empirical case study results in time use from Campo Bello, an indigenous Tsimane' community in the Bolivian Amazon. The research findings are presented along the following lines: first, the socially disposable time at the system level is discussed for different age/sex groups along their life-cycle. The second research interest entails a more holistic approach and scrutinises the number of person-hours invested in the reproduction of the four different social subsystems: the person system, the household system, the community system and the economic system. The third subsection looks into locally implemented strategies to increase the productivity of time. Finally, this chapter also argues that even if applied independently of the sociometabolic transition paradigm, the FTU approach may also serve as a useful tool for planning and monitoring the impact of development interventions.

2. Review of Time Use Studies with Special Reference to Labour Time

Time use studies have a rather long tradition in the social sciences, especially in sociology, anthropology and economics. As concerns sociology, early accounts of sociological time use dealt predominantly with exploring the social conditions of the rising working class, for which the publications *How Working Men Spend their Time* (Bevans 1913) and *Round about a Pound a Week* (Pember-Reeves 1913) provide testimony. In the early 1930s, a whole new era of work/leisure studies was launched. Among the range of emerging time diary literature, *Time Budgets of Human Behaviour* (Sorokin and Berger 1939) probably provided the most intruiging insights into sociological and psychological stimuli for daily time use. Since the 1950s, the effects of longer working hours have become increasingly analysed through the lens of comparative time use data. Probably the most ambitious multi-country time use study was the Multinational Time Use Study directed by Alexander Szalai (1972) in the mid-1960s. Since then, comparative national level studies have flourished, with Jonathan Gershuny's (2000) Multinational Time Budget Data Archive undoubtedly taking the centre stage. Today, we owe sociology a great deal for having methodologically advanced the area of time use research; especially the statistical time-budget tradition has been significant in many respects and has since been adopted by other disciplines.

In contrast to the quantitative sociological tradition, earlier anthropological studies have generally more relied on qualitatively describing the "daily round" of the communities studied. In various anthropological studies the goals of time allocation studies have largely centred on the following interests: to provide insights into the sexual divisions of labour within a given community, to point to the social limitations of labour time through the lens of culture and to measure labour efficiency and effectiveness. What we see is that the study of labour time has been an attractive feature of anthropological time use research and, in contrast to sociological endeavours, generally been more theory-led. From the 1920s onwards continuous observation or recall methods were used to record the "daily/weekly round of activities" (e.g., Malinowski 1935). More theory-led, Sahlins (1972) mobilised quantitatively available time use data and came up with the view that labour time increases as societies become more complex. A different approach to labour comes from the field of ecological anthropology. Rappaport's (1968) detailed monograph *Pigs for the Ancestors,* whilst striving to document the interdependence of cultural phenomena and biophysical variables, provides interesting data on energy expenditure during labour processes through the application of time-and-motion studies. More recent anthropological publications on time use among horticultural societies include Johnson's (1975, 2003) account on the Matsigenka of Peru and Descola's (1996) study of the Achuar ethnic group in the Ecuadorian Amazon, both of which have substantially contributed to the further refinement of time use methods. Within the field of economics, Becker (1965 in Soeftestad 1990) emphasised the value of time at the household level, instigating the so-called "New Household Economics". Many of the goods identified in the household production system cannot be expressed in monetary terms but time is used as an indirect way of measuring inputs and outputs.

More recently, human time use as a limited biophysical key resource beyond the individual level has been taken up by a small number of sustainability scientists. Within ecological economics, Pastore et al. (2003) conducted a land-time budget (LTB) analysis for various villages in rural China, examining demographic variables, land availability and land use, time availability and labour time use as well as cash flows. The LTB analysis is indeed one of the first approaches to treat land and time use as an opportunity or constraint at the social system level. The social ecologists Schandl and Grünbühel (2005) applied a comparative LTB approach for different scale levels; they analysed and compared the land-time budget of a local rural Laotian community with the national-level land-time budget of Laos. The analysis identified biophysical limitations for further socio-economic development and trade-offs in land and time resource use patterns. Finally, Schor's (2004) paper on *Sustainable Consumption and Worktime Reduction* was discussed as a strategy for sustainable development by the sociologist Proinger (2005) through an empirical analysis of labour time developments in Europe.

3. Functional Time Use: Theory, Concept and Methodology

3.1. The Theoretical Framework

Functional time use is a fairly new approach that is embedded within the sociometabolic transition studies paradigm developed over the past decade at the Institute of Social Ecology in Vienna (see Fischer-Kowalski 2003, Fischer-Kowalski and Haberl 2007, Sieferle 2001, 2003). Transition studies look at common historic and contemporary development trajectories (so-called "sociometabolic regimes") from a biophysical perspective and establish sustainability indicators at the society-nature interface that can be compared cross-culturally irrespective of biogeographical conditions. Covering large time frames, from decades to centuries, the specific research focus centres on understanding the structures and dynamics of a social system under transition (a national economy, a region or a local community) in order to determine future trends and plan suitable interventions in these social processes accordingly (Schandl and Grünbühel 2005). Historically, three different sociometabolic regime patterns can be distinguished: the hunter and gatherer regime, the agrarian regime and the industrial regime. Each sociometabolic regime is determined by a certain metabolic profile, i.e., intrinsic energetic and material flows from and to the environment, the use of particular technologies, certain population and reproduction dynamics as well as a distinct (labour) time profile. Each of these metabolic profiles generates a certain set of environmental and social impacts.

To establish the sociometabolic profile of a social system empirically, three conceptual systemic tools are applied: social metabolism, colonization, and functional time use. These tools are operationalised using what we call the MEFA framework. When we apply these three tools, we obtain a detailed metabolic profile of the system being researched, an analysis of the feedback loops shaping both, the social and the natural system, and a clear indication of the biophysical limitations the system is currently facing (in terms of material, energy, land and time constraints). The MEFA framework equally establishes an inherent link between biophysical indicators and socio-economic variables and, in doing so, sheds light on the possibilities and constraints the specific sociometabolic regime entails. It is characterised by three interrelated sets of relations that are compartmentalised as stocks and flows:

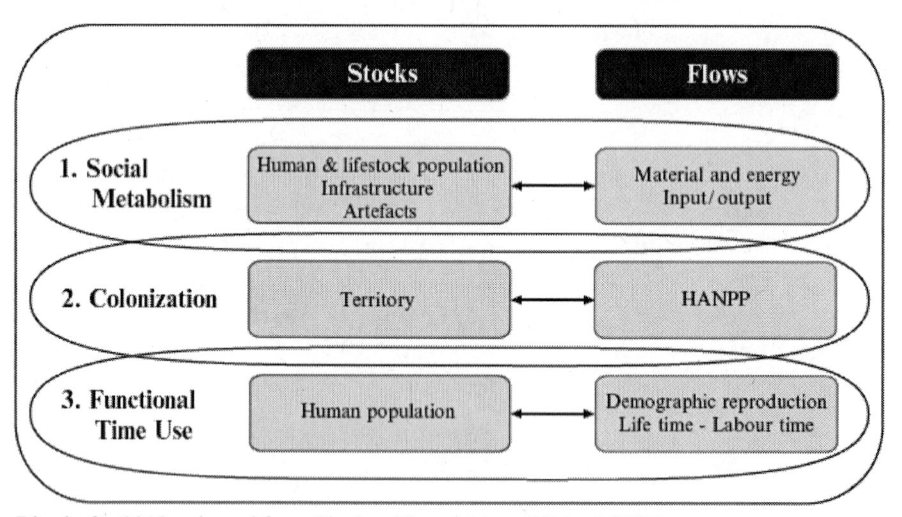

From Ringhofer 2010, adapted from Fischer-Kowalski and Haberl 2007.

Figure 1. MEFA framework with three sets of metabolic relations.

Social metabolism analyses the exchange of material and energy flows between a society and its natural environment. A society and its economy are regarded as an open system in constant physical exchange with natural systems: people (and livestock) extract primary resources and make use of them as foodstuffs, machines, buildings, infrastructure, heating and other products until they are finally returned to nature in the form of emissions and wastes or exported to other societies. Hence, the notion of social metabolism implies a new conceptualisation of a society's pressure on the environment, but also determines its dependency on other social systems (Schandl et al. 2002). Material and Energy Flow Accounting (MFA and EFA, respectively) are the two methodological tools that trace all input/output material and energy flows of a social system and establish socio-economic pressure indicators.

Colonization refers to the second set of metabolic relations within the MEFA framework. It refers to a society's deliberate interventions into natural systems in order to render it more useful for them (Fischer-Kowalski and Haberl 1998, 2007; Krausmann et al. 2003) . It analyses land use and measures the socio-economic pressures upon the environment through land cover changes. Colonizing strategies of natural systems are intrinsically linked to the exchange of energy and material. The larger the population and the larger its metabolism, the more ecosystems need to be colonized by the society in order to maintain this metabolism. In many traditional societies, agriculture is the classical strategy to colonize nature. For the colonized areas to remain of use value to the social system, continuous labour inputs are required. The expenditure of labour, including human, animal and mechanical labour, has the transforming capacity of controlling environmental systems in such a way as considered useful for humans. This impact of land use caused by the human population can be measured by comparing ecosystem patterns and processes that would be expected without human intervention with those actually visible in the presence of interventions (Fischer-Kowalski and Haberl 2007). An example of this approach is the calculation of the 'human appropriation of net primary production' or HANPP (see Vitousek et al. 1986) which assesses to which extent human land use changes the availability of energy in ecosystems.

Functional time use examines the use of time according to functional subsystems in order to examine the labour/life-time ratio of different segments of the social system. Boserup (1965, 1981) as been instrumental in linking the intensification of land use with labour time intensification. She holds the view that the workload increases as we move from hunting-gathering forms of technology towards more land use intensive forms of agriculture. The productivity of labour time, however, declines with land use intensification, since altering the nature of soils, moisture or topography (e.g. through irrigation or terracing) involves time demanding activities, both in terms of investment and maintenance. The interrelation between population growth, increased workload per worker and the intensified use of land are at the core of her agricultural intensification theory. This has been a useful point of departure for the incorporation of human time use into the theory of sociometabolic regimes.

While social metabolism and colonization have been dealt with extensively elsewhere (see Fischer-Kowalski and Haberl 2007, Schandl et al. 2002, Singh 2003), the following sections will focus on functional time use only, its methodological and conceptual base, followed by a presentation of some empirical findings on time use.

3.2. Conceptual and Methodological Considerations of Functional Time Use

Following the same systemic logic as with social metabolism, human time is seen as a limited and evenly distributed key resource at the system level: everybody has 24 hours at his/her disposal. The quantity of time or ‚stock' available in a society depends on the number of people and their reproduction rate. In other words, human time is ‚created' by demographic reproduction. Higher reproduction rates result in higher growth rates of the available human time in the social system. The same goes for life expectancy: the higher an individual's life expectancy, the higher the available time per human life. As opposed to many time use studies produced within sociology and anthropology, human time is considered an element of social functioning rather than a personal resource of individuals. Especially in traditional social systems, the metabolic exchange relations between the people and their natural environment are coordinated by certain socio-cultural time norms (e.g. sexual division of labour) that are responsible for the functioning of the society.

Concerning the 'flows' of human time, we distinguish between flows serving four functional subsystems that each need time for their reproduction: the person system, the household system, the community system and the economic system. Such a systemic analysis provides a clear view on the amount of labour time available in the whole local social system, thereby aiding our understanding of the specific opportunities and constraints a society faces in its interaction with the natural environment. At the same time, analysing the time invested in each of the functional subsystems according to age and gender sheds light on the functional differentiation and inequities within the social system, the 'social burden' a society (or some of its age/gender subgroups) is bearing (see Singh et al. 2010).

The use of these functional subsystems (largely) avoids the ambiguity of coding, as certain activities like sleeping or eating, which are physiologically necessary for basic personal reproduction, can unequivocally be categorised within the person system. What this framework also provides is a general activity and time allocation analysis, embracing all kinds of categorised activities throughout a 24 hour time span. The advantage of such a complete record of the activities performed by different categories has the advantage that 'comparative theorists are then free to define variables in accordance with their theoretical aims rather than having to accept the incommensurable figures each idiosyncratic fieldworker may choose to publish' (Johnson 1975: 307). This may be particularly useful when analysing work-leisure dichotomies that have caused tremendous ambiguity among the time use research community in the past.

Moreover, changes in time use in one subsystem have an impact on the time budget available for the other three subsystems, since the total time resources cannot exceed 24 hours per day and person. These changes in time use can take place via two strategies only: expansion/shrinkage, on the one hand, and intensification/de-intensification, on the other hand. Each set of strategies entails pressures – either social pressures on certain segments of the society or environmental pressures. Expanding time use on certain activities, for example, means reducing time use on others, e.g. expanding labour time may mean reducing sleep. In the long term, this may lead to social costs, such as conflicts or illness, which are provoked by chronic lack of sleep. In pre-industrial societies, we also see a direct link between the expansion of labour time and environmental costs, since all ways of interacting with nature are mediated through labour (see Fischer-Kowalski 2003). The more a society colonizes its environment, the more metabolic returns it can expect, but the more labour needs to be invested in order to maintain the environment in the desired colonized state. Historic hunting and gathering societies, for example, lacked the incentive to increase time investments in labour, as they largely depended on natural reproduction cycles. This direct link between the colonization of natural systems and the investment of human labour changed, however, with the onset of industrialisation when labour became conceived as separate from the worker.

With the tapping into fossil fuel resources and the industrialisation of agricultural practices, the extent of labour time no longer had a direct bearing on the environment.

Concerning the second set of strategies - intensification/de-intensification - throughout history, time-saving assets have been invented to increase the productivity and efficiency of time. Every society applies its own economic and/or socio-culturally determined strategies to increase the productivity of time. These time-saving measures, however, while they relieve the ‚labour burden' on some segments of this society, may at the same time have an adverse impact on other social groups in this system. For example, the introduction of fishing nets substantially de-intensifies the time required for fishing and equally produces higher fish returns. However, the mending of fishing nets may be socially ascribed to women only, therefore intensifying the women's workload that must be invested in the economic system. Besides, the introduction of time-saving assets may equally increase the burden on the environment. Ever more modern technologies for labour or transport efficiency increases require higher and more energy-intensive inputs on the input side; a strategy that, in the shorter and longer run, works much to the detriment of the natural environment.

3.2.1. Methodological Classifications of the Functional Subsystems

Methodologically, we analyse a social system's life time/labour time investment along four functional subsystems: the person system, the household system, the community system, and the economic system (see also Ringhofer 2010, Singh et al. 2010). Although this classification is largely coherent with what is found in sociological literature on time use, what we are interested in is to obtain a macroscopic look at time use at the social system level. While the different activities may need to be adapted depending on the specific structure of the society investigated, the main functional subsystems and their corresponding individual activity sets, however, do not change.

The *person system* functionally serves personal reproduction and includes all those activities that are not subject to a sexual division of labour. On the one hand, the person system holds all the functions that are physiologically necessary for a person's self-reproduction, such as sleeping and eating. These activities can neither be delegated to other members of the society nor 'outsourced' to specialists and are largely horizontally distributed in a population's time budget. Apart from these basic functions for personal reproduction, the person system encompasses functions for extended reproduction, such as studying, leisure activities or idling. Breaking it down into single activities, the person system comprises sleeping (SL), eating (ET), hygiene (HY), rest and idleness (ID), leisure activities (LE), and study and education (SC). Hygiene involves river bathing, the morning toilet or hair combing. The category 'rest and idleness' generally entails periods of inactivity, such as lying in a hammock or simply day-dreaming. Study and education constitutes the time spent at school and the time for doing homework or studying for exams. Leisure refers to periods of deliberate self-entertainment, such as playing with children or pets[1].

The second higher functional level is presented by the *household system*. The household system is the organisational frame and has two equally important functions to fulfil which are both indispensable for the overall running of the domestic unit: the intrinsic functions for basic day-to-day reproduction, on the one hand, and the functions that ensure the long-term

[1] With leisure it is sometimes hard to draw a distinction to household activities (such as child care) and/or communal activities (such as festivities, ritual visits to relative, etc.).

maintenance of the household, on the other hand. Contrary to the person system though, the household system is subject to a division of labour. The household system is typically organised as an exchange of unpaid labour according to the socio-cultural norms regulating age and gender roles in the local system. Time use for the household system contains the following sub-activities: care for dependents (CC), food preparation (FP), house building (HB), repair/maintenance work (MR), and domestic chores (D). Care for dependents involves child care and care for the sick and elderly. Food preparation entails all activities related to food processing such as the salting and drying of meat for conservation, the smoking of fish or the husking and peeling of rice. House building hosts the collection and preparation of wood and other forest items for the construction of infrastructure, the gathering and processing of palm leaves for roofing, the weaving of door mats to serve as walls, etc. Repair and maintenance constitutes all activities required to sustain the physical household infrastructure: the mending or fabrication of clothing, the manufacture of household artefacts such as fans or floor mats, the fixing of the roof, etc. Finally, the activity set 'domestic chores' considers shopping, the fetching of food and water, firewood collection, clothes and dish washing, and general house cleaning.

On the next higher functional level is the *community system*. It is the reference system for activities contributing to the reproduction of services on the community level, reciprocal relationships, social cohesion, politics and religion. In non-industrial societies, this system may be regarded as a predecessor of several other, more specialised systems such as politics or the judicial system (see Fischer-Kowalski et al. 2010). It subsumes public sports and games (PL), visiting friends and relatives (VS), ceremonies and festivals (RI), communal work and political participation (PO). Public sports and games may include a football match or sports competitions. The final activity set subsumes the time invested in communal work (e.g. school maintenance, clearing public pathways) and political participation (e.g. political campaigning).

Beyond the confines of household and community, we deal with the *economic system*. For our purpose, the time invested in reproducing the economic system is what we refer to as "labour time". In general terms, the economic system implies and relies upon a social division of labour beyond the confines of household and community, and usually, though not imperatively, involves monetary transactions. Economic activities include all preparatory tasks for economic investments (e.g. manufacture and preparation of working tools, general repair, handicraft for subsequent sales), as well as directly productive tasks (e.g. harvesting, fishing, hunting). The following activities are distinguished: agriculture (AC), hunting (H), fishing (F), gathering (G), trading (TD), wage work (W), kitchen garden (HG), manufacture of handicraft (MF), and animal husbandry (AN). For agriculture/horticulture (AC), the range of activities included should reflect the entire agricultural cycle from land preparation to cultivation, weeding and harvesting of crops. The time for gathering (G) may sometimes be difficult to measure since especially men do not necessarily engage in separate gathering trips but do gathering as a side activity during hunting expeditions. Trading (TD) may involve the bartering of produce or monetary transactions on the market. Wage work (W) includes all kinds of paid work, from short-term to more permanent placements. 'Kitchen garden' (HG) subsumes all activities related to the maintenance of the kitchen garden, from cultivating, watering, weeding to harvesting the local fruits or vegetables. As mentioned before, the activity set 'manufacture of handicraft' (MF) entails both, the manufacture of tools for hunting, fishing or agriculture, on the one hand, as well as the making of items for direct market sale, on the other. Finally, animal husbandry (AN) should consider both, the direct (e.g. feeding or milking) as well as indirect reproductive activities (e.g. building and fixing stables, fencing, etc.).

4. A Case Study Approach to Functional Time Use

4.1. The Study Area: The Village of Campo Bello (Bolivia)

The village of Campo Bello (231 inhabitants living in 41 households) is quite remotely situated in the Bolivian Amazon plains. It is one of some 120 indigenous Tsimane' communities scattered along the Maniqui river and lies about a day downriver from the next commercial centre. In the absence of proper roads, the community can be accessed only by canoe or motor-driven boats or simply on foot. Villagers engage in subsistence farming and forage on forest and river resources. Campo Bello has witnessed a steady population growth from 210 inhabitants in 2003 to 231 in 2005, 235 in 2006 and 250 in 2008. From the period observed (2004 to 2006) it can be deduced that roughly one third of this growth (3.8% annually) was due to a positive migration balance and two thirds to births exceeding deaths.

The conjugal household is the minimal unit of production, consumption and social reproduction. The villagers tend to live in single-family dwellings within extended family clusters. Families regularly practice *sobaqui* that is visiting relatives for extended periods that may last for several days. The production of manioc beer plays a central role in daily family life, with each extended household producing it at least once a week. Whereas only female household members are involved in the laborious four to five hour beer preparation process, men and women alike, often including neighbouring families and visitors, indulge in its consumption.

Campo Bello is characterised by both, a monetary economic system (marketing of agricultural crops, forest products and wage labour) as well as by reciprocal kinship relations of barter. Such as other communities in the area, Campo Bello's economy rests upon four main pillars. Whereas swidden agriculture takes up the central place, fishing, hunting and gathering activities are almost equally important for the villagers. Raising livestock and occasional wage labour complete the local economic profile. Slash-and-burn agriculture is practised by all households in the village and constitutes the main source of income with rice making up for 40% of all cash incomes within the community. The rice harvest is the most time and labour-intensive agricultural task in which all able-bodied family members are involved. Besides rice, the villagers also grow plantains, maize, manioc and other crops of lesser importance, such as peanuts, sugar cane, citrus and varieties of sweet potatoes. Plantains have a high economic value as they can easily be marketed all-year round. Fishing is practised throughout the year in streams, lagoons and the main river. The raising of livestock, on the other hand, is only of minor importance. While all families own at least some poultry, only one family owns cattle. Wage labour is an economic activity normally engaged in by younger male residents. With the exception of the teacher, wage opportunities for local people are confined to working as agricultural farm hands and petty labour for cattle ranchers. The contemporary Tsimane' belief system has somewhat merged its traditional spiritual domain with Christian elements that have been introduced by missionaries fairly recently. Nonetheless, much of the Tsimane' world is still charged with supernatural significance. The Tsimane' sense of community is also reinforced through cheerful communal feasts. The people of Campo Bello clearly enjoy such recreational gatherings and prepare for them with enthusiasm. Still largely secluded and self-contained, the village is becoming growingly exposed to outside influences. The village has witnessed a number of development projects introduced by the local administration and non-governmental agencies.

4.2. The Research Framework

The aim of the empirical case study among the Tsimane' was a general description of their sociometabolic profile by means of analysing their use of material and energy resources, describe their land use patterns and examine their life time/labour time profile (see Ringhofer 2007, 2010). The latter had three specific sub-aims: (1) based on a demographic analysis, to obtain a general description of the ‚socially disposable labour time' of the different age/sex groups in Campo Bello. This aim was based on the thesis that especially in traditional social systems, capabilities and capacities are not purely a function of biologically based variables like age and gender, but more so culturally transmitted and socially ascribed (e.g. through the sexual division of labour). At the same time, the overall socially disposable labour time in a social system depends on the number of people living in the system and their demographic reproduction rates. (2) The second aim was an analysis of the person-hours invested in the reproduction of the four different functional sub-systems. Specific research interests were the womens' and childrens' labour contributions to the economic and household system and their respective sub-activities. And, what are the current and future challenges related to these findings? (3) A third interest centred on the discussion of local strategies for increasing the productivity of time. These findings were thought to reveal the time and effort contributed by the ‚less visible' household members such as children, women and/or the elderly.

4.3. Data Collection in the Field

The time use data were gathered using mainly observational methods (continuous observation and random visits/spot checks) as well as self-reporting methods (household surveys) mainly for cross-checking. The data were collected between September 2004 and February 2005, followed by additional observations in April and May 2006 in order to capture seasonal variations. The household samples were selected according to demogaphic characteristics (selection of various age/sex categories), migratory backgrounds and household composition.

As for continuous observation of individuals, at different random days in 2004 and 2005, total of 18 individuals[2] were each observed for a 14 hour daytime period (6 a.m. to 8 p.m.). This observation was repeated for seven individuals in 2006. Average activity profiles were thus calculated on the basis of a total of 25 person days spread over almost the entire annual

[2] 6 married men (age ranges between 21 and 58), 6 married women (age ranges between 18 and 54), 3 girls and 3 boys (age ranges between 6 and 13). For toddlers and the elderly population, estimates were resprted to which were consequently cross-checked with interview data and general, but more informal, observation.

cycle (except for June and July when no samples were taken)[3]. To increase data reliability and validity, additional spot checks were carried out. A non-random person was selected, who were visited four different times throughout the same daily round, taking discrete notes of what he/she was engaged in for a 15 min period each time. In so doing, a time allocation period of 1 hour could be documented. This sample method was repeated for a total number of 14 active adults aged from 25 to 45 (7 men and 7 women) and 14 children aged from 5 to 12, from which an additional 14 hour person-day could be derived. To sum up, the total of 112 spot check observations resulted in 2 full person-days which were consequently added to the pool of samples, thereby arriving at a total of 27 person days. In addition to direct observation and spot checks, time use samples were complemented with household surveys. As people were asked about the main activities they engage in during the course of a week, this method proved particularly useful for getting a better idea of the duration and frequency of (especially) productive activities. A total of 11 interviews were conducted and cross-checked with other empirical data. Finally, for the study of labour time inputs for the main agricultural activities, a focus group was organised. The meeting was held in the local school building with 18 women and men constituting the group. The participants were asked about the number of work days required to do all the different tasks within the entire rice production process.

For data collection two different notebooks were used. One was a codebook containing various behaviour codes in the form of two-letter acronyms, various field jottings, diagrams, interviews and time-space-maps. Descriptions of observed behaviour were also written in longhand on special code sheets and were coded each night. The second notebook served more as a personal memo book and contained all kinds of observations, 'off the record' contemplations, and field diary entries.

4.3.1. Some Methodological Challenges

Some of the methodological problems encountered were the lack of night time sampling, the difficulty with measuring multiple and discontinuous behaviours[4], as well as, at certain instances, a clear distinction between activities related to economic food provision and a household's food preparation. As far as the first goes, the time spent during the night time hours is based on grounded estimates. Another challenge that surely surges at some stage of time use studies is the typological problem of multiple and discontinuous behaviours. People in fact engage frequently in several overlapping activities. This was particularly noticeable in the case of household tasks, when women engage in general household chores at the same time, such as breastfeeding and tending the fire. Confronted with this problem plus the practical unfeasibility of timing the sequence of some activities (e.g., hunting and gathering), White's (1976) advice was taken up who accounted half of the period to each activity. On occasion though, when the dominant activity was obvious, at least in my subjective

[3] It should be noted that my samples do not include any 14 hour observation of toddlers and small children below the age of 6. The main drawback was the fact that I could not observe a small child unaware. Also, my sample population does not include any elderly residents above the age of 60, as the elderly village population was usually more apprehensive in participating in the time use study. Here is probably where the drawbacks of this research method become apparent, since direct observation, by definition, lacks a systemic sampling procedure.

[4] Another challenge is how to account for travel time. While this may differ depending on the local context, in my case study it was decided to add travel to the activity it was associated with since distances (to gardens and fallow fields, neighbours, etc.) were relatively short.

perception, I only accounted for the sequence of the primary activity. With regard to the often discontinuous operations that constitute household tasks, for example, I generally had to fall back on overall estimates.

The final and probably most taxing challenge was the functional distinction between economic food provision and a household's food preparation. This may especially be the case when activities are performed out of the usual surrounding (e.g., what if manioc tuber is peeled directly in the field where it is uprooted? Is it food preparation time or part of a woman's agricultural activities?) or when commodities are manufactured which are used for both, the household as well as the socio-economic system (e.g. the manufacture of a mortar and a pestle for husking rice, part of which gets sold at a later stage). The solution I decided on was regardless of the spatial performance of tasks, any task related to food processing (i.e. a woman's peeling of tubers in the field) was accounted for as belonging to the food preparation process. As concerns the manufacture of household items for direct food production (such as mortar and pestle for rice husking), the time invested was subsumed under the household system (despite eventual partial selling of rice). Only the manufacture of directly productive hunting or fishing equipment, as well as handicraft clearly destined for later selling, was hence to be subsumed within the economic system.

4.4. Findings

4.4.1. Socially Disposable Labour Time at the System Level

Looking at the socially disposable labour times by age/sex group aims to focus on the specific capacity and capability constraints faced by each of these groups within a certain life-cycle period[5].

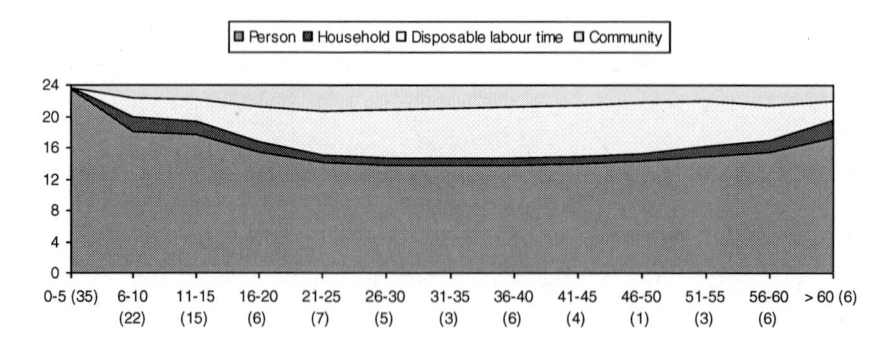

From Ringhofer 2010.

Figure 2. Male time use by age group, Campo Bello, 2004, 2006.

[5] To determine the disposable labour time available in Campo Bello, the average duration of each activity was allocated according to the four functional subsystems. By so doing, a time aggregate for each individual subsystem was obtained by sex. These times were subsequently allocated among the age/sex categories to arrive at a 24 hour period for each age group. The time available for the reproduction of the economic system was termed the 'socially disposable labour time'. In order to arrive at the disposable annual labour time of the different age groups within the community, the disposable daily labour time was multiplied by the amount of people within the age range and the 'work' days of the year. For 'work' days, a total 300 were estimated per year, accounting for festive days, days away from the community, and occasional sick days.

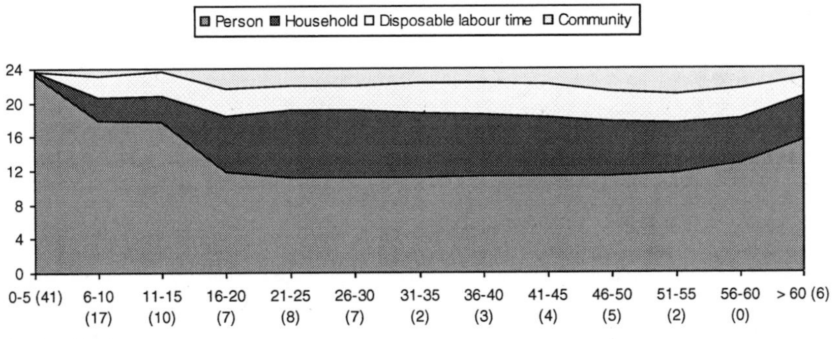

From Ringhofer 2010.

Figure 3. Female time use by age group, Campo Bello, 2004, 2006.

With the Tsimane' the transitional process for children from completely dependent recipients of parental time to more active economic producers starts at a relatively early age - some time around the age of 4 or 5. The age group 0 to 5 year olds with the highest number of individuals though (for both sexes) only has limited (physical) resources to contribute to the system's labour time. The second hightest labour time contributors in terms of numbers would be the 6 to 10 year olds (22 boys/17 girls) and indeed they present an important workforce in terms of domestic chores, child care and light agricultural tasks. But besides the physical constraints it is the educational demands that limit this age group's disposable labour time. School classes take up 4 hours daily and most children attend regularly[6].

For both sexes, this age range represents a crucial socialisation period. Boys generally aid with house building and maintenance work and engage in agricultural activities, while girls aid their mothers in sewing clothes and, most importantly, care for younger siblings. The sexual division of labour takes place rather gradually and, at least in the initial stages of this socialisation process, is not imposed too stringently. By the ages 11 to 15, children are turning into adolescents - physically and socially. Round about the age of 12, a boy starts to cultivate his own agricultural fields, even if this seems to be more of an educational activity. With physical capacity constraints diminishing, educational demands still present the most limiting factor for the disposal of more labour time. In 2004, the proportion of boys and girls from 11 to 15 still attending school classes accounted for almost 80%.

For the Tsimane' girls, the transition to married life is more abrupt than for boys. By the age of 16 or 17, most girls are married or have an infant. Boys this age, however, may engage in erratic wage labour away from the community and those who remain in the village begin to work in agriculture in earnest, often tending several active fields at the same time. From the ages 21 to 25, the investment of male labour is to a large extent used up in outside wage labour. Some are pressured by former employers, as often the accumulation of debts from previous labour engagements forces them to continue with this kind of work. In a Tsimane' man's lifecycle, this is probably the most flexible and 'freest' time of his life, while a woman's time resources are largely used up by reproductive activities for the household system. With small children to take care of, a woman almost exclusively has to bear the time costs of child rearing. It is in fact one of the most time-consuming and difficult stages of a

[6] The first school was built in 1993 and the consciousness for the need of education has been reinforced by various education campaigns in the area.

woman's life. If the husband is away on temporary labour, a woman of this age not only bears the reproductive workload, but also assumes the productive burden to provide enough food for her infants.

The reproductive workload for women starts to decrease steadily over the following years as older children gradually step in and take over some of the activities. One important way for children to contribute their time and effort is to tend younger siblings, thereby imposing fewer time demands on their mothers. When this is the case, mothers are freed to dedicate their time to more productive activities such as gathering or agriculture. Men, on the other hand, still dedicate some of their time resources to occasional wage labour activities while the largest fraction of their working time though is used up by agricultural activities. The following years are the most productive for both sexes in terms of agricultural labour investments. This is due to the fact that older children are useful farmhands, and add considerably to the household's labour force. The empirical data show the limited number of elderly population segments, especially women. There are only 6 women above the age of 50 and surprisingly no women between 56 and 60. The absence of elderly women though, who are an important contributor to household maintenance labour, adds again to the ‚labour burden' of the younger women in the household.

This discussion reveals the importance of examining the demographic profile of the entire social system in detail, rather than looking only at an individual's capabilities. In theory, the potential contribution of labour may be highest in an age group that is free from physical, educational, and social constraints. In practice, however, the actual contribution of labour ultimately depends on the number of people constituting this age group. But this also works the other way round. If we look at the 6 to 10 year olds that comprise the second largest number after the toddlers, this age group would indeed be able to provide a substantial amount of labour if only aggregate numbers are scrutinised. Nonetheless, they are largely constrained by physical limitations as well as the educational demands that have become strongly embedded in the local culture in recent years. On the other hand, 35 to 50 year olds, although largely free from physical, educational and other social restraints, are equally limited in their potential contribution to the economic system due to their low numbers.

The findings therefore show the limited availability of people in their most productive years, coupled with high numbers of individuals in lower productive ranges, most of whom are economic dependents that add to a woman's time demands. Also, a man's absence from the family due to outside wage labour puts an additional burden on a young woman's time, as she must increase her own time investment in order to compensate for that of the absentee. Yet due to socio-cultural restrictions not all of the work ascribed to men can be taken over by a women (e.g. hunting), even if she was still able to expand her workday. In order to prevent food or nutritional shortages for her and her family, the extended family network is likely to step in, to a certain extent providing a 'safety net' for these periods of (especially) female hardship.

4.4.2. Time Investments in All Functional Subsystems

General Time Investments per Adult and Per Inhabitant

Table 1 shows that 55% of the available daily time of adults and more than three quarters of the available daily hours of all inhabitants[7] goes into the reproduction of the person system. The economic system accounts for the second largest time consumer and requires almost 5 hours daily from each adult in the community.

Table 1. Comparison of time use, daily hours per adult and per inhabitant, Campo Bello 2004, 2006

Daily hours[8]	Average adult 16-60	%	Average inhabitant	%
Population size	91		231	
Number of children 0-15			137	
Person System	13.21	55%	18.18	76%
Sleeping	7.90		10.28	
Eating	1.59		2.19	
Hygiene	0.77		1.21	
Rest and Idleness	2.43		2.10	
Leisure Activities	0.14		1.50	
Studying and Education	0.16		0.90	
Household System	3.79	16%	2.11	9%
Care for Dependents	1.59		0.84	
Food Preparation	1.07		0.48	
House Building	0.26		0.10	
Repair/Maintenance Work	0.34		0.24	
Domestic Chores	0.64		0.45	
Economic System	4.69	20%	2.46	10%
Agriculture/Horticulture	2.53		1.08	
Animal Husbandry	0.02		0.05	
Hunting	0.46		0.26	
Fishing	0.35		0.28	
Gathering	0.17		0.22	
Trading	0.43		0.19	
Wage Work	0.27		0.10	
Handicraft	0.41		0.29	
Community System	2.32	10%	1.25	5%
Public Sports and Games	0.09		0.34	
Visiting Friends and Relatives	1.56		0.66	
Ceremonies and Festivals	0.39		0.14	
Community and Political Participation	0.27		0.10	
TOTAL	24		24	
daily working time Household + Economic System	8.48		4.57	

adapted from Fischer-Kowalsi et al. 2010.

The largest time fraction is invested in agriculture/horticulture while foraging and fishing activities barely amount to 1 hour of an adult's day. Cash producing economic activities (trading, wage work and the production of saleable handicraft) account for about 1 hour a day. Next in terms of time investment comes the household system which requires almost 4 hours or 16% of the available daily time of adults for its upkeep. Contrary to the person system, activities for the day-to-day reproduction of the household may be delegated to other

[7] For all children age 0 to 5, in lack of better evidence, we assumed that all their 24 hours were spent on the person system.

[8] Standard Deviations for adults amounted to 1.5 hrs for the person system, 3.2 hrs for the household system, 1.9 hrs for the economic system and 5.6 hrs for the community system. This high variability is substantially reduced to within gender-homogenous samples.

household members, thereby alleviating one's workload. Finally, we find that the community sysem is allocated the least daily time, accounting for only 10% of the available daily time of adults and a mere 5% of the available daily hours of all inhabitants. Notwithstanding, the cultural importance of visiting relatives and friends - the so-called *sobaqui* – is still reflected in the peoples' time use profile, constituting more than two-thirds of all time investments in the community system.

If we now sum up the daily labour hours invested for the reproduction of both - the household and economic system - we arrive at 8.48 hours for adults and 4.57 for all inhabitants.

Gender Differences in Time Use

This section analyses the gender differences in time invested in the household and economic system.

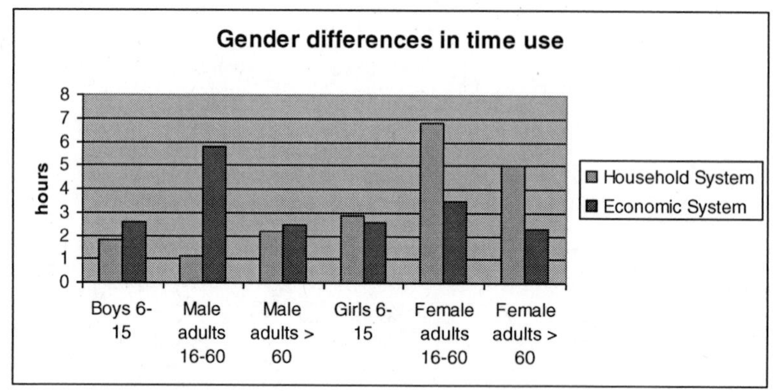

Adapted from Fischer-Kowalsi et al. 2010.

Figure 4. Gender differences in time use, Campo Bello 2004, 2006.

Generally, we find that Campo Bello's male population contributes relatively little to the reproduction of the household system, leaving the lion's share to the women. The time invested by the elderly female population is also quite substantial (5 hours), accounting for almost the same amount of person-hours as contributed by the entire male population (boys and adults). Their daily workload for the household system goes particularly into child care, food and manioc beer preparation and the manufacture of floor mats and other indispensable household appliances, thereby relieving substantially the daily workload for the younger women in the household.

While the household system is largely a female domain, women also contribute quite significantly to the economic workload: female adults[9] work 5.8 hours daily (as compared to 8.3 hours invested by their male counterparts) and are a particularly important workforce in agricultural/horticultural activities (especially manioc and rice production) as well as fishing and food gathering. This difference in labour input is less visible for the children aged 6 to 15, yet tendencies in the same direction may be observed[10]. Boys already contribute about an

[9] Includes female adults 16 to 60 and females >60.

[10] With the Tsimane', a pronounced sexual division of labour starts at about the age of 9 or 10. When younger, little boys are also involved in child care activities or engage in the food production process.

hour less per day than girls to the day-to-day reproduction of the household, particularly in child care and food preparation. At the same time though, both sexes invest the same amount of daily hours (2.6 hours) in economic activities: girls already start to become active in food gathering and fishing at an early age, while boys rather invest their time resources in agricultural tasks and the fabrication and manipulation of hunting and fishing gear. As a result, females can invest less time in the person system which constitutes not only the basic metabolic functions for personal reproduction (sleeping, eating) but also the functions for extended reproduction such as studying and leisure. Detailed empirical data show that females not only sleep less but also invest less time in studying, rest and idleness. In the long run, this time use pattern may impinge on the women's health and also lead to periods of social unrest or conflict.

Children's Share of Labour Time

Befitting a largely traditional agricultural community, at the time of research around 60% of the entire village population were below the age of 16 and a mere 5% were beyond 60. Hence we find a heavy bias towards infants and youths coupled with a fairly low life expectancy. Due to this phenomenon it is not surprising to find that the children's share in the community's overall time budget accounts for 61%.

Table 2. Daily time distribution children as compared to the whole population, Campo Bello 2004, 2006

	Daily time distribution children/all inhabitants in %
Person System	
Children 6-15	0.75
Children 0-5	1.00
All children	0.88
All inhabitants	0.76
Household System	
Children 6-15	0.09
Children 0-5	0.00
All children	0.04
All inhabitants	0.09
Economic System	
Children 6-15	0.11
Children 0-5	0.00
All children	0.05
All inhabitants	0.10
Working time: Household and Economic System	
Children 6-15	0.20
Children 0-5	0.00
All children	0.09
All inhabitants	0.19
Population System	
Children 6-15	0.28
Children 0-5	0.33
All children	0.61
All inhabitans	1.00

adapted from Fischer-Kowalsi et al. 2010.

Hence we find that the children of Campo Bello (6 to 15) invest a substantial amount of their day in working, starting at the age of 4 or 5 to engage in "enabling labour"[11] activities, performing physically undemanding tasks like carrying bowls of water, fetching items or shooing chickens. In fact, children invest about the same share of their day in labour as an average inhabitant, and only one third less than a working age adult (aged 16 to 60). 30% of the total labour hours performed at the community level (incl. the household and economic system) are contributed by children – this is quite a substantial contribution (see Fischer-Kowalski et al. 2010).

These numbers may partly be explained through the socially ascribed marriage among the Tsimane' community. Especially girls tend to marry early, at around the age of 12 or 13, when they start assuming the productive tasks that correspond to an adult. This pattern is changing, however, as the village is becoming increasingly connected to the outside world through state-funded and private development programmes which all to various extents emphasise the value and importance of education and studying. Thus, as regular schooling is becoming more embedded within the Tsimane' culture, early marriage patterns are also likely to change.

Local Strategies to Increase the Productivity of Time

Finally, examining Campo Bello's current strategies to increase the productivity of time was done through the lens of cash investments.

What we see is that quite substantial amounts of cash are spent on technological 'amplifiers' (see Fischer-Kowalski 2007: 11) like rice seeders and agricultural tools to relieve human labour inputs in agriculture (Table 3). All households spend money on basic tools that are necessary for agricultural production. Without the indispensable machete, for example, no fields could be cleared or plantains harvested. The introduction of rice seeders has cut the workload tremendously during the planting stage, in fact by almost 90%[12]. Also, while the traditional rice cultivation method requires the input of more people, manual rice seeders are employed by one person only. At the time of research only 23 households were in possession of such a device. Yet contrary to other tools, rice seeders are frequently passed between families, even if not related by blood. But if we take a gender-segregated look in terms of labour efficiency gains we find that women do not necessarily benefit to the same extent as their male counterparts. Rice seeders merely substitute manual sowing, an activity largely undertaken by men. Other crop management labour tasks like weeding and harvesting, however, which are both predominantly a woman's domain, are not reduced by this technology.

To increase the productivity of hunting time, shotguns and rifles have largely taken precedence over the use of more traditional hunting devices. As hunting is an exclusively male activity, women only benefit indirectly (in terms of higher game returns) from these technological amplifiers. Nylon fishing nets are another item which entail time productivity gains. With such a net, substantially more fish can be caught in a much shorter time frame.

---

[11] The term is borrowed from Cain (1980) as it frees other household members to engage in economic activities that are directly productive.

[12] Using the traditional dibble stick for sowing, 1 ha of rice production has been calculated at 108 person-days. With the application of a rice seeder, a total of 96 person-days was calculated for the entire production cycle. This means that 12 days of hard labour are saved if a rice seeder is used at the planting stage.

Apart from higher fish returns, time productivity gains generated by fishing nets largely benefit the men in the community.

Table 3. Cash investments in Campo Bello, 2004

	Nr. of items	US$/per item	Total US$	Function	
				Time-saving	Socialisation
Labour amplifiers					
Rice seeder	23	5.4	125	x	
Machete, axe, spade	176	6.0	1,063	x	
Shotgun	34	18.1	616	x	
Fishing net	21	10.9	228	x	
Transport amplifiers					
Bicycle	17	21.8	370	x	
Status symbols					
Radio	34	9.7	329		x
Watch	24	7.3	174		x
Clothes, shoes	n.a.	6.0	302		x

(from Ringhofer 2010).

Women still engage in fishing using traditional armoury like hooks and lines or machetes. At the same time though, the mending of fishing nets, however, is predominantly assigned to women, thereby adding to their ‚labour burden' rather than reducing it. Finally in terms of transport amplifiers, the use of a bicycle has become a popular means of commuting within and between neighbouring villages. A bicycle equally provides an opportunity for transporting agricultural products (e.g., rice and plantains) to the market, and in doing so, also increasing the efficiency of travel time. All 17 bicycles at the time of study were exclusively owned by men and some of whom would spend considerable time and effort in repair and maintenance. Again, women do not directly benefit from these transport amplifiers.

5. Conclusion

5.1. Factual Conclusions

What have we learnt from this analysis in terms of opportunities, challenges and labour time squeeze for the community of Campo Bello?

Examining the system's disposable labour time as a social rather than individual resource shows some interesting results. First, the potential contribution of labour time may be highest in age groups that are free from physical, social and educational constraints. In the community, however, we find a limited number of people in their most productive years, while the age group with the highest number of boys and girls are infants and toddlers who do not contribute to labour but are economic dependents of their parents', especially their mothers', time. Notwithstanding, there is evidence that the more children are added to the family, the less are the time costs of child rearing on the mother's time resources, since older children can step in and take over some of the chores. By the age of 5 or 6, children of both sexes become economically active, engaging first in skillfully undemanding labour. The culturally prescribed division of labour only starts gradually and by the age of 8 or 9, boys become more actively involved in directly productive labour, while girls start dividing their labour time between household maintenance activities and, to a lesser extent, more directly productive tasks. For many girls, the transition from being a pupil to becoming a wife and a mother seems fairly abrupt. Men, on the other hand, tend to engage in wage labour away from the community. In their absence, others have to increase their workload, adding to their own labour demands. This is particularly felt by young, married women, who, in the absence of their husbands, need to take over more productive tasks. For some activities, this would mean increasing her workday; often to the detriment of sleep or other functions for personal reproduction.

Let us now consider the findings for the time investments in the functional subsystems. First, if we account for the labour input into the economic system only, we arrive at 4.69 h/d for the average adult population which is 20% of all ‚live' hours of this population segment available in Campo Bello. This means an annual (economic) working time of 1,711 hours per adult person which compares to the annual labour time of the economically active population in the US and Japan: 1,800 hours per year (Groningen database 2005). Though if we add to the daily economic working time also the labour invested in the household system, we arrive at 8.48 daily working hours for adults and 4.57 labour hours for all inhabitants. Whereas in modern economies, much of the household labour may be ‚outsourced' to other institutions (e.g. child care), this is not the case with traditional agrarian societies.

A gender-segregated perspective informs us of the ‚labour burden' borne by the female population. Adult women invest more than three times as many daily labour hours as their male counterparts in the reproduction of the household system. The elderly female population contributes substantially to child care, manioc beer preparation and other minor enabling labour activities. In their absence, these efforts have to be contributed by the mother or older daughters, adding to their ‚labour burden'. But adult women are equally important contributors to the economic system; they account for almost two-thirds of the labour time invested by adult men. The lion's share of their labour is invested in agricultural activities. Compared to other studies of agricultural time use, e.g. the indigenous Matsigenka from the Peruvian Amazon (see Johnson 2003), adult women in Campo Bello provide more than twice as much agricultural labour throughout the year.

Children's contribution to the community's labour time is also high. 30% of the total labour performance in Campo Bello is contributed by children. Hence, it is not surprising that there is a strong bias towards children, in fact 60% of the entire community population are below the age of 16. Boys and girls get involved at an early age in enabling household maintenance activities, including child care and food preparation. It is noteworthy that boys start to move away from the day-to-day running of the household at around the age of 9 or 10, while girls in the same age group continue to invest their labour time in fairly equal shares between the household and economic system. The numbers in Table 2 reveal that the boys' (aged 6 to 15) input in the household system totals close to 2 hours, while girls in the same age group invest about 1 hour more per day. At the same time though, both sexes contribute the same amount of daily labour in the upkeep of the economic system. As they get older, the boys invest this , time gain' in more personal rest, leisure as well as occasional wage work.

Finally, the people of Campo Bello apply rice seeders as a labour-saving device within the laborious rice cropping cycle. As opposed to traditional methods for rice sowing, this technology saves in fact about 12 labour days. This efficiency gain, however, is mainly enjoyed by men, since women's labour contribution to rice growing largely consists in weeding, harvesting and husking processes. Also, the introduction of nylon fishing nets undoubtedly increases productivity gains, but repair and maintenance of nets is predominantly assigned to women.

Are Time Demands on the Subsystems Likely to Change in the Future?

To start with the person system, there does not seem to be much leeway for changes in time use. Functions for basic reproduction like sleeping and eating are both activities that cannot be delegated to others. As concerns the time inputs for extended personal reproduction, childrens' schooling takes up about 4 hours every day, a time that could otherwise be used for labour activities. But parents are well aware of the benefits of schooling and there is a general consensus that children will be less likely to be exploited by future employers. The introduction of school classes has also changed a child's time demands on the mother. For a 4 hour period every day, mothers are free to engage in a range of activities that would not have been feasible otherwise. At the same time though, children cannot contribute to other tasks during these morning hours. Time invested in schooling is hardly likely to increase, since further educational opportunities in the village are non-existent and it is not common practice to send children away for further education.

Let us look at the time demands on the household system. Care for dependents takes up most of a woman's time resources and, in light of demographic growth rates, is likely to increase. Whereas no formal institutions exist to 'outsource' the work of child care, as there would be in modern societies, the presence of elderly women in the household has an enormous impact on alleviating the workload of a young mother. However, there is only a limited number of elderly women and in fact no women between the age range 56 to 60. As long as life expectancy rates remain low while population growth continues at the current rate, and wage labour opportunities for men become more popular, young mothers will be increasingly faced with growing labour pressures in the reproductive and productive sphere. In light of steady population growth and the absence of labour-saving household technologies (e.g. gas cookers or rice peeling machines), time investments for food production are also likely to increase. House building and maintenance activities are also not likely to change as a change fro traditional to more resistant building materials would mean the investment of additional economic resources, which are currently not available to most families.

Time demands on the community system are likely to increase as a result of a growing exposure to the regional market economy and cultural adaptation processes to the national society. This is expressed through the growing importance allocated to the celebration of national holidays, birthdays and regular village feasts and the general high status given to market goods.

As for changing time demands on the economic system, I will focus on agriculture as the main economic activity in terms of time. One option would be an intensification of time use through labour-saving technologies (e.g. chainsaws for field opening and chemical fertiliser to reduce need for weeding) for the different crop production stages. While the use of chemical fertilising is not culturally accepted in the Tsimane' traditional ecological land use and tenure system, there is a strong desire for chainsaws among the local men. These technologies will undoubtedly find their way into the community within the next years, thereby relieving the workload of men substantially. Again, we find that women will hardly (or only indirectly) benefit from these technological innovations. The other option for changing time use is the expansion/shrinkage of time investments in certain activities. What would the current options for shifting labour time within the economic system in favour of agriculture be? Fishing, hunting and gathering take up one third of all time inputs for the average individual in the community. Simply shifting time resources would not be feasible since most agricultural tasks require physical capabilities and capacities that cannot be provided by children or women. Fishing, for instance, may require some skill, yet not necessarily involves the use of heavy equipment. Similar to gathering, these activities are also suitable for children. If we consider that most of a child's day is taken up by studying, playing, child care, rest, eating, fishing and gathering, then time resources for agricultural labour for this age stratum remain fairly limited. Likewise, some agricultural tasks call for a certain skill level as well as physical stamina, both of which boys and girls may lack.

Reaching beyond the economic system, one of the possibilities (except for reducing some of the leisure time in the person system) would be to decrease time investments in the community system. This would mostly impinge on visiting and socialising with kin and neighbours, an activity that is deeply ingrained in the local social fabric and equally reinforces social cohesion and reciprocity. With the Tsimane' though, both norms are deeply ingrained cultural assets that ensure day-to-day living. Also, the expansion of the agricultural workday may mean a reduction of sleep at agricultural peak times that would be felt by adults particularly. Nonetheless, a likely expansion of agricultural production time is hampered by limited marketing facilities. For the time being, Campo Bello remains largely remote and lacks the adequate transport facilities to market centres. At various times of the year, the people have to rely on the market coming to them rather than vice versa. As far as intensification is concerned, the main constraint is the lack of economic resources.

5.2. Methodological Conclusions for "Development in Practise"

When practicing development, one must be aware that all kinds of interventions cause (intended and unintended) impacts on the target systems, or at least certain parameters of it. From the above empirical analysis we have learnt the importance of acquiring local knowledge of socially ascribed time use patterns and sexual labour division before starting to intervene. In the absence of such knowledge, even well-intended gender-sensitive development projects may lead to adverse (short- or long-term) impacts in terms of increasing the social costs and labour pressures on most most vulnerable beneficiary groups.

In such a light, the FTU methodology may be used as a tool for observing changes in time use patterns. In the context of development projects, it may be applied as a baseline to ascertain the situation prior to the intervention, and as a monitoring tool for observing the changes in time use during interventions and even afterwards. In summary, here are some methodological conclusions that underline the usefulness of the FTU methodology in the context of development:

(1) *FTU provides a detailed time profile for all segments of society:* As FTU data entail a holistic approach to time use, they provide a more detailed picture of the whole system's time use as compared to recall methods. Also, women and children are generally less visible than male household members. This sampling method therefoe ensures that otherwise invisible time use behaviour gets revealed.
(2) *FTU increases reliability and validity as compared to self-reported assessments*: Self-reported assessments, the typically applied method for baselines prior to development interventions, are often biased as people tend to remember their own behaviour selectively, in terms of cultural models of significant activities. Self-reports on working time may also be underestimated when opportunity costs of labour are low and when there is no clear distinction between working and non-working time which is quite common in tradional households. Furthermore, self-reports by male household members may tend to underestimate the involvement of children and elderly household members in productive activities, as in some cultures their labour contribution does not get the same consideration as the labour time invested by adults. Also, recall methods may also be biased as a whole in that they emphasise 'events' over 'non-events'. This is because discrete acts are easier to count. A record of no activity can however be potentially interesting (e.g., the amount of leisure time available to some segments of society).
(3) *FTU data collection is not particularly labour intensive and may be combined with the collection of other relevant monitoring data.*

REFERENCES

Bevans, G. E. (1913). *How working men spend their spare time*. New York: Columbia University Press.

Boserup, E. (1965). The conditions of agricultural growth. *The economics of agrarian change under population pressure*. Chicago: Aldine/Earthscan.

Boserup, E. (1981). *Population and technology*. Oxford: Basil Blackwell.

Cain, M. T. (1980). The economic activities of children in a village in Bangladesh. In H. P. Binswanger (Ed.), *Rural household studies in Asia* (pp. 218–247). Singapore: Singapore University Press.

Descola, P. (1996). *In the society of nature: A native ecology in Amazonia*. Cambridge: Cambridge University Press.

Gershuny, J. (2000). *Changing times: Work and leisure in post-industrial societies*. Oxford: Oxford University Press.

Fischer-Kowalski, M. (2003). Socio-ecological regimes, time use and the environment. Presentation at the second international conference of the International Society for Industrial Ecology (ISIE), hosted by the University of Michigan, *Ann. Arbor.*, 29th June – 2nd July 2003.

Fischer-Kowalski, M. (2007). Ageing, time use and the environment. Presentation at the workshop: Research foresight for environment and sustainability – *megatrends and surprises*, EEA Copenhagen.

Fischer-Kowalski, M., and Haberl, H. (1998). Sustainable development: Socio-economic metabolism and colonization of nature. *International Social Science Journal*, 158 (4), 573–587.

Fischer-Kowalski, M., and Haberl, H. (2007). Conceptualizing, observing and comparing socioecological transitions. In M. Fischer-Kowalski, H. Haberl (Eds.), Socioecological transitions and global change: *Trajectories of social metabolism and land use* (pp 13–62). Cheltenham, UK, Northampton, USA: Edward Elgar.

Fischer-Kowalski, M., Singh, S. J., Ringhofer, L., Grünbühel, C. M., Lauk, C., and Remesch, A. (2010). Sociometabolic regimes in indigenous communities and the crucial role of working time. *A comparison of case studies.* Institute of Social Ecology, Vienna: Working Paper 121

Harvey, A. S., and Pentland, W. E. (1999). Time use research. In W. E. Pentland, A. S. Harvey, P. M. Lawton and M. A. McColl (Eds.), *Time use research in the social sciences* (pp. 3–14). New York, Boston, Dordrecht, London, Moscow: Kluwer Academic/Plenum Publishers.

Johnson, A. (1975). Time allocation in a Machiguenga community. Ethnology, 14 , 310–321.

Johnson, A. (2003). Families of the forest: *The Matsigenka Indians of the Peruvian Amazon.* Berkley: University of California Press.

Krausmann, F. Haberl, H., Schulz, N. B., Erb, K. H., Darge, E., and Gaube, V. (2003). Land-use change and socioeconomic metabolism in Austria. Part I: *Driving forces of land-use change*: 1950–1995. Land Use Policy, 20(1), 1-20.

Pastore, G., Giampetro, M., and Ji, L. (1999). Conventional and land-time budget analysis of rural villages in Hubei province, China. *Critical Review in Plant Sciences*, 18 (3), 331–357.

Pember-Reeves, M. (1913). *Round about a pound a week.* London: Bell.

Proinger, J. (2005). Arbeitszeit und nachhaltige Entwicklung in Europa: *Ausgleich von Produktivitätsgewinn in Zeit statt Geld?* Institute of Social Ecology, Vienna: Working Paper 77

Rappaport, R. A. (1968). Pigs for the ancestors: *Rituals in the ecology of a New Guinea people.* New Haven: Yale University Press.

Ringhofer, E. (2007). The Tsimane' in their environment: *a socio-ecological analysis of the environmental relations of an indigenous community in the Bolivian Amazon.* Institute of Social Ecology, Vienna: PhD thesis

Ringhofer, L. (2010). Fishing, foraging and farming in the Bolivian Amazon. On a local society in transition. Dordrecht, Heidelberg, London, New York: Springer Science + Business Media B.V.

Sahlins, M. (1972). *Stone age economics.* London: Tavistock.

Schandl, H., and Grünbühel, C. M. (Guest Eds.). (2005). Southeast Asia in Transition. *International Journal of Global Environmental Issues*, 5 (3/4) pp 115–118.

Schandl, H., Grünbühel, C. M., Haberl, H., and Weisz, H. (2002). Handbook of physical accounting. measuring bio-physical dimensions of socio-economic activities. MFA-EFA-HANPP. Vienna: Federal Ministry of Agriculture and Forestry, *Environment and Water Management.*

Schor, J.B. (2004). *Sustainable consumption and worktime reduction.* Johannes Kepler University, Linz: Working Paper 0406.

Sieferle, R. P. (2001). *The subterranean forest. Energy systems and the Industrial Revolution* . Cambridge: The White Horse Press.

Sieferle, R. P. (2003). Sustainability in a World History Perspective. In B. Benzing and B. Herrmann (Eds.), *Exploitation and Overexploitation in Societies Past and Present* (pp. 123–142). Münster: LIT.

Singh, S. J. (2003). In the sea of influence: *A world system perspective of the Nicobar islands.* Lund: Lund University.

Singh, S.J., Ringhofer, L., Haas, W., Krausmann, F., Fischer-Kowalski, M. (2010). *Local Studies Manual: a researcher's guide for investigating the social metabolism of rural systems.* Institute of Social Ecology, Vienna: Working Paper 120.

Soeftestad, L. (1990) Time allocation studies: a tool in planning and impact analysis of development projects. In A. Rahman, S. Huq, and G. Conway (Eds.), *Environmental aspects of surface water systems of Bangladesh: an introduction* (pp. 24-46). Dhaka: University Press Limited.

Sorokin, P., and Berger, C. (1939). *Time-budgets of human behaviour.* London: Harvard University Press.

Szalai, A. (1972). *The use of time: Daily activities of urban and suburban populations in twelve countries.* The Hague: Mouton.

Vitousek, P. M., Ehrlich, P. R., Ehrlich, A. H., and Matson, P. A. (1986). Human appropriation of the products of photosynthesis. *BioScience*, 36 (6), 368–373.

White, B. (1976). Population, involution and employment in rural Java. *Development and Change*, 7 , 267–290.

In: Social Indicators: Statistics, Trends...
Editor: Candace M. Baird

ISBN 978-1-61122-841-0

Chapter 4

GENOA INDEX OF DEPRIVATION (GDI): AN INDEX OF MATERIAL DEPRIVATION FOR GEOGRAPHICAL AREAS

E. Ivaldi and A. Testi
University of Genoa – Department of Economy and Quantitative Methods, Genoa, Italy

ABSTRACT

The existence of an inverse association between socioeconomic status and the incidence of most diseases is well-established in literature: higher rates of morbidity and mortality have been reported among lower socioeconomic groups in many European countries.

The relation between socioeconomic factors and health inequality may be proved at the individual level, or at the geographical area level. In this paper we follow the second stream of literature, i.e studies on deprivation relating the state of disadvantage suffered by an individual, with the living conditions of the area where the individual resides. Deprivation underlines the characteristics of a group (that is, the population living in a defined geographical area) by measuring similarities and dissimilarities of the individuals forming that group.

Knowledge of deprivation indexes is, therefore, very important for resource allocation: according to equity's considerations, more deprived areas should be assigned a larger amount of resources.

The first part of the proposed chapter examines, in a historical perspective the more commonly used deprivation indexes, i.e. the ones proposed by Jarman, Carstairs, Townsend, MATDEP and SOCDEP the Index of Multiple Deprivation (IMD 2000) developed by the U.K. Department of the Environment, Transport and the Regions. The second part presents an index of material deprivation which has been applied to "small areas" of the city of Genoa (GDI).

INTRODUCTION

The relationship between socioeconomic factors and health inequality may be proved at the individual level as well as the geographical area level. In this paper we follow the second stream of literature, studies on deprivation relating the state of disadvantage suffered by an individual to the living conditions of the area where that person resides. Deprivation highlights the characteristics of a group (that is, the population living in a defined geographical area) by measuring the similarities and dissimilarities of those individuals making up that group. Knowledge of deprivation indexes is therefore very important for resource allocation since, considering equity, more deprived areas should be assigned a larger amount of resources.

In the first part of this paper, some well-known and commonly used deprivation indexes are examined in a historical perspective i.e. the ones proposed by Jarman, Carstairs, Townsend; the MATDEP, SOCDEP and Index of Multiple Deprivation (IMD 2000) developed by the U.K. Department of the Environment, Transport and the Regions. The second part of the paper presents an index of material deprivation which has been applied to "small areas" of the city of Genoa, Italy (GDI).

PART 1. A REVIEW OF THE LITERATURE

The existence of an inverse association between socioeconomic status and the incidence of most diseases is well-established in literature as higher rates of morbidity and mortality have been reported among lower socioeconomic groups in many European countries [Fuchs 2004]. This association may reflect poor living conditions as well as other possible determinants such as genetic factors or social exclusion [Boyle et al, 1999], though all these factors can be approximated by personal income [Carstairs et Morris, 1991]. The relation between socioeconomic factors and health inequality may be proved at the individual level [Deaton, 2003], or geographical area level [Fuchs, 2004]. In this paper we follow the second stream of literature, studies on deprivation relating the state of disadvantage suffered by an individual to the living conditions of the area where that individual resides. This view is based on the assumption that, equity considering, more deprived areas require a larger amount of resources [Judge and Mays 1994a 1994b; Buckingam and Freeman 1997].

Deprivation highlights the characteristics of a group (that is, the population living in a defined geographical area) by measuring similarities and dissimilarities of those forming that group. Similarities may affect not only material conditions but social and cultural ones as well.

Deprivation indexes are defined referring to a small, well specified geographical area where they "measure the proportion of households…with a combination of circumstances indicating low living standards, or a high need for services, or both" [Bartley and Blane, 1994]. Consequently, deprivation indexes point out the close relationship that exists between deprivation and territory. This relationship creates two problems, the first one concerning the definition of territory, the second of index interpretation.

Firstly, with regard to the definition of territory, the term "small area" has been used in literature [Bartley and Blane 1994; Carr Hill et. al 2002, Carstairs, 2000, Salmond et

Crampton, 2002 Boyle et al. 1999]. However, this definition is not completely clear and unambiguous since indexes are commonly calculated in the UK using electoral wards (in Scotland "pseudo-postcode sector") which include about 2000 households (in 1991)[1] , but there are also proposals for using enumeration district (the smallest geographical unit in a census), consisting of about 200 households [Crayford et al, 1995; Barnett et al. 2001; Gilthorpe et al 2003].

Secondly, the use of measures based on geographic areas rather than individual conditions causes the implicit assumption of equality among people living in the same area. The results must be carefully interpreted since "not all deprived people live in deprived wards, just as not everybody in a ward ranked as deprived are deprived themselves" [Townsend et al, 1988]. Though this is a relevant issue, it is impossible to obtain individual measures of deprivation. Consequently, indexes for small areas should identify an "environmental" component underlying social differences like a proxy of unknown individual characteristics. This hypothesis requires that the geographical area be rather small [Jarman, a].

Deprivation indexes are quite simple, inexpensive instruments to measure the socioeconomic conditions of areas of residence because they are generally made up of census indicators which are easily available, combined using different types of statistical data [Bartley et Blane, 1994]. For these reasons, deprivation indexes are widely used in epidemiology and public health studies [Macintyre et al 2002; Carr Hill et al 2002; Davey Smith et al., 2001; Salmond et Crampton, 2002] and have been developed in the United Kingdom [Carstairs et Morris, 1991; Jarman, 1984; Scottish Executive,1999, DETR 2000; Davey Smith et al., 2001; Forrest et Gordon, 1993; Gordon et al 1997;] as well as many other countries in the world (Barnett et al., 2004; Benach et Jasui, 1999; Buckingham et al. 1997; Crampton et al, 1997; Hales et al., 2003; Khelleher et al., 2002, Smits et al, 2002, Sutton et. Al. 2002, Biggeri et al 1998; Rapiti et al 1999; Cadum et al. 1999; Michelozzi et al. 1999; Valerio et al. 2000; Quaglia et al. 2005; Vercelli et al 2006; Quaglia et al 2010; SLTo 2004; Costa et al. 2004; Spandonaro et al. 2004; Brenna, 2007; Costa et al. 2009; Smits et al 2002; Toreshei et al 2004].

1.1. The Jarman Underprivileged Area Score (UPA 8)

The Underprivileged Area Score 8 (UPA 8), proposed by Jarman in 1983, was not originally made to measure deprivation but to take account of the social factors, derived from census data, that affect the workload of General Practitioners in England and Wales [Jarman *a*]. Since 1988, it had been used by the Department of Health and Social Security in the review of RAWP (resource allocation working party) formula, in order to make additional payments to General Practitioners for each patient living in a deprived area. In 1995 the Department of Health set three bands of deprivation payment corresponding to Jarman scores of 30, 40 and 50. Each patient residing in an electoral ward with a Jarman score between 30 and 40 attracted an additional annual payment of £5.85, which increased to £10.20 for each patient residing in an electoral ward with a Jarman score of 50 or more [Crayford et al, 1995]. UPA 8 was also employed in the analysis of admission rates to mental illness hospitals [Carstairs and Morris 1991].

The eight variables in the index are:

1. X_1 = pensioners living alone as a percentage of all residents in households
2. X_2 = children aged under five years as a percentage of all residents in households
3. X_3 = people in households of one person over 16 and one or more children as a percentage of all residents in households
4. X_4 = people in households headed by a person in socioeconomic group 5 (unskilled manual workers)[1] as a percentage of all residents in households
5. X_5 = people aged 16 or more unemployed as a percentage of economically active adults
6. X_6 = people in households living at more than 1 person for room as a percentage of all residents in households
7. X_7 = people aged 1 or over with a usual address one year before the census different from the present usual address as a percentage of all residents in households
8. X_8 = people in households headed by a person born in the New Commonwealth as a percentage of all residents in households

Note that selected variables, originally taken from a 1981 census data, could be divided into two different categories as they reflect both socioeconomic conditions and demographic subgroups.

The index could be expressed as follows:

$$\text{Let } T_1 = \arcsin\sqrt{\frac{X_1}{100}},\ T_2 = \arcsin\sqrt{\frac{X_2}{100}},\ \ldots,\ T_8 = \arcsin\sqrt{\frac{X_8}{100}}$$

and

$$z_1 = \frac{t_1 - \mu_{T_1}}{s_{T_1}},\ z_2 = \frac{t_2 - \mu_{T_2}}{s_{T_2}},\ \ldots,\ z_8 = \frac{t_8 - \mu_{T_8}}{s_{T_8}}$$

the Jarman index is given by the weighted sum of z_i

$$UPA\ 8 = \sum_{i=1}^{8} z_i w_i$$

[1] In U.K. exists a "Registrar General's Social Scale" (renamed in1990 "Social Class based on Occupations", actually to be replaced by the "National Statistics Socio-economic Classifications") which divides people up into seven different groups according to occupations, listed below:

I Professional occupations II Managerial and technical occupations IIIN Skilled non-manual occupations IIIM Skilled manual occupations IV Partly skilled occupations V Unskilled occupations VI Armed forces. [www.hewett.norfolk.sch.uk/curric/soc/class/reg.htm].

The weights .applied (table 1), just like selected variables, emerged from a survey of general practitioners. A sample was made up of one in ten general practitioners in the U.K, who were asked to weigh (on a scale from zero to 9) various census factors according to the degree to which these factors increased their workload or pressure on the services they provided. The average weights were used [Jarman b].

The index uses an angular transformation (arcsine transformation) and standardization. The arcsine transformation is given by

$$T = \arcsin\sqrt{\frac{X_i}{100}}$$

where the square root is applied to a decimal value, ranging from zero to one[3]. Firstly, this transformation achieves the normalization of the data, so they become more or less normally distributed; otherwise, standardization could not correctly proceed. In addition, this type of transformation serves the purpose of bringing variance back to a situation of homogeneity, causing variations more relevant to the extremes of the scale than to the centre [Freeman and Tukey 1950].

Standardization that expresses each variable in terms of its mean and standard deviation in the specific area is used because "if this were not done then items with longer scales would have more weight than those with shorter scales in the overall score" [Bartley and Blane 1994]. The larger the value of the overall score, the larger the deprivation suffered by the population of interest.

With reference to its use in admission rate analysis of psychiatric hospitals, this measurement has been criticized by Glover. In his study commissioned by the Department of Health, aimed at developing an *ad hoc* index *(the Mental Illness Needs Index),* he noted that UPA 8 explained only 23% of the variance between districts and that two components (elderly living alone and children under five) had very poor predictive capacity [Glover 1998].

Table 1. Jarman Index Variables and Weights

Variables	Weights
X_1	$w_1 = 6,62$
X_2	$w_2 = 4,64$
X_3	$w_3 = 3.01$
X_4	$w_4 = 3,74$
X_5	$w_5 = 3,34$
X_6	$w_6 = 2,88$
X_7	$w_7 = 2,68$
X_8	$w_8 = 2,50$

1.2. The Townsend Index of Deprivation

This measure was developed by Townsend [Townsend *et al*, 1988], under commission of the *Northern Regional Health Authority* in order to analyze health measures within the Northern region (counties of Cleveland, Cumbria, Durham, Northumberland, Tyne and Wear [Phillimore et al, 1994]), with particular reference to inequalities in health. In accordance with the author's wishes, this index is a measurement of material deprivation. Material deprivation is distinguished from social deprivation, as Townsend himself stated: "Material deprivation entails the lack of goods, services, resources, amenities and physical environment which are customary, or at least widely approved in the society under consideration. Social deprivation, on the other hand, is non-participation in the roles, relationship, customs, functions, rights and responsibilities implied by a member of a society and its sub-groups. Such deprivation may be attributed to the affects of racism, sexism and ageism…" [Townsend *et al*, 1988].

The Townsend index is also commonly used in epidemiological analysis [Carstairs and Morris 1991] and, like the UPA 8, encompasses unemployment, suitable for summarizing a lack of material resources and economic confidence, and overcrowding, a variable reflecting material life conditions. What appears innovative in this index is the insertion of car and house ownership, intended as a proxy related to wealth and current income. In this case the four, un-weighed indicators are:

1. X_1 = percentage of unemployed, economically active people
2. X_2 = percentage of households with more than one person per room
3. X_3 = percentage of households with no car
4. X_4 = percentage of households not owner-occupied

Townsend points out that the four selected variables, originally obtained from a 1981 census solely reflecting socioeconomic circumstances, represent the state or condition of deprivation and are hence referred to as "direct indicators" of deprivation. On the contrary, "indirect indicators" of deprivation represent the victims of those conditions or states such as the elderly, ethnic minorities and single parents [Townsend 1987]. Townsend stresses that belonging to these categories is not, in itself, an indicator of deprivation, though many people in these categories are indeed deprived. In selecting indicators, it is of utmost importance to consider the form of deprivation that has to be measured and not the status of the individuals suffering from it [Townsend *et al* 1988].

The index is calculated as follows:

Let $T_1 = \log(X_1 + 1);\ T_2 = \log(X_2 + 1);\ T_3 = X_3;\ T_4 = X_4$

and

$$z_1 = \frac{t_1 - \mu_{T_1}}{s_{T_1}};\ z_2 = \frac{t_2 - \mu_{T_2}}{s_{T_2}};\ z_3 = \frac{t_3 - \mu_{T_3}}{s_{T_3}} \text{ and } z_4 = \frac{t_4 - \mu_{T_4}}{s_{T_4}}$$

being μ_{T_i} $i=1,\ldots,4$ and s_{T_i} $i=1,\ldots,4$ the means and the standard deviations for the whole area of interest.

Townsend index is given by the un-weighted sum of the z_i:

$$Townsend\ Index = \sum_{i=1}^{4} z_i$$

Note that the unemployment and overcrowding variables are transformed using a log-transformation, which achieves several effects. Log-transformations are, in fact commonly used to stabilize variances, make relationships linear and reduce skewness. In addition, this type of transformation allows more normal distributions to be obtained, especially in the case of a large, positive asymmetry [Osborne 2002].

Negative values of the overall Townsend scores reflect less deprived areas, positive values reflect more deprived areas.

1.3. The Carstairs Deprivation Index

This index was created by Carstairs and Morris in 1991 to evaluate existing health inequalities within the population of Scotland. Also well known as the SCOTDEP, it is very similar to the Townsend index and differs from it only in the presence of variables which pertain more to the situation in Scotland. The SCOTDEP, also used in epidemiological analysis, is based on the combination of four socioeconomic variables originally derived from a 1981 census. The variables were chosen on the basis of previous works which examined health and deprivation in the areas of Glasgow and Edinburgh. In accordance with the author's wishes, each of the indicators selected are representative or determinant of material disadvantage [Carstairs and Morris 1991].

Two of the variables are the same as used by Townsend though unemployment is restricted to males (considering the low rate of female employment in Scotland) and being in a low social class substitutes housing tenure. This choice is justified by the author's observation that "being in a low social class...indicates earnings at the lower end of the income scale...Housing tenure does not feature in our list of indicators since this is considered to be of lesser value in Scotland which has a higher proportion of its housing stock in the public sector and lesser variation between areas than occurs in England and Wales" [Carstairs and Morris 1991]. So they concluded that " the variable would not have acted as a discriminator between large sections of the population" [Morris and Carstairs 1991].

The variables selected are listed below:

1. X_1 = persons in private households living at a density of >1 person per room as a proportion of all persons in private households
2. X_2 = proportion of economically active males who are seeking work

3. X_3 = proportion of all persons in private households with the head of household in social class four or five
4. X_4 = proportion of all persons in private households with no car

Note that "unlike a number of other measures considered, all four variables are calculated on the basis of individuals not households; this is considered preferable for the purpose of the analysis of events which relate to individuals but in practice the differences from using the two approaches are likely to be small" [Carstairs and Morris 1991].

The SCOTDEP is an un-weighted combination of four standardized variables:

let $z_1 = \frac{x_1 - \mu_{X_1}}{s_{X_1}}$, $z_2 = \frac{x_2 - \mu_{X_2}}{s_{X_2}}$, $z_3 = \frac{x_3 - \mu_{X_3}}{s_{X_3}}$ and $z_4 = \frac{x_4 - \mu_{X_4}}{s_{X_4}}$

being μ_{X_i} $i=1,\ldots,4$ and s_{X_i} $i=1,\ldots,4$ respectively the means and the standard deviations for the whole area of Scotland, the index is given by:

$$SCOTDEP = \sum_{i=1}^{4} z_i$$

The larger the score, the greater the deprivation suffered by the area of interest.

The extended distribution of the index was subdivided into seven categories, determined on the basis of standard deviation distribution, that give way to a "new" variable called the DEPCAT (deprivation category). DEPCAT 7 identifies the greatest deprivation, DEPCAT 1 highest affluence.

1.4. The MATDEP and SOCDEP

In 1993, Forrest and Gordon [Forrest and Gordon 1993] developed two different measures of deprivation. Following the distinction between material and social deprivation explicitly stated by Townsend, the MATDEP is designed to measure material deprivation, the SOCDEP social deprivation. On this basis all the variables included in the MATDEP are "direct indicators" of deprivation, representative of the deprivation state, whereas those for the SOCDEP are "indirect indicators", and represent those suffering the condition. The variable unemployment, although classified by Townsend as a direct indicator, represents an individual condition and hence can be considered similar to an indirect indicator. Both indexes use 1991 census data.

Variables included in the MATDEP are:

1. . X_1 = percentage of household with more than one person per room

2. X_2 = percentage of households lacking or sharing use of a bath/shower and/or indoor WC
3. X_3 = percentage of household with no central heating
4. X_4 = percentage of household with no car

The index is formulated as follows:

let $\max(X_i),\ i=1,\ldots,4$ the maximum values for each indicator in the whole area of interest, the overall score is given by the un-weighted sum of each x_i divided by its maximum, which is

$$MATDEP = \sum_{i=1}^{4} \frac{x_i}{\max(X_i)}.$$

Variables included in the SOCDEP are:

1. X_1 = percentage of unemployed, economically active population.
2. X_2 = percentage of economically active, unemployed 16-24 year olds.
3. X_3 = single parent households as a proportion of all households.
4. X_4 = percentage of households containing a single pensioner.
5. X_5 = percentage of households containing a person with a limiting long-term illness.
6. X_6 = percentage of households containing dependants only (e.g. single pensioners with long term illnesses)

The SOCDEP score is, like the MATDEP, the sum of the un-weighted, standardised scores for each variable, so being $\max(X_i),\ i=1,\ldots,6$ the maximum values for each indicator in the whole area of interest,

$$SOCDEP = \sum_{i=1}^{6} \frac{x_i}{\max(X_i)}$$

Both indexes are therefore sums of values between zero and one. Consequently, there are four maximum theoretical scores for the MATDEP and six for the SOCDEP, both corresponding to the greatest deprivation.

1.5. The Index of Multiple Deprivation 2000 (IMD 2000)

The Index of Multiple Deprivation 2000, commissioned in 1998 by the Department of the Environment, Transport and the Regions (DETR), was developed by the Department of Social Policy and Social Work at the University of Oxford in order to supply local authorities with useful information [DETR 2000]. This is an area level, innovative, detailed index that reviews and updates the 1991 Index of Local Conditions (1991 ILC) and 1998 Index of Local Deprivation (1998 ILD). The IMD 2000 is made up of six separate "domains" of deprivation, listed below:

1. Income
2. Employment
3. Health Deprivation and Disability
4. Education, Skills and Training
5. Housing
6. Geographical Access to Services.

The index is based on the premise that deprivation is made up of separate dimensions, each one reflecting different aspects of deprivation. For this reason an appropriate index is calculated for each dimension: indexes are made up of a number of indicators statistically robust, up to date and available at a ward level for the whole of England. Above all, each index should directly measure a major aspect of the dimension of deprivation under consideration [DETR 2000].

Methodology to calculate the index is complex, but the main points can be summarized as follows:

1. Income and Employment index are presented as a simple rate, so "if a ward scores 38,6 in the Income Domain, this means that 38,6% of the ward's population are income deprived,...and is it possible to say that Ward X with a score of 40% is twice deprived as Ward Y with a score of 20%" [DETR 2000]
2. the other four indexes are obtained by combining indicators using factor analysis
3. then for each index a rank of one is assigned to the most deprived ward, and a rank of 8414 is assigned to the least deprived ward.

The IMD 2000 uses 32 indicators taken from a great number of data sources[4], among which some previously untapped sources stand out, such as the Department of Social Security benefits data and University and Colleges Admission Service (UCAS) data. Note that most of the indicators can be regularly updated simply because they are not derived from census data alone, which would quickly become outdated [DETR 2000].

The six separate indexes are then combined into an overall index as follow:

1. Indexes scores are transformed to a standard distribution, using exponential transformation
2. Then indexes are summed after the weights listed below have been applied[5]

1. Income [25%];

2. Employment [25%];
3. Health Deprivation and Disability [15%];
4. Education, Skills and Training [15%];
5. Housing [10%]
6. Geographical Access to Services [10%];

Again, the greater the IMD 2000 score, the more deprived the ward, and the overall index is then ranked in the same way as the Domain Indices.

Furthermore, six summarizing measures of the IMD 2000 have been produced at district level; they focus on different aspects of multiple deprivation and give local authorities information pertaining to the form of deprivation suffered in their area of interest.

Table 2. Indexes of deprivation

	Jarman (UPA 8)	Townsend	Carstairs	MATDEP	SOCDEP
Primary application	Allocating resources to GP's	Analysis of inequalities in health	Analysis of inequalities in health		
Further application	Analysis admission rates to psychiatric hospitals	Epidemiological analysis	Epidemiological analysis		
Purpose(Y)	GP's workload	Material deprivation	Material deprivation	Material deprivation	Social deprivation
Independent variables (X)					
X_1 Elderly alone	√				√
x_2 Children under 5	√				
x_3 single parent households	√				√
X_4 Household social class 5	√				
x_5 Unemployment	√	√	√ (Male)	√	√ √ (Youth)
X_6 Overcrowding	√	√	√	√	
x_7 Moved	√				
x_8 Ethnic minorities	√				
x_9 Households x no car		√	√	√)	
x_{10} Housing tenure		√			
x_{11} Households social classes 4 or 5			√		
x_{12} Households x no amenity				√	
x_{13} Households x no central heating				√	
x_{14} Households x limiting long-term illnesses					√
x_{15} Households x dependants only					√
Index formulation	Additive	Additive	Additive	Additive	Additive
Weights	Yes	No	No	No	No
Transformation used	*	Log of 2 x	None	None	None
Standardization	Yes	Yes	Yes	No	No
Normalization	No	No	No	Yes	Yes
Data sources	Census	Census	Census	Census	Census

1.6. A Comparison of Deprivation Indexes

Table 2 summarizes the indexes reviewed, with the exception of the IMD 2000 (excluded for its particular typology).

These indexes present two common characteristics:

1. they are made up of variables which identify a condition of disadvantage
2. their formulation is additive

All the selected variables appear to be correct in describing a state of disadvantage. The question is to establish the methodological reasons underlying their selection.

Given that the problem of data availability limits the choice of available indicators from a census, it must be kept in mind that all indexes are constructed leaving aside a universally accepted definition of the dependent variable which has to be measured.

This is why Jarman (who was not primarily interested in measuring deprivation) solves this problem adopting a consensual approach while Townsend links primary care needs to a concept of material deprivation, which he himself defines theoretically and distinguishes from social deprivation, thereby also making a distinction between direct and indirect indicators of deprivation.

Carstairs, Forrest and Gordon follow the line traced by Townsend, but point out differences which, on the one hand, include the need of taking "face validity" into account (as we have already seen, this is Carstairs's reason for considering the male gender only in unemployment and excluding housing tenure), and on the other hand mark the non-existence of a well defined theoretical reference basis (mentioning, for example, the double meaning of unemployment included in the SOCDEP).

In the choice of indicators, further limitation is due to statistical considerations, so highly inter-correlated variables and indicators with poor predictive capacity need to be excluded.

With reference to variables concretely used, note that although indexes could be re-calculated by using more recent census data, exogenous changes that occur with the passing of time could diminish the significance of some variables (e.g. car ownership, at present, seems to be less relevant as a proxy for income).

Weights are applied only to the Jarman index (again, on the basis of a consensual approach), while in other indices the same weight is given to each indicator, probably because it does not seem possible to accurately evaluate influences different determinants have on deprivation.

The use of transformations meets statistical needs, although this has been criticized (in the case of Jarman) since it "obscures the original policy intent" [Carr Hill and Sheldon 1991].

Variables are standardized or normalized: first solution seems to be preferable, simply because it is possible to give an unambiguous meaning to zero value, which indicates an average situation of deprivation.

PART 2. AN INDEX OF DEPRIVATION FOR GENOA (GDI): A PROPOSAL

2.1. Materials and Methods

The aim of this paper is to propose an index of deprivation following the British examples. It was decided to develop a material deprivation index, which represents a neutral objective measure, independent from the consequences of the individual standard of life [Testi et Ivaldi, 2009]. Thus among the indexes presented above, the ones of Towsend and Carstairs were taken into consideration. They do not appear, however, completely appropriate in describing deprivation in today's society. Some variables are obsolete, for instance "car ownership", while others are not meaningful in Italian society, such as "social class". Consequently, a new index has been proposed.

First of all, the definition of a small geographic unit [Reijneveld et al 2000] for the deprivation index to be calculated was required. This unit is commonly called a "small area" . In the present paper, geographical areas have been identified through so-called Urban Units (UUs), into which the city of Genoa has been divided. UUs presently represent the smallest areas able to satisfy the need for population homogeneity and data availability at the same time. The relationship between health inequalities and socioeconomic conditions is studied with reference to the 71 *UUs* of the city of Genoa: each Unit has an average population of about 9,500 people.

Secondly, the variables included in the index must be chosen. This choice is strictly related to the concept of material deprivation and the availability of reliable and updated data. The variables should be, as said above, "direct" measures of deprivation [Townsend et. al.1988]. Variables reflecting demographic sub-groups, such as ethnic minorities and elderly people living alone, were therefore excluded. The chosen variables are the following: i) unemployment, ii) housing ownership, iii) overcrowding, iv) low education level.

Unemployment represents a state of economical insecurity and lack of resources; housing ownership could be intended as a proxy for wealth, while overcrowding has been inserted for its potential capacity to synthesize living conditions.

The fourth variable, "low education level", is used as a proxy to represent social position and indirectly gives information about current income.

The choice of the variables has been limited to the ones derivable from census data, updated at a municipal level when possible. Consequently, some potentially relevant variables were excluded if unavailable at UU level.

The four variables selected were quantified as indicated below (2001 census):

1. X_1 = % of unemployed people compared to active (Unemployment)
2. X_2 = % of households living in rented houses (Housing ownership)
3. X_3 = *a*verage number of people per room (Overcrowding)
4. X_4 = % of people with secondary education (8 years) or lower (Low education level)

An additional index was computed, summing the partial indicators referring to each variable selected.

Due to the non-normality of original distributions[6], the use of a transformation capable of achieving an approximately normal distribution for each variable is required [Jarman, Townsend et al, Carstairs and Morris, Cadum et al]. The Box Cox method [Box and Cox 1964] was used to find an appropriate transformation [Bland et al. 1996].

This method turns to a family of power transformations given by

$$x(\lambda)=\frac{(x^{\lambda}-1)}{\lambda} \qquad \lambda \neq 0$$

$$x(\lambda)=\ln(x) \qquad \lambda = 0$$

and it plans, in order to select the value of parameter λ, to use the value which, given an observations vector $\mathrm{X}=x_1,x_2,\ldots,x_n$, maximizes the logarithm of the likelihood function

$$f(x,\lambda)=-\frac{n}{2}\ln(\sigma^2_{X(\lambda)})+(\lambda-1)\sum_{i=1}^{n}\ln(x_i)\cdot$$

After variables have been transformed, z-scores were calculated for each observation. These are obtained by subtracting the mean of Genoa from the observed transformed value and dividing the result by the standard deviation of Genoa.

2.2. Results and Discussion

The variables for measuring deprivation were drawn from the Census Data (Statistical and studies Department - Municipality of Genoa, Italy). In Table 3, the mean and standard deviations of the four variables measuring socioeconomic conditions are reported.

Table 3. Variables describing socioeconomic conditions of the city of Genoa

	Housing ownership (% rented houses)	Overcrowding (# of people per room)	Unemployment (% unemployed compared to active)	low education (% people with secondary education or lower)
mean	24.77	0.55	8.56	64.09
S.D.	7.35	0.07	2.29	13.52

The index has been calculated for all UUs within the city of Genoa as explained above.

The index scores range from -5,80 to 13,80. The distribution does not exhibit absolute normality, because a positive asymmetry exists (skewness 0,652).

Index values have been ranked: a rank of 1 was assigned to the most affluent UU and a rank of 71 to the most deprived.

In order to better distinguish between different levels of deprivation, the index distribution has been divided into six categories determined on the basis of standard deviation. Category 1 (very affluent) identifies less deprived UUs; on the contrary, Category 6 (great deprivation) contains UUs characterized by strong deprivation.

Table 4. Class boundaries and deprivation categories

Number	Deprivation categories	Boundaries	# of UUs
1	Very affluent	(-5.80;-σ)	13
2	Affluent	(-σ;-σ/2)	6
3	Not deprived	(-σ/2; 0)	15
4	Low deprivation	(0;+σ/2)	20
5	Middle deprivation	(+σ/2; σ)	11
6	High deprivation	(σ; +13.80)	6

Table 5. Deprivation scores and deprivation classes

ID	UU	Index Score	Category
64	Lido	- 5,80	1
39	S. Vincenzo	- 5,74	1
38	Manin	- 5,71	1
62	Albaro	- 5,70	1
37	Castelletto	- 5,63	1
65	Puggia	- 5,63	1
63	San Giuliano	- 5,34	1
41	Foce	- 4,78	1
40	Carignano	- 4,78	1
68	Quartara	- 4,07	1
42	Brignole	- 4,01	1
36	San Nicola	- 3,92	1
70	Quinto	- 3,26	1
66	Sturla	- 2,80	2
67	Quarto	- 2,63	2
61	San Martino	- 2,56	2
7	Pegli	- 2,38	2
56	Bavari	- 1,89	2
69	Castagna	- 1,69	2
71	Nervi	- 1,57	3
8	Multedo	- 1,42	3
27	Belvedere	- 1,42	3
1	Crevari	- 1,35	3
30	San Teodoro	- 1,31	3
58	Apparizione	- 1,21	3
9	Sestri	- 0,98	3
47	Marassi	- 0,87	3
43	S. Agata	- 0,86	3
25	San Gaetano	- 0,68	3

Table 5. (Continued)

ID	UU	Index Score	Category
26	Sampierdarena	- 0,64	3
28	S. Bartolomeo	- 0,44	3
60	Chiappeto	- 0,38	3
44	S. Fruttuoso	- 0,16	3
48	Forte Quezzi	- 0,07	3
32	Oregina	0,04	4
31	Lagaccio	0,05	4
34	Maddalena	0,70	4
6	Castelluccio	1,10	4
15	Rivarolo	1,14	4
19	Morego	1,15	4
4	Palmaro	1,18	4
59	Borgoratti	1,21	4
50	San Pantaleo	1,26	4
46	Fereggiano	1,26	4
11	Calcinara	1,36	4
12	Borzoli Ovest	1,41	4
35	Molo	1,50	4
21	Pontedecimo	1,52	4
55	Prato	1,53	4
10	S. G. Battista	1,57	4
23	Campi	1,59	4
14	Certosa	1,64	4
29	Angeli	1,65	4
57	S. Desiderio	1,67	4
45	Quezzi	2,06	5
2	Voltri	2,08	5
49	Parenzo	2,28	5
13	Borzoli Est	2,46	5
24	Campasso	2,52	5
53	Molassana	2,58	5
54	Doria	2,82	5
33	Prè	2,90	5
51	Montesignano	2,93	5
20	S. Quirico	3,22	5
22	Cornigliano	3,27	5
5	Pra'	3,62	6
16	Teglia	3,73	6
18	Bolzaneto	5,48	6
52	S. Eusebio	5,56	6
17	Begato	5,82	6
3	Ca' Nuova	13,80	6

Table 4 shows the definition of classes and boundaries. Note that the classes are unequal; they were not, in fact, designed to ensure equality of numbers within classes but to retain the discriminatory features of the distribution. Other methods of determining the boundaries of classes (e.g. septiles or quintiles) would not affect substantial changes in the general patterns observed.

According to the above mentioned criteria, results for each UU are presented in table 5: index score, ranking and category number. The first column lists the UU Census Identification number.

From the methodological point of view, the index distribution for the 71 UUs has a mean of zero and a standard deviation of 3,36. This value of the standard deviation is due to the existence of a correlation between selected variables, as shown in table 6. In particular, a rather strong linear relationship exists between low education level and housing ownership.

Table 6. Correlation matrix

	Housing ownership	Overcrowding	Unemployment	Low education
Housing ownership	1			
Overcrowding	,311(**)	1		
Unemployment	,728(**)	,394(**)	1	
Low education	,343(**)	,511(**)	,691(**)	1

** Correlation is significant at the 0.01 level (2-tailed).

Finally, a deprivation map of the city of Genoa, representing the UUs (identified by their ID number), is obtained (Figure 1).

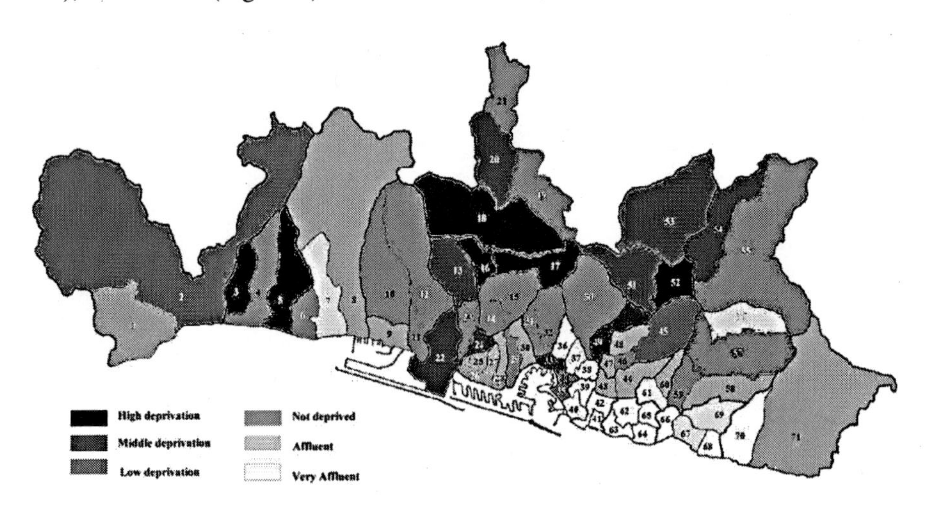

Figure 1. Deprivation classes in Genoa.

According to what may be considered as "face validity", the most affluent areas are concentrated in the southeast, near the sea. The most deprived UUs are in the industrial or ex-industrial areas where numerous council houses are dislocated.

A rigorous validation was required in order to use the index in the resource allocation. Following past experiences [Haynes et al. 1999; Testi et Ivaldi, 2008; Van Lenthe et al, 2005

Gordon et al 1995; Quaglia et al 2005; Quaglia et al 2010; Vercelli et al. 2006], correlation between index and mortality was studied. Death records referring to the two years analyzed in this paper were collected from the Mortality Registry of Genoa (http://registri.istge.it/). A three-year average was carried out.

Standardized Mortality Ratios (SMR) for all causes were calculated for each UU. SMR measure relative risk, which is the probability of death for people living in a specified UU related to the same probability calculated in a reference group, which is the city of Genoa.

SMR could be interpreted as a measurement of increase/decrease of the probability of death compared to the reference group. They have been calculated for people aged 0-64 and over 65. Remember that SMR=1, which means that the deprivation category does not influence the risk of premature mortality, whereas if it is <1 or >1, socioeconomic conditions decrease or increase, respectively.

The results are substantially encouraging because they confirm index effectiveness in explaining variations of the socioeconomic circumstances within Genoa. The predictor role of the socioeconomic circumstances with respect to variations in mortality patterns seems verified.

Table 7 shows that this happens particularly for the people aged 0-64. The association between deprivation classes and *SMR* is very strong: Living in the most deprived area implies a high differential of premature dying risk, in fact, the ratio between SMR of the most deprived category to the most affluent was about 64%.

Table 7. Correlation between mortality and deprivation

Deprivation class	SMR
	Male-Female 0-64
1 Very affluent	0.83
2 Affluent	0.79
3 Not deprived	0.95
4 Low deprivation	1.03
5 Middle deprivation	1.10
6 high deprivation	1.47

The Pearson Correlation between GDI and SMR for the age class 0-64 is 0,622 (2001), showing that more than 50% of premature deaths are due to socioeconomic conditions coeteris paribus.

2.3. Conclusions

The analysis developed is based on the hypothesis that the demand for social and health services depends not only upon the supply of "individual risk" factor and "availability effect", but also on "ecological risk" factors [Lancaster et al 2002]; . For this reason, people living in a geographical area with certain characteristics have specific needs, all conditions being equal

[Sloggett et al 1994]. In other words, the features of the residence area, such as an unhealthy environment, unfavorable residential conditions, unsatisfactory transport services, a generally disadvantaged economic situation, could even influence individual risk and therefore require *ad hoc* readjustment interventions/actions. As a result, the analysis and assessment of deprivation situations is aimed at contributing to the restoration of equity, adapting the allocation of resources taking into consideration the diverse socioeconomic conditions that distinguish different regions. The inequalities to be removed are not only those referring to health indicators (different mortality and morbidity), but also, more generally, those that reduce the opportunities of a better quality of life; participating in society, being able to enjoy a better urban environment and so on.

Deprivation indexes on a geographical basis seem to be a good starting point because, being calculated on a regional basis, they are probably able to integrate information about that part of private welfare that depends on social organization type and culture, generally on all the factors that may be summed up in the characteristics of a certain region. The model used to assess the disadvantages typical of different geographical areas has been chosen considering the traditional, well-established models in the UK. After a review of the main indicators proposed in literature, we were led to the formulation of a deprivation index (GDI). This index, applied to a Genoese reality, appeared to be useful in explaining the mortality differentials among the municipality's different urban units/entities. The proposal for decision makers in the social and health field is therefore to use the index to integrate present criteria for resource allocation so that it is more consistent with actual socioeconomic risk situations on a regional basis. It is worth mentioning that an allocation of resources that takes into account these differentials could meet not only ethical requirements aimed at increasing equity, but also mere efficiency requirements: the removal of obstacles to express oneself at one's best, in the meaning of Sen's capability approach, actually allows for the removal of obstacles to economic development as well.

It is possible to distinguish various fields in which the availability of deprivation indicators allows us to study phenomena more in depth and could be functional to better intervention planning, especially for indicators calculated not only for the Genoa municipality but the whole region of Liguria. An interesting application is the explication of the hospitalization rates' differentials in different regions, which could be explained by diverse socioeconomic conditions, all other conditions being equal. Another use could be the exploitation of overall knowledge pertaining to the socioeconomic conditions in the different geographical areas, in order to deepen existing synergies also among various intervention areas, mainly in the area of social-health care. Joint intervention and cooperation among regional, health and municipal administrations are of increasing necessity in order to arrange effective, integration systems of various types of services; social, health and combined social-health care. In this framework, deprivation indicators could be a suitable means of highlighting the potential welfare burden of an area and the need for social aid, thus analyzing the aspects of social-health integration between the municipalities and public health service providers (Asl) [Sheldon et al. 1992; Brenna 2007]

In the end, it is worth mentioning that the proposed index could be further improved, trying to favor the connection among different administration databases, already effective in other regions, also thanks to the widespread application of new information and communication technologies. The analysis should be mainly refined from two points of view. The first regards the *small area* of reference, deepening the relationship of the dimension of the considered area, the indicator's significance and its explicative ability through suitable sensitivity analyses. The second concerns broadening the analysis to indirect variables as well, allowing for material deprivation measures and social ones to be combined.

REFERENCES

Barnett R., Moon G. Kearns R. (2004), Social inequality and ethnic differences in smoking in New Zealand, *Social Science et Medicine*, 59:129-143.

Barnett S., Roderick P, Martin D, Diamond I. (2001), A multilevel analysis of the effects of rurality and social deprivation on premature limiting long term illness, *J. Epidemiology Community Health*; 55: 44-51.

Bartley, M., et Blane, D. (1994). Commentary: Appropriateness of deprivation indices must be ensured. *British Medical Journal*, 309, 1479.

Benach, J., et Yasui, Y. (1999). Geographical patterns of excess mortality in Spain explained by two indices of deprivation. *Journal of Epidemiology and Community Health,* 53, 423-431.

Biggeri A., Benvenuti A., Merler E., Nardulli M., Olmastroni L., (1998), La mortalità per condizione socioeconomica e professionale nello studio longitudinale toscano. Comuni di Livorno e Firenze, *Informazioni Statistiche, settore Studi e Ricerche* n° 5 Maggio.

Bland J, Altman D. (1996) Statistics Notes: Transforming data. *British Medical Journal*; 312: 770.

Boarini, R. et M. Mira d'Ercole (2006), Measures of Material Deprivation in OECD Countries, OECD Social Employment and Migration Working Papers, No. 37, OECD Publishing.

Box G., Cox D. (1964) An analysis of transformations (with discussion), *Journal Royal Statistic Society B*, 26, 211-252.

Boyle P, Gatrell A, Duke-Williams O. (1999) The effect on morbidity of variability in deprivation and population stability in England and Wales: an investigation at small-area level. *Social Science et Medicine* 49:791-799.

Boyle P, Gatrell A, Duke-Williams O. (2001) Do area-level population change, deprivation and variations in deprivation affect individual-level self–reported limiting long-term illness?, *Social Science et Medicine* 53 795-799.

Boyle, P., Gatrell, A., et Duke-Williams, O. (1999). The effect on morbidity of variability in deprivation and population stability in England and Wales: an investigation at small-area level. *Social Science et Medicine* 49, 791-799.

Brenna E. (2007) La ponderazione della quota capitaria in base a fattori di deprivazione. Suggerimenti per l'Italia dall'esperienza scozzese, *Politiche Sanitarie* 8, n°2: 65:76.

Buckingham K, Freeman P. (1997), Sociodemographic and morbidity indicators of need in relation to the use of community health service: observational study, *British Medical Journal*, 315: 994-996.

Buckingham K, Freeman P. Sociodemographic and morbidity indicators of need in relation to the use of community health service: observational study. *British Medical Journal* 1997; 315: 994-996.

Cadum E, Costa F, Biggeri A, Martuzzi M. (1999), Deprivazione e mortalità: un indice di deprivazione per l'analisi delle disuguaglianze su base geografica, *Epidemiologia e Prevenzione*; 23: 175-187.

Costa G., Cislaghi C., Caranci N.; (2009) Le disuguaglianze sociali di salute. Problemi di definizione e di misura Salute e Società, Franco Angeli, 1, pp. 6.

Carr Hill R, Sheldon T. Designing a deprivation payment for general practitioners: the UPA(8) wonderland. *British Medical Journal* 1991; 302: 393-396.

Carr Hill R., Jamison J., O'reilly D., Stevenson M., Reid J. (2002), Risk adjustment for hospital use using social security data: cross sectional *small area* analysis, *British Medical Journal*, 324: 390.

Carstairs V. (2000), Socio-economic factors at area level and their relationship with health: In Elliott, P., Wakefield, J., Best, N., Briggs, D. (Eds.). Spatial Epidemiology methods and applications (pp. 51-68). Oxford University Press.

Carstairs, V., et Morris, R. (1991). Deprivation and Health in Scotland. Aberdeen: Aberdeen University Press.

Costa G., Spadea T. Cardano M. (2004), Diseguaglianze di salute in Italia, *Epidemiologia e Prevenzione*, 28:3-15.

Crampton, P., Salmond, C., et Sutton, F. (1997). NZDep91 Index of Deprivation Research Report No. 5. Wellington: Health Services Research Centre.

Crayford T, Shanks J, Bajekal M, Langford S. (1995) Analysis from inner London of deprivation payments based on enumeration districts rather than wards, *British Medical Journal*; 311: 787-788.

Davey Smith, G., Whitley, E., Dorling, D., et Gunnel, D. (2001). Area based measures of social and economic circumstances: cause specific mortality patterns depend on the choice of index. *Journal of Epidemiology and Community Health*, 55, 149-150.

Deaton A. (2003), Health, Inequality and Economic Developmentr, Journal of Economic Literature, XLI, 113-158.

Department of environment, transport and the regions (DETR), (2000), Indices of Deprivation 2000, *Regeneration Research Summary,* Vol. 31, 3-42.

Department Of Environment, Transport And The Regions. Indices of Deprivation 2000. *Regeneration Research Summary.* N. 31; 2000.

Forrest, R., et Gordon, D. (1993). People and Places: a 1991 Census atlas of England. SAUS. University of Bristol.

Freeman M, Tukey J. *Ann. Math. Statist.* 1950; 21, 607-611.

Fuchs V.R. (2004), Reflections on the socio-economic correlates of health, *Journal of Health Economics*, 23: 653-661

Fuchs, V. (2004). Reflections on the socio-economic correlates of health. *Journal of Health Economics,* 23, 653-661.

Gilthorpe M. Wilson R. (2003), Rural/urban differences in the association between deprivation and healthcare utilisation, *Social Science et Medicine*, 57, 11;2055-2063.

Glover G, Robin E, Emami J, Arabscheibani G. A Needs index for mental health care. *Soc Psychiatry Psichiatr Epidemiol* 1998; 33: 89-96.

Gordon D. (1995) Census Based Deprivation Indices: Their Weighting and Validation, *Journal of Epidemiology and Community Health,* 49 (Suppl 2), S39-S44.

Gordon D., Pantazis C., (1997), *Breadline Britain in the 1990s*, Ashgate Publishing Limited, England.

Hales, S., Black, W., Skelly, C., Salmond, C., et Weinstein, P. (2003). Social deprivation and the public health risks of community drinking water supplies in New Zealand. *Journal of Epidemiology and Community Health*, 57, 581-583.

Haynes R. Gale S. (1999), Mortality, long-term illness and deprivation in rural and metropolitan wards of England and Wales, *Health Place*, 5; 301-312.

Jarman B. Underprivileged areas: validation and distribution of scores. *BMJ* 1984; 289: 1587-92.

Jarman, B. (1983). Identification of underprivileged areas. *BMJ,* 1983, 286, 1705-09.

Judge K, Mays N. Equity in health care. *BMJ* 1994; 309: 673.

Judge K, Mays N. Equity in the NHS Allocating resources for health and social care in England. *BMJ* 1994; 308: 1363-1366.

Kelleher, C., Timoney, A., Friel, S., et McKeown, D. (2002) Indicators of deprivation, voting patterns and health status at area level in the Republic of Ireland. *Journal of Epidemiology and Community Health*, 56, 36-44.

Lancaster G, Green M. (2002), Deprivation, ill-health and the ecological fallacy, *Journal Royal Statistic Society A*, 165, Part 2, 263-278.

Macintyre S, Ellaway A, Cummins E. (2002), Place effects on health: how we can conceptualise, operationalise and measure them?, *Social Science and Medicine* 55:125-139.

Mackenbach Johan P, Bos Vivian, Andersen Otto, Cardano Mario, Costa Giuseppe, Harding Seeromanie, Reid Alison, Hemström Orjan, Valkonen Tapani, Kunst Anton E (2003). Widening socioeconomic inequalities in mortality in six Western European countries. *Int. J. Epidemiol.* Oct 2003; 32(5):830–837

Michelozzi P., Perucci C., Forastiere F., Fusco D., Ancona A., Dell'orco V., (1999), Differenze sociali nella mortalità a Roma negli anni 1990-1995, *Epidemiologia e Prevenzione*, 23: 230-238.

Morris R, Carstairs V. Which Deprivation? A comparison of selected deprivation indexes. *Journal of Public Health Medicine* 1991; 13: 318-326.

Osborne J. Notes on the use of data transformations. *Practical Assessment, Research et Evaluation* 2002; 8(6).

Phillimore P, Beattie A, Townsend P. Widening inequality of health in northern England, 1981-91. *BMJ* 1994; 308: 1125-1128.

Quaglia A, Vercelli M, Lillini R, Mugno E, Coebergh JW, Quinn M, Martinez-Garcia C, Capocaccia R, Micheli A, and the ELDCARE Working Group. Socio-economic factors and health care system characteristics related to cancer survival in the elderly. A population-based analysis in sixteen European countries. *Crit. Rev. Oncol. Hemat.* 2005; 54:117-128.

Quaglia A, Lillini R, Casella C, Giachero G, Izzotti A, Vercelli M, Liguria Region Tumour Registry. The combined effect of age and socio-economic status on breast cancer survival. *Crit .Rev. Oncol. Hematol.* 2010 Mar 12. [Epub ahead of print].

Rapiti E., Perucci C., Agabiti N., Ancona C., Arcà M., Di Lallo D., Forastiere F., Miceli M., Porta D., (1999), Disuguaglianze socioeconomiche nell'efficacia dei trattamenti sanitari. Tre esempi nel Lazio, *Epidemiologia e Prevenzione*, 23:153-160.

Reijneveld S, Verheij R, De Bakker D. (2000), The impact of area deprivation on differences in health: does the choice of geographical classification matter? *Journal Epidemiology Community Health*; 54: 306-313.

Salmond, C., et Crampton, P. (2002). Heterogeneity of deprivation within very small areas. *Journal of Epidemiology and Community Health,* 56, 669-670.

Scottish Executive Health Department, *Fair Shares for All,* 1999 Report of the National Review of Resource Allocation for the NHS in Scotland, July.

Sheldon T., Carr-Hill R., (1992), Resource Allocation by Regression in the National Health Service: a Critique of the Resource Allocation Working Party's Review, *Journal of the Royal Statistical Society*, 155, Part 3, 403-420.

Sloggett A, Joshi H. (1994), Higher mortality in deprived areas: community or personal disadvantage?, *British Medical Journal*; 309:1470-1474.

SLTo (a cura di P. Baldi, A. Biggeri, A. Barchielli) (2004), *Studio Longitudinale Toscano, Condizione socio-economica e ricovero ospedaliero a Firenze*, Regione Toscana, Firenze

Smits J., Westert G. Van Den Bos G. (2002), Socioeconomic status of very *small area*s and stroke incidence in the Netherlands, in *Journal Epidemiology Community Health*, 56:637-640.

Smits, J., Westert, G., et Van Den Bos, G. (2002). Socioeconomic status of very small areas and stroke incidence in the Netherlands. *Journal of Epidemiology and Community Health,* 56, 637-640.

Spandonaro F., Mennini F.S., Atella V. (2004), Criteri per l'allocazione regionale delle risorse per la sanità, *Politiche Sanitarie*, 5, 1, 2004.

Sutton M., Gravelle H., Morris S., Leyland A., Windmeijer F., Dibben C:, Muirhead M., 2002 Allocation of Resources to English Areas (AREA). Individual and small area determinants of morbidity and use of healthcare resources. *Report to the Department of Health*. Edinburgh: Information and Statistic Division.

Testi A., Ivaldi E. (2009), Material versus social deprivation and health: a case study of an urban area, *The European Journal of Health Economics*: Volume 10, Issue3; pp 323–328.

Torsheim T., Currie C., Boyce W, Kalnins I. Overpeck M. Haughland S. (2004) Material deprivation and self-rated health: a multilevel study of adolescents from 22 European and North American countries, *Social Science et Medicine*, 59:1-12.

Townsend, P. (1987). Deprivation. *Journal of Social Policy* 16,2, 125-146.

Townsend, P., Phillimore, P., et Beattie, A. (1988). Health and deprivation: inequality and the North. London: Croom Helm.

Valerio M, Vitullo F. (2000) Sperimentazione di un indice di svantaggio sociale in Basilicata, in *Epidemiologia e Prevenzione*; 24: 219-223.

Van Doorslaer E. (1997), Socioeconomic inequalities in health: Measurement, computation*Journal of Econometrics*, 77, (1), 87-103.

Van Lenthe, F J, Borrell, L N, Costa, G, Diez Roux, A V, Kauppinen, T M, Marinacci, C, Martikainen, P, Regidor, E, Stafford, M, Valkonen, T (2005). Neighbourhood unemployment and all cause mortality: a comparison of six countries. *J. Epidemiol. Community Health* 59: 231-237.

Vercelli M, Lillini R, Capocaccia R, Micheli A, Coebergh JW, Quinn M, Martinez-Garcia C, Quaglia A, and the ELDCARE Working group. Cancer survival in the elderly: Effects of socio-economic factors and health care system features. *Eur. J. Cancer* 2006; 42:234-242.

In: Social Indicators: Statistics, Trends...
Editor: Candace M. Baird

ISBN 978-1-61122-841-0

Chapter 5

SOCIAL CAPITAL INDICATORS AND ENVIRONMENTAL POLICIES FOR PROTECTED AREAS

Nikoleta Jones*[1]*, Marina Proikaki and Panayiotis G. Dimitrakopoulos
Department of Environment, University of the Aegean,
Mytilene, Greece

ABSTRACT

Social capital is an important factor influencing several issues both in individual and collective level. Various indicators have been presented in the relevant literature for its measurement. The most commonly known are: social trust, institutional trust, social networks and social norms. The aim of the chapter is to analyze social capital indicators and to underline their connection with the development of environmental policies. Specifically the influence of social capital indicators on different environmental policy instruments will be presented. Through this analysis the importance of exploring social capital during the formation of environmental policies and the need to develop measurement techniques for this purpose is highlighted. The above issues will also be explored taking as an example environmental policies for the protection of areas with high biodiversity value.

1. INTRODUCTION

Social capital may be regarded as one of the most influential terms of sociology in the past decade (Portes, 2000). Bourdieu (1986) was one of the first theorists who analyzed the term 'social capital' emphasizing the benefits deriving for individuals from their participation in social networks. Following Bourdieu (1986), James Coleman (1988, 1990) examined social capital both in an individual and a collective level. Coleman analyzed social capital

[1] Correspondence: jones@env.aegean.gr.

focusing on the connections developed among different entities of a community (Coleman, 1990). He also underlined the importance of social capital as a collective resource for a community (Coleman, 1990). Finally, Robert Putnam (1993, 2000) made the term 'Social capital' widely known. Putnam studied social capital empirically both in Italy (Putnam, 1993) and in the United States (Putnam, 2000) and connected it with the efficiency of democratic institutions, development and collective action. Specifically, in his book '*Bowling alone: the collapse and revival of American Community*' (Putnam, 2000) he analyzed the declining aspects of social capital in the USA while in Italy he attempted to identify and explain differences between South and North Italian regions based on social capital measurements (Putnam, 1993).

The wide use of social capital and its introduction to other scientific fields is attributed to the recognition of its numerous consequences. In this context, social capital has been linked to individual health (e.g. Poortinga, 2006) employment status (e.g. Aguilera, 2002; Halpern, 2005, p.45; Zhao, 2002), academic achievement (Sandefur et al., 2006), management of natural resources (e.g. Jones, 2006; Pretty, 2003) and economic development (Woodhouse, 2006). In order to investigate the influence of social capital significant research focuses on its measurement. This is mainly conducted with the use of quantitative social research methods and in particular through the distribution of questionnaires to a representative sample of a community.

The aim of this article is to contribute to the discussion for the quantitative measurement of social capital by indicating the main sets of variables which may be used for this purpose. Furthermore, the utilization of these indicators for the development of environmental policies is highlighted taking also as an example the case of protected areas management. The chapter is divided in five main parts. In the next section the main theories and definitions concerning social capital are presented. In the third part, the indicators used for the measurement of social capital are analyzed along with a statistical technique which may be applied. In the fourth part, the connection of social capital indicators with environmental policies are described followed by the main links with protected areas management. In the final part, means of improving social capital measurement are discussed.

2. Social Capital

2.1. Main Theorists of Social Capital

Several definitions of social capital have been proposed in the relevant literature (Bourdieu, 1986; Bowles and Gintis, 2002; Coleman, 1990; Fukuyama, 2001; Portes, 1998; Woolcock and Narayan, 2000) each of them identifying different components. Jacobs (1961) analyzed social capital emphasizing social networks promoting trust, cooperation and security. Loury (1977) emphasized the benefits that each person gains and how these can be used in order to improve individual human capital (in Coleman, 1990: 300).

Despite these initial theories, Bourdieu was one of the first analysts who systematically investigated the term 'social capital' and introduced it in the field of social and political sciences (Portes, 1998; Narayan and Cassidy, 2001; Adam and Roncevic, 2003). Bourdieu claimed that it is impossible to study the structure and functioning of a society without taking into consideration all forms of capital (Bourdieu, 1986). Specifically, Bourdieu (1986:248) determined social capital as *'the aggregate of the actual or potential resources which are linked to possession of a durable network of more or less institutionalized relationships of mutual acquaintance or recognition'.* The definition of Bourdieu emphasizes two main issues. Firstly, it focuses on individuals' voluntary participation in social networks and claims that they deliberately participate in these networks in order to build 'stocks' of social capital (Portes, 1998). Secondly, social capital refers to mutual knowledge and recognition and it is transformed in a 'symbolic' capital (Bourdieu, 1986).

Regarding Coleman, he introduced the term 'social capital' in American Sociology (Portes, 1998) and connected it with issues of human capital and individual educational level (Coleman, 1988). According to Coleman '*social capital is defined by its function. It is not a single entity, but a variety of different entities having two characteristics in common: They all consist of some aspect of social structure, and they facilitate certain actions of individuals who are within the structure*' (Coleman, 1990: 302). Thus, Coleman, regards that elements of social capital may be utilized for the benefit of individuals (Portes, 2000). However, he examined social capital also from a collective aspect attributing to it three main characteristics (Coleman, 1990): a. Social capital can not be transferred as private goods; b. The number of individuals benefited from the existence of social capital exceed those who are trying for its creation and development; c. Individuals decisions influencing the formation of social capital also affect a wider group not involved in this procedure.

Although the contributions of Bourdieu and Coleman on social capital literature are important, the most influential theorist of the past two decades in this field is Robert Putnam. Putnam conducted two empirical studies, in Italy and USA (Putnam, 1993, 2000) investigating the development of social capital. His definition of social capital refers to (Putnam, 1993: 167) '*features of social organization, such as trust, norms and networks that can improve the efficiency of society by facilitating coordinated actions*'. The definition proposed by Putnam identified specific elements of social capital thus significantly facilitating future empirical research. Similar to other analysts (e.g. Fukuyama, 2001) he regards 'trust' as one of the most important components of social capital (Putnam, 2000: 137) referring mainly to trust developed among members of the community and connects it both with social norms and social networks of a society (Putnam, 1993:. 171). Putnam also regards 'generalized norms of reciprocity' as very important. These norms refer to the action of 'giving and taking' among community members (Putnam, 2000: 21): '*I'll do this for you without expecting anything specific back from you, in the confident expectation that someone else will do something for me down the road*'. Thus, in cases where higher levels of social trust are presented more actions of reciprocity will take place.

Concerning social networks, Putnam (1993) emphasizes the role of both formal and informal networks. However he underlines the role of horizontal networks of voluntary participation as they link citizens with the everyday activities of their community (Putnam, 1995b). Dense horizontal networks may increase cooperation among citizens and thus facilitate the resolution of collective problems and contribute to the efficiency of governance (Putnam 1993, 1995a). On the other hand, horizontal networks involving entities with similar roles and power are not beneficial for the development of social capital of a community. Finally, Putnam regards social capital both as 'a public and a private good' (Putnam, 2000: 20) with significant benefits in individual and collective level (e.g. better governance, less corruption and reduced criminality) (Putnam, 1993: 167; Portes, 2000).

2.2. Forms of Social Capital

2.2.1. Cognitive Social Capital

Several definitions of social capital have been presented in the relevant literature. In order to better understand the variety of elements included in 'social capital', we can divide them in two main categories: cognitive and structural elements (Grootaert and Bastelaer, 2002).

Cognitive social capital refers mainly to social norms, values and trust. Social or interpersonal trust is one of the most important components of social capital (Newton, 2001). It influences collective actions of individuals (Putnam, 1993) and may be divided in generalized trust and particularized trust (Uslaner and Conley, 2003). The former refers to trust towards individuals in general whereas the latter refers to trust towards specific social groups such as family, friends and neighbors.

A second element included in cognitive social capital is trust in institutions. These institutions refer mainly to institutions which facilitate the functioning of a community. Several institutions may be included in this category such as political and international institutions. The level of trust in these actors is highly connected with their efficiency in managing public issues (Kim, 2005).

Both social and institutional trust are connected with the existence of social norms in a community. Putnam (1993) analyzes norms of reciprocity referring mainly to the actions of an individual expecting that in the future some other member of the society will also proceed to a different action, beneficial for the individual (Putnam, 2000; Onyx and Bullen, 2000). According to Coleman (1990) these norms may be regarded as a type of obligation determining what is right and wrong in a community. However, in order these norms to function properly, collective motives should overcome individual ones (Coleman, 1990: 311).

2.2.2. Structural Social Capital

Regarding structural elements of social capital, these refer mainly to issues of social organization and social networking in a community (Uphoff, 1998). The importance of social networks has been underlined by several researchers prior to the expansion of the social capital theory. The work of Granovetter (1973) is very important concerning the analysis of social networks and their functioning in a community.

In the context of social capital, social networks have been extensively analyzed. Putnam (1998) divided social networks in two main categories. Firstly organized formal networks, referring mainly in participation to activities of non-governmental organizations (individuals may participate as members or volunteers). Secondly, the case of informal networks referring to non-organized collectivities such as friends, family and colleagues and in general any type of networking it is not in an organized context.

Apart from social networks, in the context of structural social capital several other issues may be included referring to the level of civic participation, interest in politics and participation in activities connected with collective issues in general.

2.2.3. Bonding, Bridging and Linking Social Capital

A different categorization of social capital is based on the type of social networks. The first format is '*bonding*' social capital (Putnam, 2000: σελ. 22) referring to social networks developed between the same social group such as family or friends (Woolcock and Narayan,

2000). Secondly, *bridging* social capital (Putnam 1995b; 2000: 22) refers to networks developed between different social groups facilitating the flow of information among them. A third category is *linking* social capital (Woolcock, 1998). The basic difference of linking social capital is that it examines networks of non-homogeneous groups based on their level of power and resources (Halpern, 2005: 25; Cramb, 2005; Woolcock and Narayan, 2000) such as connections between governmental actors or groups of citizens.

2.3. Consequences of Social Capital

Social capital has often been used as an explanatory parameter both in individual and collective level. A main assumption is that in communities with higher levels of social capital there is tendency to have better governance, a strong civil society, an efficient political system and also higher economic development (Putnam, 1993; Knack and Keefer, 1997; Newton, 2001). Furthermore, social capital influences the level of voluntary cooperation among citizens minimizing individualistic behaviour and the cost of cooperation (Boix and Posner, 1998; Ostrom, 2000; Putnam, 2000: 135; Maloney et.al., 2000; Van Schaik, 2002; Woolcock and Narayan, 2000; Arnold, 2003). Thus, communities with higher stocks of social capital present a higher probability of initiating collective actions for the protection of the common good. Also, social norms and compliance of citizens with these norms minimize the need for control from the state (Adler and Kwon, 1999). Finally, dense social networks facilitate coordination and communication in the context of social and political decisions (Putnam, 1995a), enhance the creation of civil society organizations (Rotberg, 1999; Fukuyama, 2001; Newton, 2001) and improve the quality of information disseminated among members of a community (Adler and Kwon, 1999).

Due to the positive consequences resulting from social capital it has been connected with several social, economical and political issues. It is regarded as a useful parameter to investigate the reasons of failure or success of certain economic and political activities in regional and national level (Maloney et. al., 2000; Woodhouse, 2006; Knack and Keefer, 1997; Whiteley, 2000). Several studies have also been presented, connecting social capital with the health sector (e.g. Kritsotakis and Gamarnikow, 2004; Poortinga, 2006; Araya et al., 2006; Sundquist and Yang, 2007; Rostila 2007). Furthermore, social capital has been linked to environmental issues as it is assumed that communities with higher stocks of social capital can manage their natural resources in a more sustainable manner (Pretty, 2003; Rydin and Pennington 2000; Jones et al., 2009a; Wagner and Fernandez-Gimenez, 2008).

Apart from collective benefits, social capital is regarded as a beneficial asset also in individual level. Indicative connections refer to employment (Zhao, 2002; Aguilera, 2002), income level (Boxman et al., 1991; Parks-Yancy, 2006) and educational achievements (Coleman, 1988; Sandefur et al., 2006). Furthermore, individuals with higher stocks of social capital present more responsible environmental behaviour and they tend to participate in activities aiming on the protection of the environment (Jones, 2010a,b).

Although the majority of the literature emphasizes the positive consequences of social capital, several negative implications have also been observed. Putnam (1993, 2000) referred to the negative consequences due to externalities. Social capital may be beneficial for a specific social group while having significant negative impacts on other social groups (Portes, 1998; Adler and Kwon, 1999; Paxton, 1999; Fukuyama, 2001; Ostrom, 2000). Thus, social capital may be both social and unsocial (Krishna and Shrader, 2002; Levi, 1996) and may be characterised as 'good' and 'bad' social capital depending on its consequences.

3. MEASURING SOCIAL CAPITAL

In order to measure social capital the most common technique is the distribution of questionnaires. However, additional techniques may be applied depending on the aims of the research. These include qualitative social research methods and also measurement of indicators in macro level. This section will emphasize on the indicators used for the measurement of social capital in questionnaires.

3.1. Social Trust

Social trust (or interpersonal) may be regarded as the most important element of social capital (Fukuyama, 2001; Putnam, 1993, p.167). The most common question for measuring social trust is: 'Most people can be trusted or you can't be too careful' (e.g. Paxton, 1999). This type of question is included in several social surveys such as the European Social Survey (ESS), the European Values Survey (EVS) and the Eurobarometer (European Commission) thus permitting its utilization in several studies with comparative perspective (e.g. Jones et al., 2009b).

Table 1. Social trust

Level of measurement	Indicator	Reference
Generalized indicators	Most people can be trusted or you can't be too careful	Paxton (1999); Newton and Norris (2000); Beugelsdijk and van Schaik (2005); Newton, 2001
	Most people try to be fair or try to take advantage of you	Paxton (1999); Narayan and Cassidy (2001)
	Most people try to be helpful or care for themselves	Paxton (1999); Narayan and Cassidy (2001)
Particularized indicators	Trust in family members Trust in fellow nationals Trust in neighborhood/ village/city/ community	Whiteley (2000); Grootaert et al. (2004) ; Narayan and Cassidy (2001) ; Woodhouse (2006); Green and Fletcher (2003)

A main problem of this question is that it is too general and consequently does not explore the level of trust for different social groups in a community. For example, there may be a different level of trust between a group of neighbours and the people of the same region of the respondent. In this case, the level of particularized trust for a specific social group can be investigated (Uslaner and Conley, 2003). In this context, some researchers have proposed the exploration of the level of trust on different social groups such as family and fellow-nationals (Whiteley, 2000; Narayan and Cassidy, 2001) or towards the individuals of a community, a village, a city or a neighborhood (Narayan and Cassidy, 2001; Woodhouse, 2006). Nevertheless, if social capital is seen as a collective characteristic of a community (and not as an individual characteristic) then the selection of the generalized format may be appropriate. Apart from the 'typical' question of trust, some additional questions may be used as social capital indicators (Table 1). Indicative examples are the corresponding questions of fairness and helpfulness ('Most people try to be fair' or 'Most people try to be helpful'). All of these questions may be answered either in a dichotomous format ('Most people can be trusted or you can't be too careful'), or in a Likert scale (where, for example, 0 refers to low trust and 10 to high trust - as in the ESS).

3.2. Institutional Trust

Another element included in the measurement of social capital refers to the level of trust in institutions. Although several studies of measurement connect institutional with social trust, it should be underlined that they investigate different issues (Newton, 2001) and may not have equal impact on the total stock of social capital. In order to measure this component of social capital, questions regarding the level of trust on different institutions (either dichotomous or on a Likert scale) are created (Table 2). The most commonly used questions are the ones which refer to political institutions such as the national government and parliament, the political parties and politicians. A second category refers to institutions of law and order. These institutions may include the legal system, the armed forces or the police. The third type concerns international institutions, such as the European Parliament, the NATO and the United Nations. Finally, several other institutions may be included in a social capital survey depending on the aim of the study (e.g. National Security System, National Health System, Educational System, Trade Unions).

Table 2. Institutional Trust

	Type of Institutions	Reference
Political Institutions	National parliament, National government, Local and regional government	Paxton (1999); Newton and Norris (2000); Van Oorschot et al. (2006)
Law and Order	Justice system, Judges, Police, Armed forces, Army	Newton and Norris (2000); Van Oorschot et al. (2006); Hjollund and Svensen (2003)
Religious	Church	Paxton (1999); Newton and Norris (2000); van Schaik (2002)
Educational	Educational system	Paxton (1999); Newton and Norris (2000)
Private and Non-Governmental	Large companies, NGOs	Newton and Norris (2000)
Media	Press	Newton and Norris (2000) Van Schaik (2002)
International	European Union, United Nations, NATO	van Schaik (2002)

3.3. Social Networks

Regarding the measurement of social networks these are usually divided in formal and informal depending on the type of connections investigated (Putnam, 1998; Putnam et al., 2000). Formal networks refer primarily to the involvement of individuals in organized social groups such as non-governmental and non-profitable organizations. Indicative examples are the bowling leagues, used in Putnam's study in the United States (Putnam, 2000) and environmental organizations. In order to investigate the density of formal networks it is common to ask respondent whether they are a member in a list of organizations presented in the questionnaire (e.g. Newton and Norris, 2000; van Oorschot et al., 2006). However, while constructing the questionnaire there is a possibility of omitting organizations which imply important formal networks for the respondent (de Ulzurrun, 2002). An important distinction is between passive and active participation (Beugelsdijk and van Schaik, 2005). Passive participation refers to the membership of individuals in organizations whereas active participation refers to volunteerism. Consequently, an addition in the questionnaire may investigate whether the respondent is a volunteer in the listed organizations (Table 3) (e.g. Green and Fletcher, 2003; Hjollund and Svensen, 2003).

Participation through the involvement on issues of the local community may also be explored (Onyx and Bullen, 2000) while several studies have also investigated participation through the contribution of money (e.g. Grootaert et al., 2004; Narayan and Cassidy, 2001). Finally, through a different set of questions the characteristics of an organization may also be investigated, such as religion or gender (Krishna and Shrader, 2002; Narayan and Cassidy, 2001) or even the necessary knowledge in order to be a member of an organization (Grootaert et al., 2004; Krishna and Shrader, 2002).

Table 3. Formal Social Networks

	Indicator	Reference
Individual level	Membership to an organization	Newton and Norris (2000); Beugelsdijk and van Schaik (2005); Woodhouse (2006) Groot et al. (2007)
	Volunteer to an organization	Hjollund and Svensen (2003); Beugelsdijk and van Schaik (2005); Van Oorschot et al. (2006); Green and Fletcher (2003)
	Contribution of money	Grootaert et al. (2004) ; Hjollund and Svensen (2003)
	Hours of volunteer work	Grootaert et al. (2004)
Characteristics of Organization	Members of the organization are of the same gender, family, religion	Krishna and Shrader (2002); Narayan and Cassidy (2001)
	Knowledge required in order someone to participate	Krishna and Shrader (2002); Grootaert et al. (2004)
	Cooperation of the organization with other organizations	Grootaert et al. (2004)
	Most important funding source of the organization	Grootaert et al. (2004)
	Type of organization	Onyx and Bullen (2000)

3.4. Civic Participation

In order to capture the level of civic participation the most common question used is whether an individual has voted on previous national or local elections (Green and Fletcher, 2003; Grootaert et al., 2004; Hjollund and Svensen, 2003; Narayan and Cassidy, 2001). In addition, the frequency of political conversations with friends (van Oorschot et al., 2006) and the level of interest on political issues (Jones et al., 2009b) have also been utilized. Similarly investigation of the actual participation has been proposed, measured through the level of influence on local decisions (Green and Fletcher, 2003), the frequency of attending local meetings and public hearings (Grootaert et al., 2004) or participation in election campaigns (Hjollund and Svensen, 2003) (Table 4).

Apart from the level of political participation, several studies investigate collective activities in a wider context (Table 4). In particular, a researcher may explore the willingness of individuals to participate on certain collective activities (Narayan and Cassidy, 2001; Woodhouse, 2006) and the possibility of enforcing 'punishments' towards citizens who do not participate in actions for the common good (Grootaert et al., 2004; Narayan and Cassidy, 2001). On the other hand, several questions investigate involvement in individual level (e.g. Narayan and Cassidy, 2001; Woodhouse, 2006). This may also be explored through the presentation of specific actions with significant influence on the common good (e.g. collecting litter of a neighbour or contribution of time/money for a program with significant benefits for the community) (Hjollund and Svensen, 2003; Krishna and Shrader, 2002; Onyx and Bullen, 2000).

Table 4. Civic participation

Indicator	Reference
Frequency of talking for politics	Van Oorschot et al. (2006)
Watching political news on media	Van Oorschot et al. (2006)
Participation in protest march	Hjollund and Svensen (2003)
Level of influence on local political decisions	Green and Fletcher (2003); Grootaert et al. (2004)
Action for the resolution of collective problems	Green and Fletcher (2003)
Participation in last national/local elections (vote)	Green and Fletcher (2003); Hjollund and Svensen (2003)
Participation in local council	Grootaert et al. (2004) Narayan and Cassidy (2001)
Participation in public hearing/ deliberation	Grootaert et al. (2004) Narayan and Cassidy (2001)
Meeting or contact/person of political influence	Grootaert et al. (2004) ; Narayan and Cassidy (2001) ; Hjollund and Svensen (2003)
Participation in election campaign	Hjollund and Svensen (2003)

3.5. Norms of Reciprocity

According to Coleman (1988) a social norm may be a type of social capital. Similarly, Putnam (1993) underlined the importance of norms of reciprocity for the formation of social capital in a community. Nevertheless, social norms are not often included in social capital measurement studies. A possible mean of measuring social norms is through the inclusion of questions where respondents evaluate certain actions concerning the level of approval. Such actions have been included in the international surveys of ESS and EVS. Van Oorschot et al. (2006) used EVS questions concerning the claim of false benefits, not taking receipt in order to avoid tax, someone lying for his personal interest and bribing. Respondents indicated how justifiable these actions were regarded. A different type of question has been included in the questionnaires of Green and Fletcher (2003) and Hjollund and Svensen (2003) where a situation of loosing a wallet is presented and the respondent valuates the possibility of the wallet being returned. Several similar questions may be created depending mainly on the aim of the study and the community where the survey is conducted (e.g. Jones, 2010b).

3.6. Statistical Analysis of Social Capital Indicators

Apart from simple descriptive statistics, including frequencies and mean scores, the measurement of social capital has been significantly developed in the past years. This is also due to the fact that social capital is a multi-dimensional concept and thus its measurement should be based in statistical techniques which may combine different variables and create aggregate indicators.

For this purpose techniques based on factor analysis have been applied in the relevant literature (e.g. van Oorschot et al., 2006; Jones, 2010b). Specifically, in Confirmatory Factor Analysis the researcher determines a model of connections between the variables and tests how well this model fits the data. Thus, a main advantage of the CFA is that it permits the combination of variables in certain factors and in sequence these factors can be aggregated in one final factor. An indicative example of these models is presented in Figure 1. In this case, three variables measuring social trust are combined in one factor named *SOCIAL TRUST*. Similarly, other variables are combined thus creating three additional social capital factors (*INSTITUTIONAL TRUST*, *SOCIAL NETWORKS* and *SOCIAL NORMS*). These new factors are then connected with one final factor measuring *SOCIAL CAPITAL*. Through this procedure a specific score of social capital is estimated for each unit of the data (e.g. individual) which can also be regarded as a 'stock' of social capital. The final variable measuring social capital is in a continuous format and thus it can be introduced in regression analysis and correlations with other variables.

Although CFA is a very useful technique, it is important that the researcher selects the appropriate technique based on the type of data available (e.g. Joreskog and Moustaki, 2006). Through the model, factor loadings may also be estimated revealing the strength of the connection between latent variables and the final factors. These factor loadings may be interpreted similar to correlations. Higher factor loadings (closer to 1) indicate a stronger connection between two variables. Finally, a researcher should also check all the indicators of goodness of fit of the model provided by the statistical program utilized (e.g. LISREL).

4. Social Capital and the Environment

4.1. The Connection of Social Capital with Environmental Issues

The literature connecting social capital with environmental policy and management has significantly increased in the past decade (Pretty, 2003; Jones, 2010a,b). A general assumption is that communities with higher stocks of social capital will also manage natural resources in a more sustainable manner (Pretty, 2003). Furthermore, individuals with higher stocks of social capital also present more responsible environmental behavior and are also more environmentally active (Jones, 2010a,b). In order to understand the significant consequences of social capital with natural resources management and in sequence with protected areas it is important to investigate the influence of each social capital parameter.

Firstly, *social trust* is regarded as one of the most influential indicators for environmental behavior (Wagner and Fernandez-Gimenez 2008) and also perceptions for environmental policies (Jones, 2010b). It is connected with the perception on how other people in a community will act when managing public goods. In communities with high levels of social trust individuals regard that their fellow citizens will act for the protection of the common good and thus will manage their natural resources in a sustainable manner (Pretty, 2003; Jones et al., 2009a; Corral-Verdugo and Frias-Armenta 2006).

Secondly, *social norms* may be utilized in order to explain individuals' behavior towards natural resources. Specifically, in communities where there is a general tendency to comply with social norms, there is also a tendency to follow norms connected with the management of natural resources (Jones et al., 2009a). Social norms may be either formal or informal. The former refers to environmental regulations imposed from the state while the latter concerns means of actions and types of behavior proposed from a community which have been developed in the long-term in a community. An indicative example is the social norm of paying taxes. In communities where tax evasion is very frequent it is also expected that there will be high levels of non-compliance with other social norms including also those connected with environmental issues. Furthermore, social norms are also linked with the level of external control imposed through penalties or social exclusion (Pretty, 1998).

Thirdly, *institutional trust* is connected with the perceived level of effectiveness concerning environmental management projects. For example, in cases of environmental policies where the responsible actor is the state, the level of trust towards governmental institutions (e.g. Ministry of Environment) is expected to influence citizens' perceptions concerning the efficiency of a proposed policy (Jones et al., 2009a). Thus, institutional trust is linked with the level of acceptance of an environmental policy from citizens (Jones, 2010b; Cvetkovich and Winter, 2003) and also with their environmental behavior during the stage of policy implementation (Beierle and Cayford 2002; Jones et al. 2009a).

Fourthly, *social networks* and the level of civic participation are also connected with environmental issues. Specifically, social networks have two very significant functions: They determine the flow of information for environmental issues (Jones, 2006) and they increase the level of environmental activation. Regarding their role as transmitters of information in communities with dense social networks, the flow of information for environmental issues is more easily distributed. This information may refer to practices of environmentally responsible behavior, changes from imposed from an environmental policy or the reasons that a policy is applied. Social networks are also connected with the level of environmental awareness (Cramb, 2005) and the level of acceptance of an environmental policy from citizens (Jones et al., 2009a; Jones, 2010b). Regarding their influence on citizens' activation, social networks function also as means of enforcing public participation. In communities where dense social networks exist high level of civic participation may occur for the resolution of environmental problems (e.g. environmental protest, voluntary work for environmental issues). However, it should be mentioned that specific forms of social networks may have a significant negative influence. Indicative examples are the vertical and clientelistic networks (Putnam, 1993) which may be developed in a community. Such networks may distribute information only to certain parts of a community while in some cases non-responsible environmental behavior may be promoted.

4.2. Utilizing Social Capital Indicators for the Management of Protected Areas

Taking into consideration the important links between social capital and the environment, in the present section management of protected areas will be used as an indicative example revealing the need of measuring social capital during environmental policy decision-making.

Management of protected areas is a challenging task. For this purpose several policy instruments have been applied such as the formation of protected zones and activities permitted in them, payment fees or co-management frameworks (Hajkowicz, 2008). Despite the policy instrument selected, the designation of protected areas is often accompanied by significant changes for the local community. This is mainly connected with changes in the everyday life of a community such as agricultural and recreation activities (Oltremari and Jackson, 2006; Weladji and Tchamba, 2003; Dimitrakopoulos et al, 2010). Thus, prior to the designation of a protected areas and the creation of specific management frameworks it is important to explore social factors influencing the level of acceptance of environmental policies (Jones, 2010; Jones et al, 2009a). In this context, the investigation of local social capital may significantly contribute to the formation of efficient environment policies for the protection of areas of high biodiversity value.

Concerning *social trust*, the level of trustworthiness among citizens is linked with perceptions regarding environmentally responsible behavior (Pretty, 2003). As a consequence, social trust will increase the level of acceptance of an environmental management scenario (Petts, 1998; Logan and Nekerle, 2008). Especially in the case of market-based policy instruments, such as users' fee in national parks, social trust is a necessary requirement. This is mainly due to the connection of social trust with the free-riding phenomenon (Jones et al., 2009a). Free-riders refer to the situation were individuals avoid the costs of a policy but enjoy the benefits deriving from its implementation (Olson, 1965). Thus, when implementing such policies it is essential that citizens regard that all of their fellow citizens will pay for the specific fee. Furthermore, the designation of protected areas is often accompanied by the creation of zones where specific regulations apply. In such cases social trust will determine citizens' perceptions concerning the level of compliance of their fellow citizens with these restrictions and the level of acceptance of an environmental policy. On the contrary, when there is distrust among citizens then there is belief that fellow citizens will act based on individualistic motives and thus may not confront with new regulations. Apart from governmental management, social trust is also important in the case of participatory management. Participatory management (co-management) refers to the situation were the management of the area is the responsibility of several entities representing different social groups (e.g. governmental actors, citizens, non-governmental organizations, international institutions) (Kruse et al, 1994; Pretty and Ward, 2001). As a consequence, participatory management necessitates good cooperation of all entities involved and thus high levels of social trust are essential.

A similar influence is expected from *social norms*. Norms are very important due to their connection with the free-riding phenomenon (Olson, 1965). In communities were citizens tend to comply with social norms, a higher level of compliance is expected. Furthermore, the existence of strong social norms protecting the common good will facilitate the implementation of environmental policies as members of a community co-operate for the protection of the natural resources (Primmer and Karppinen, 2002; Thogersen, 2007).

Regarding the influence of *institutional trust* this is equally important for the effective development of policies for protected areas. Specifically, it is important that there is a high level of trust in institutions formulating an environmental policy (Petts, 1998). It is important that citizens trust the actors involved in the decision-making processes and regard that all decision are based on the common good of the community. Thus, high levels of trust imply also a high reliability for the effectiveness of a proposed policy and a higher level of acceptance and cooperation is expected from citizens. Furthermore, during the creation of protected areas, often a new institution is created responsible for its management. It is important that this institution is regarded by citizens as reliable in order to accept its' decisions (Petts, 1998; Owen and Videras, 2007). Thus, significant effort should be conducted focusing on the building of trust towards this institution, in order to achieve an effective management.

Finally, regarding social networks, their role both as channels of information and means of environmental activation are important. Networks are essential during the implementation of softer policy frameworks, such as participatory management (Jones et al., 2009b; Badin and Crona, 2009; Jones et al., 2009a). In order to achieve a high level of participation several entities of the community should be involved in decision-making and management processes. In communities where social networks are very low, information on important issues will not be provided and easily distributed. This information concerns means of participation, reasons that participation is necessary, the goals of a policy and also the changes brought with this policy (Grootaert, 1998). Thus, co-management frameworks cannot be implemented without dense social networks and in consequence citizens' participation. The importance of social networks should also be underlined in the case of more regulatory frameworks. Specifically, it is important that in very restrictive policies citizens are informed on the goals of a policy and the reasons justifying the implementation of such measures. This level of information may be transmitted quicker through social networks both of bonding and bridging social capital and will significantly influence the level of acceptance of an environmental policy (Pretty and Ward, 2001).

5. CONCLUSION

The aim of the present chapter was to present the main indicators for measuring social capital and to highlight its importance for the development of environmental policies. The several links underlined reveal that it is essential to explore social capital in order to identify how it may influence the development and implementation of an environmental policy. However, a social capital assessment technique has not been developed for this purpose. In this context, some suggestions may be mentioned concerning the measurement of social capital and means of improvement, thus facilitating future research for the formation of appropriate instruments for the measurement of relevant indicators.

Regarding social networks, one may claim that they have been extensively analyzed in the relevant literature concerning issues both for their type and density. However, further improvements are necessary for the investigation of informal networks, mainly due to the higher difficulty in determining them. A facilitation tool in this effort is the application of qualitative techniques prior to the creation of the questionnaire. Through these techniques a researcher may identify several informal networks and their level of importance and select those to be investigated through the questionnaire.

Regarding the measurement of social trust there is a wide use of certain questions. However when constructing a social capital questionnaire, a researcher should consider the possibility that these questions may be emphasizing the conceived level of trustworthiness in the community and not the actual level of trust (Newton, 2001). In addition, there is a need for specification of the level of trust for different social groups (e.g. people of the same region, family, friends). This is important due to the significant changes on the level of trust towards different social groups and for the exploration of differences attributed to the density of social networks.

Furthermore, although the construction of the questions for measuring institutional trust is comparative easy, there is a difficulty in selecting the institutions to be investigated. One of the criticisms on Putnam's study in the US (Putnam, 2000) was that several institutions were omitted from his study (Paxton, 1999). The selection of the institutions should be based on the aim of the study and also on the community where the study is conducted. In this context, a pre-survey with qualitative techniques may reveal significant findings for the importance of each institution thus facilitating significantly the researcher.

A different set of questions refers to the level of compliance to social norms. Through the previous analysis it was indicated that although norms are regarded an important component of social capital, they have not be analyzed in extend in the relevant literature. In addition, several commonly used questions refer to formal norms created from the state. For example, bribing public officials is a felony in most countries and consequently individuals' answers are influenced from the existence of penalization. On the other hand, social norms which are informally created and are connected to issues of the common benefit have been underestimated in the literature of measuring social capital. Several examples of such norms may derive from the field of public goods and particularly the theories of collective action (Olson, 1965) and should also be included in a questionnaire when measuring social capital.

Through these suggestions, measurement of social capital may be improved. These measurement instruments should be included in the policy decision-making and development process in order to identify possible interactions with social. Through these interactions, changes in proposed environmental policies may be conducted which will significantly increase the level of effectiveness of an environmental policy in general and the management of protected areas specifically.

REFERENCES

Adam F., Roncevic B. (2003). Social capital: recent debates and research trends. *Social Science Information* 42:155-183.

Adler P.S. and Kwon S.-W. (1999). Social capital: The good, the bad and the ugly. Working paper available at www.ssrn.com.

Aguilera, M.B. (2002). The impact of social capital on labor force participation: Evidence from 2000 Social Capital Benchmark Survey. *Social Science Quarterly*, 83, 853-874.

Araya R., Dunstan F., Playle R., Thomas H., Palmer S., Lewis G. (2006). Perceptions of social capital and the built environment and mental health. *Social Science and Medicine* 62:3072-3083.

Arnold M. (2003). Intranets, Community, and Social Capital: The Case of Williams Bay. *Bulletin of Science Technology and Society* 23:78-87.

Badin O., Crona B.I., (2009), The role of social networks in natural resource governance: What relational patterns make a difference? *Global Environmental Change*, Volume 19, (3), pp: 366-374.

Beierle T.C., Cayford J. (2002). Democracy in practice. *Public participation in Environmental Decisions*. Washington D.C.: Resources for the Future.

Beugelsdijk, S., and Schaik, T.V. (2005). Differences in Social Capital between 54 Western European Regions. *Regional Studies*, 39, 1053-64.

Boix C., Posner D.N. (1998). Social Capital: Explaining Its Origins and Effects on Government Performance. *British Journal of Political Science* 28:686-693.

Bourdieu, P. (1986). The forms of capital. In: J.G. Richardson (ed.), *Handbook of Theory and Research for the Sociology of Education* (pp.241-258). New York: Greenwood Press.

Bowles, S., and Gintis, H. (2002). Social capital and community governance. *The Economic Journal*, 112, F149-F436.

Boxman E.A.W., de Graaf P.M., Flap H.D. (1991). The impact of social and human capital on the income attainment of Dutch managers. *Social Networks* 13:51-73.

Coleman J.S. (1990). Foundations of Social Theory. Cambridge, MA: Belknap Press of Harvard University Press.

Coleman, J.S. (1988). Social Capital in the creation of human capital. *The American Journal of Sociology*, 94, 95-120.

Corral-Verdugo V., Frias-Armenta M. (2006). Personal normative beliefs, antisocial behavior, and residential water conservation. *Environment and Behavior* 38:406-421.

Cramb R.A. (2005). Social capital and soil conservation: evidence from the Philippines. *The Australian Journal of Agricutural and Resource Economics* 49:211-226.

Cvetkovich G., Winter P.L. (2003). Trust and social representations of the management of threatened and endangered species. *Environment and Behavior* 35:286-307.

De Ulzurrun, L.M.D. (2002). Associational membership and social capital in comparative perspective: A note on the problems of measurement. *Politics and Society*, 30, 497-523.

Dimitrakopoulos P.G., Jones N., Iosifides T., Florokapi I., Lasda O., Paliouras F., Evangelinos K. (2010). Local Attitudes on protected areas: Evidence from three Natura 2000 wetland sites in Greece. *Journal of Environmental Management,* 91, 1847-1854.

Fukuyama, F. (2001). Social capital, civil society and development. *Third World Quarterly*, 22, 7-20.

Granovetter, M. (1973). The strength of weak ties. *American Journal of Sociology*, 78, 1360-79.

Green, H. and Fletcher, L. (2003). Social capital harmonised question set: A guide to questions for use in the measurement of social capital. Social and Vital Statistics Division Office for National Statistics, September 2003. Retrieved 14 November 2006 from http://www.statistics.gov.uk/socialcapital.

Groot, W., van der Brink, H.M., van Praag, B. (2007). The compensating income variation of social capital. *Social Indicators Research*, 82, 189-207.

Grootaert C., (1998). Social capital, The missing link. *World Bank, Social capital Initiative Working Paper,* Washington DC: The World Bank.

Grootaert, C. and van Bastelaer, T. (2002). Social capital: From definition to measurement. In: Grootaert, C. and van Bastelaer, T. (eds.) (2002). Understanding and measuring social capital: A multidisciplinary tool for practitioners. *The World Bank*: Washington D.C.

Grootaert, C., Narayan, D., Jones, V.N., Woolcock, M. (2004). Measuring social capital: An integrated questionnaire. *The World Bank*: Washington D.C.

Hajkowicz., (2008), Supporting multi-stakeholders environmental decisions. *Journal of environmental Management*, Volume88, (4), pp: 607-614.

Halpern, D. (2005). *Social capital.* Cambridge UK, Polity Press.

Hjollund, L., and Svendsen, G.T. (2003). Social capital: *A standard method of measurement. Working paper* No. 00-9, Aarchus School of Business, Department of Economics.

Jacobs J. (1961), The Life and Death of Great American Cities, New York, Random House.

Jones. N. (2010a). Environmental activation of citizens in the context of policy agenda formation and the influence of social capital, *The Social Science Journal*, 47, 121-136.

Jones N. (2010b). Investigating the influence of social costs and benefits of environmental policies through social capital theory. *Policy Sciences*, 43, 229-244

Jones N., Sophoulis C.M., Iosifides T., Botetzagias I., and Evangelinos I.K. (2009a). The influence of social capital on environmental policy instruments, *Environmental Politics*, 18(4), 595-611.

Jones N., Malesios C., and Botetzagias I. (2009b). The influence of social capital on willingness to pay for the environment among European citizens, *European Societies*, 11(4), 511-530

Jones, N. (2006). The role of social capital in environmental policy and management. *International Journal of the Interdisciplinary Social Sciences*, 1, 163-168.

Joreskog, K. G. and Moustaki, I. (2006). Factor Analysis of Ordinal Variables with Full Information Maximum Likelihood, accessed online December 12, 2006, http://www.ssicentral.com/lisrel/techdocs/ orfiml.pd.

Kim J.Y. (2005). "Bowling together" isn't a cure-all: The relationship between social capital and political trust in South Korea. *International Political Science Review* 26:193-213.

Knack, S., and Keefer, P. (1997). Does social capital have an economic pay-off?. *Quarterly Journal of Economics,* 112, 1251-88.

Krishna, A. and Shrader, E. (2002). The social capital assessment tool: Design and Implementation. In: C. Grootaert and T. van Bastelaer (eds.) Understanding and measuring social capital (pp. 17-40). Washington D.C.: The World Bank.

Kritsotakis G., Gamarnikow E. (2004). What is social capital and how does it relate to health? *International Journal of Nursing Studies* 41:43-50.

Kruse J., Klein D., Braund S., Moorhead L., Simeone B., (1994), Co-management of natural resources: A comparison, of two Caribbean management systems. *Human organization*, Volume 57, (4), 1998, pp: 447-458.

Levi M. (1996). Social and unsocial capital: A review essay of Robert Putnam's Making Democracy Work. *Politics and Society* 24:45-55.

Logan S., Wekerle G.R., (2008) Neoliberalizing environmental governance? Land, trusts, private conservation and nature on the Oak Ridges Moraine. *Geoforum*, Volume 39, (2009), pp: 595-611.

Loury G. (1977), "A dynamic theory of racial income differences" in Women Minorities and Employment Discrimination, P.A.Wallace and A. Lemund Eds, Lexington Books, Lexington MA.

Maloney W., Smith G., Stoker G. (2000). Social capital and urban governance: Adding a more contextualized "top-down" perspective . *Political Studies* 48:802-820.

Narayan, D., and Cassidy, M.F. (2001). A dimensional approach to measuring social capital: development and validation of a social capital inventory. *Current Sociology*, 49, 59-102.

Newton, K. and Norris, P. (2000). Confidence in public institutions: Faith, culture, or performance? In: R. Putnam and S.J. Pharr (eds.). Disaffected democracies: *What's troubling the trilateral countries* (pp. 52-73). Princeton NJ: Princeton University Press.

Newton, K. (2001). Trust, social capital, civil society, and democracy. *International Political Science Review*, 22, 201-214.

Olson, M. (1965). The logic of collective action: Public goods and the theory of groups. Cambridge MA, Harvard University Press.

Oltremari J.V., Jackson R.G., (2006), Conflicts, perceptions and expectations of indigenous communities associated with natural areas in Chile, *Natural areas Journal*, Volume 26, (2), pp:121-36.

Onyx, J. and Bullen, P. (2000). Measuring Social Capital in Five Communities. *Journal of Applied Behavioral Science*, 36, 23-42.

Ostrom E. (2000). Collective action and the evolution of social norms. *Journal of Economic Perspectives* 14:137-158.

Owen A.L., Videras J., (2007), Trust, Cooperation and implementation of sustainability programs: The case of Local Agenda 21, *Ecological Economics*, Volume 68, (1-2), pp: 259-272.

Parks-Yancy R. (2006). The effects of social group membership and social capital resources on careers. *Journal of Black Studies* 36:515-545.

Paxton, P. (1999). Is social capital declining in the United States? A Multiple Indicator Assessment. *American Journal of Sociology*, 105, 88-127.

Petts J. (1998). Trust and waste management information expectation versus observation. *Journal of Risk Research* 1:307-320.

Poortinga, W. (2006). Social capital: An individual or collective resource for health? *Social Epidemiology*, 62, 292-302.

Portes, A. (1998). Social capital: Its origins and applications in Modern Sociology. *Annual Review of Sociology*, 24, 1-24.

Portes, A. (2000). The two meanings of social capital. *Sociological Forum*, 15, 1-12.

Pretty J., Ward H., (2001). Social Capital and the environment. *World Development*, Volume 29, (2), pp: 209-227.

Pretty, J. (2003). Social capital and the collective management of resources. *Science*, 302, 1912-1914.

Pretty, J. (1998). "Participatory learning in rural Africa: towards better decisions for agricultural development" in Participation and the Quality of Environmental Decision-Making, Coenen, F.H.J.M., Huitema, D. and O'Toole L.J., eds, Kluwer Academic Publishers, Dordrecht, pp. 251 266

Primmer E., Karppinen H., (2010). Professional judgment in non-industrial private forestry: Forester attitudes and social norms influencing biodiversity conservation. *Forest policy and economics,* Volume 12, (2), pp: 136-146.

Putnam, R., with Leonardi, R.and Nanetti, R.Y. (1993). Making Democracy Work: Civic traditions in modern Italy. New Jersey: Princeton University Press.

Putnam R. (1995a). Bowling Alone: America's Declining Social Capital. *Journal of Democracy* 6:65-78.

Putnam R. (1995b). Tuning in, Tuning out: The strange disappearance of social capital in America. *Political Science and Politics* 28:664-683.

Putnam, R. (1998). Foreword. Housing Policy Debate, 9.

Putnam, R. (2000). Bowling alone: The collapse and revival of American community. New York: Simon and Schuster Paperbacks.

Putnam, R., Pharr, S.J., Dalton, R.J. (2000). Introduction. What's troubling the trilateral democracies. In: R. Putnam R. and S.J. Pharr (eds.). Disaffected democracies. *What's troubling the trilateral countries?* (pp. 3-31). Princeton, New Jersey: Princeton University Press.

Rostila M. (2009). Social capital and health in European welfare regimes: a multilevel approach. *Journal of European Social Policy* 17:223-239.

Rotberg R.I. (1999). Social Capital and Political Culture in Africa, America, Australasia, and Europe. *Journal of Interdisciplinary History* XXIX:339-356.

Rydin Y., Pennington M. (2000). Public Participation and Local Environmental Planning: the collective action problem and the potential of social capital. *Local Environment* 5:153-169.

Sandefur, G.D., Meier, A.M., Campbell, M.E. (2006). Family resources, social capital and college attendance. *Social Science Research*, 35, 525-553.

Sundquist K., Yang M. (2007) Linking social capital and self-rated health: A multilevel analysis of 11,175 men and women in Sweden. *Health and Place* 13:324-334.

Thogersen J., (2007), Norms for environmentally responsible behavior: An extended taxonomy. *Journal of Environmental Psychology*, Volume 26, (4), pp: 247-261.

Uphoff N. (1998). Understanding social capital: Learning from the analysis and experience of participation. In: Seregeldin I., Dasgupta P., editors. *Social Capital.* Oxford: Oxford University Press.

Uslaner E.M., Conley R.S. (2003). Civic engagement and particularized trust: The ties that bind people to the ethnic communities. *American Political Research* 31:331-360.

van Oorschot W., Arts, W., Gelissen, J. (2006). Social capital in Europe. Measurement and Social and Regional Distribution of a Multifaceted Phenomenon. *Acta Sociologica*, 49, 149-176.

van Schaik, T. (2002). Social capital in the European Values Study Surveys. Paper presented at the OECD-ONS International Conference on Social Capital Measurement (London, OECD).

Wagner C.L., Fernandez-Gimenez M.E. (2008). Does community-based collaborative resource management increase social capital? *Society and Natural Resources* 21:324-344.

Weladji R.B., Tchamba M.A., (2003), Conflicts between people and protected areas within the Benoue Wildlife Conservation Area, North Cameroon. *Oryx* 37, (1), pp: 72-79.

Whiteley, P.F. (2000). Economic growth and social capital. Political Studies, 48, 443-466.

Woodhouse, A. (2006). Social capital and economic development in regional Australia: A case study. *Journal of Rural Studies*, 22, 83-94.

Woolcock, M. (1998). Social capital and economic development: Toward a theoretical synthesis and policy framework. *Theory and Society*, 27, 151-208.

Woolcock, M., and Narayan, D. (2000). Social capital: Implications for development theory, research and policy. *World Bank Research Observer*, 15, 225-249.

Zhao, Y. (2002). Measuring the social capital of laid-off Chinese workers. *Current Sociology*, 4, 555-571.

In: Social Indicators: Statistics, Trends…
Editor: Candace M. Baird
ISBN 978-1-61122-841-0

Chapter 6

WHAT AGRO-PROCESSING CAN DO TO THE SOCIAL CONDITIONS OF RURAL SUBSISTENT FARMERS: THE CASE OF *MILENOVISI* ASSOCIATION IN GHANA

Frank S. Arku[1], Cynthia Arku[2] and John-Engelbert Seddoh[3]

[1] Faculty of Development Studies, Presbyterian University College, Ghana, Akuapem Campus

[2]Department of Educational Policy Studies, University of Alberta, Edmonton, Canada

[3]Department of Management Studies, University of Cape Coast, Ghana

ABSTRACT

Many developing countries have formulated their poverty reduction strategies taking into account their development priorities, resource base and aid from the international community. Ghana's poverty reduction strategy, for example, has it to assist rural farmers to add value to their food crops so that they can benefit from relatively better returns. With the assistance of the government, farmers are increasingly processing raw cassava locally into gari (i.e., cassava grains) making it a less perishable food. While agro-processing is becoming a popular strategy to reduce poverty, an understanding of how its impact on households is important in tweaking development initiatives for better results on poverty reduction. Thus, we examined how the government–assisted gari processing is changing social conditions of rural women and their households involved within the Eastern Region of Ghana. Findings from the case study of *Milenovisi* gari processing Association demonstrated that, not only did the women's incomes improve; they were also able to afford food and health costs, and contributed to funerals and religious activities, although they faced difficulties with transportation and credit facilities. Their local political leader and families significantly influenced women's decision to be involved in this initiative. Consequently, we propose increased use of families as medium for recruiting and passing along skills to potential beneficiaries. Also, we argue that agro-

[1]. fsarku@gmail.com
[2]. cbanner2005@yahoo.ca
[3]. jseddoh2000@yahoo.com

processing initiatives need to be accompanied with credit facilities, and that tackling transportation barriers which create additional workload and health problems for the women on top of the already labor intensive task of processing gari, is critical for achieving greater impacts.

Keywords: *poverty reduction, agro-processing, women, social conditions, Ghana*

INTRODUCTION

The poor are not homogeneous. Poverty can be categorized based on the poor's control over flows and assets over time (Hulme and Shepherd 2003; IDRC, 2004; Otero and Rhyne, 1994; Smith, 2005). There are two categories of poverty differentiated by their severity, namely absolute/ultra poverty, and relative poverty. Absolute poverty is a condition in which human beings live in a state of deprivation with a minimal social functioning as a result of meager incomes or a lack of access to basic human needs, including food, safe water, sanitation, health, shelter, education, and information (Amarendra, 1998; Jackson, 1972; Riddell and Robinson, 1995). According to Townsend (1984), absolute poverty is demonstrated by extreme incidents such as disability, death, and withdrawal of participation in common social roles and relationships. Absolute poverty can be referred to as "extreme consumption poverty", "dollar poverty", or a "standard" dollar a day poverty (IFAD, 2001). Ultra poverty is very similar to the concept of absolute poverty except that the ultra poor are always deficient in minimum food and nutrient requirements. They are also described as the "poorest" of the poor (Jackson, 1972; Riddell and Robinson, 1995). Relative poverty on the other hand is rooted on perceptions. It is ones inability to attain a given contemporary standard of living based on the socio-cultural and economic levels of a particular society (Amarendra, 1998). Jackson (1972: 13) indicates that as society becomes more organized and complex, flow and stock requirements for adequate functioning in the new social set up increase and consequently an individual's or a household's relative position in the community is likely to change over time. Thus, one may be poor but not necessarily facing poverty in a relative sense. According to Amarendra (1998: 314), it may be possible to eradicate absolute poverty, but it will never be possible to eradicate relative poverty. And that poverty in developed countries deals with relative poverty. However, developed countries such as Canada, Australia, New Zealand, and the USA that have seen an erosion in their welfare system in recent years are also concerned with absolute poverty (Segal, 2006; Wilson, 1996). For the purpose of this paper emphasis is placed on absolute poverty.

Efforts to reduce poverty have taken many forms. Investing in income generating work is one of the several ways that poor households and communities can improve their lives in multi-dimensional ways. Earlier analysis of what is poverty has focused on income and consumption levels. Now, there is a shift from this quantitative analysis to qualitative ways of measuring it taking into account people's own voices, their subjective views and criteria (Chant, 2006). Poverty which is also viewed within a gender perspective is against the notion that men and women have identical needs. Thus, feminists defining poverty put emphasis on:

- conceptualizing and defining poverty with a gender perspective;
- how gender impacts the measurement of poverty;
- understanding the uneven distribution of poverty between men and women; and
- understanding how economic empowerment of women can influence poverty.

The United Nations Decade for Women occurring from 1975 to 1985, which sought to discover and expose the reasons why women suffer a greater incident of poverty than men, has influenced the growing range of poverty analysis. Literacy and education attainment, discrimination in labor markets and unequal gender division of work at home are said to account for the inequalities limiting women's access to material resources (Chant, 2006).

With the increasing understanding of poverty issues, the analysis of poverty using an income approach is considered inadequate. For example, people with low incomes may not see it as a problem if they reside in adequate shelter with access to services, including medical care. They can be described as having a healthy base of 'assets'. The assets they have may not be economic or physical, such as savings, tools, natural resources, but may include education, skills and social capital.

In poor agro-based rural communities of Africa where people have skills for agriculture as their main source of livelihood, utilizing their natural resources and skills for agricultural development is critical to reducing their poverty. Efforts to increase productivity by making irrigation, fertilizer and appropriate technology available to the poorest rural small-scale and landless farmers and farm workers continue to be pursued. This is in anticipation that this can enable them to expand their output, sales and produce for their subsistence with less effort and cash costs. This reasoning partly triggered the Green Revolution which aims to get the best technology to farmers so that they can produce three or four times more than they would otherwise produce (Rijsberman, 2003).

Accompanying the Green Revolution is the surge of agro-processing that gives more value to agricultural produce. Agro-processing, described as transforming raw agricultural produce into forms that attract greater value for the market, is deemed a pro-poor intervention. Several governments are increasingly developing their agro-processing sector given the impact it has on lessening post-harvest loses of perishable produce, creating employment, and offering better sale value for agricultural produce and incomes.

In Zambia, for example, this sector with an indigenous business structure uses significant quantities of local raw materials. And can improve access to food and incomes for the poor who depend on agriculture for their livelihood in a more sustainable way. This sector in Zambia has seen increased productivity because of new technology and competition that has encouraged processors to diversify their range of products. However, income levels are still very low and difficulty to meet basic needs such as education and health exist, although this has expanded employment (Daka, 2008). As part of its poverty reduction strategy, the government of Ghana increased access to agro- processing equipment from 24% in 2003 to 42% in 2004, exceeding its target of 30%. But post harvest loses are still in a high of over 30% (Ghana National Development Planning Commission, 2005).

Interestingly, women are active participants in this sector that is yet to realize its full benefits. The role of small low or intermediate technology entrepreneurs and female entrepreneurs in the agro-processing and catering services in local markets in African countries cannot be over emphasized (Sautier *et al.*, 2006). Women who are obtaining capital for income generating activities through micro-finance have often invested their loans in agro-processing. A study of women lenders of micro-loans from Bogoso Fiaseman Rural Bank in Ghana (i.e., private company) showed that they used their loans for farming oil palm, palm oil processing, cooked food services and petty trading. They were able to better contribute to their children's school costs, increasingly made decisions together with their spouses and fewer conflicts occurred within the household as women were able to financially assist with meeting household needs (Arku and Arku, 2009).

But it is unclear how the government of Ghana-supported gari processing projects meant to address poverty in agro-based rural communities is doing; how this project recruits beneficiaries and how it is changing their social conditions is under-researched. Thus, the goal of this study was to understand any socio-economic changes that women involved in government-assisted gari processing projects are seeing in themselves and their households, and to determine ways to improve the benefits of such initiatives. Specific study objectives were:

- To assess how participants are recruited into the gari processing project.
- To determine the project's impacts on social conditions among rural households.
- To determine ways to better improve social conditions of rural people through agro-processing initiatives.

METHODOLOGY

A case study approach along with questionnaire, key informant interviews and participants observation were employed in this study. A government assisted gari processing association in rural Ghana, named *Milenovisi* in Korkonu was chosen as the case. This association consists of 30 female members and 3 male volunteers who assist with the running of the association as executive[4]. All the 30 women association members participated in the questionnaire administered by the research team, since most of the women could not read and write English or express themselves in writing in ways that would significantly contribute to the research objectives. The leaders of the association including the men were involved in key informant interviews to obtain historical data and insights into the association's performance over the years.

Data collected were analyzed using Statistical Package for Social Scientists (SPSS). Data from open ended responses, key informant interviews and participant observation served as supporting evidence to results from the statistical analysis such as descriptive statistics and tests of difference.

BACKGROUND OF STUDY COMMUNITIES AND PROJECT

Located in the Akuapem North District of the Eastern Region of Ghana with a population of about 1000, Kokornu is about 15km from the Region's capital, Koforidua. Residents are

[4] The leadership includes a chairperson, secretary, treasurer, porter, and organizer and a contact person.

mainly adults as the young people have migrated elsewhere to continue their education after elementary school and barely returned because of a lack of employment opportunities they wish to have. In every 5 households in Korkonu, there were about two children between 1 month and 10 years. The Eastern Region is largely inhabited by Akans (the largest tribe in Ghana); however, over 95% of residents in Kokornu are Ewes who trace their lineage to communities in Ghana's Volta Region. The remaining are Akans and people of other tribes. Christianity is the most common religion.

Processing Cassava into Gari

Cassava is a root crop that can be eaten in various forms serving as a common food in many Ghanaian households. It can be eaten with sauce or stew after boiling it or the boiled cassava can be pounded into paste (locally known as fufu) and eaten with soup. Raw cassava paste is also used in combination with corn dough or flour to make a dish. But a less perishable food from cassava is gari.

Making gari is a labor intensive process. First, the cassava is peeled and grinded into paste. The fluid from the cassava paste is squeezed out. This is done by placing a heavy metal or material on the cassava paste in a sack. The paste loses its fluid when it is placed under this kind of pressure for a few days, after which it is dried. The dehydrated cassava paste is further dehydrated by cooking it over fire while constantly stirring it until it turns into dry grains.

The Government-Assisted Gari Processing Association in Korkonu

Gari processing was the main economic activity in Korkonu at the time of the study. Prior to their involvement in gari processing, the people were into subsistence farming. They sold raw cassava surpluses from their farms to earn incomes. Inadequate ready markets, poor demand from consumers and unfavorable prices , coupled with keen competition to sell raw cassava led to decline in their incomes. Post harvest losses grew over time as the surpluses not sold went bad due to inadequate preservation facilities. Adding value by processing the raw cassava into less perishable forms such as gari became an alternative option. With gari processing, cassava farmers do not have to sell cheaply during bumper harvests for the lack of preservation facilities. In addition to their farm surpluses, the gari processors buy more cassava from the market and/or other farmers to make the gari in commercial quantities. High demand by urban dwellers and increasing export of gari has lifted the face of gari processing, making it a major economic activity among the people.

Their efforts at making a living on this activity since 1962 attracted public interest. In the early 1990s, the 31st December Women's Movement aimed at empowering women sought to support them to grow this venture. Their partnership with them was short-lived due to a change in government which brought on new priorities. And for over a decade the association was running as an informal group of gari processors. In June 2006 the area's local political leader, precisely Assemblyman[5] mobilized the women making cassava paste and gari to form

[5] He performs the responsibilities of communicating the needs and aspirations of his community to politicians at either the District or Municipal levels who have the decision-making capabilities to take action using resources

Milenovisi Association - with 33 members at the time of this study. The Ministry of Agriculture provided better yielding varieties of cassava sticks for planting and extension services to the *Milenovisi.* Since their gari making process is a heavy-duty work and yet lacked any form of mechanization, the government provided one machine for grinding the cassava. The association established a shed along with mud stoves and other facilities that the members took turns to use for cooking the gari. They make a contribution of 0.5 kg of gari selling at 0.5 Ghana Cedi ($ 0.36 U.S[6] at the time of the study) after every use of the facility. The leadership of their association sells the gari and places the money in a fund that is loaned to members on as-needed-basis and for maintaining their machinery. The loans to members ranged from 100 - 200 Ghana Cedi ($ 71-143 US) with no interest charges and a repayment period of one to two months. However, this repayment period is often extended for members who have difficulty completing payment by the end of their term in order not to discourage them from borrowing. At the time of this study, the government was building a shed with stoves so that they can have better access whenever they wish to cook their gari.

In spite of the meager price they sell gari, perhaps not commensurate with the labor they put into this activity, the association seems to have no difficulty selling the gari because of abundant market for it in boarding schools and local markets where middle-men/women come to buy from them in large quantities. The women generally make the gari during and following the bumper harvest to be sold all year round.

FINDINGS

Respondents Background

Almost half of the respondents (43%) had no formal education. The rest have had some learning experience with elementary (27%) and, middle and high schools (33%). Over two-thirds of the women were married. Most of them have between three to five dependants. They largely were in the ages of 20-49 years, with 35-39 years being the largest age group (Table 1). In addition to gari processing, about 73% of the women reported that they engaged in other income generating activities, including petty trading and farming.

Table 1. Respondents' ages

Age groups	Respondents	Percentage
20-24	6	19.9
25-29	5	16.7
30-34	2	6.7
35-39	8	26.7
40-44	5	16.7
45-49	3	10.0
50 and above	1	3.3

from the central government and revenue from the locale. He is not an employee of the government. The assemblyman is also the secretary of the Milenovisi in Kokornu.

[6] $1.4 US is equivalent to GH □ 1

Recruitment and Men's Involvement

A few of the respondents reported having been involved with gari processing for over 10 years, while over 90% have been involved for one to 9 years (Table 2).

Table 2. Duration of involvement

Years	Percentage
1-3	46.7
4-6	40.0
7-9	3.3
10 years and over	10.0

The majority of the women are on their own in this gari work. Seventy percent of married women indicated that their husbands did not help them with the gari work, compared to 30% who said their husbands were involved. The men who helped their wives with the gari work performed several tasks including: weeding of the cassava farms; harvesting of the cassava; carrying of the cassava and firewood from farms to the houses; and frying/cooking of the cassava dough into the gari. Some of them supported their wives financially. For those husbands who did not help, their wives were of the view that it was because they were either absentee husbands working in cities or were engaged in another sector and did not have time to be involved with their wives' work.

While several of the women (36.7%) joined the project voluntarily, others were involved because they received information on it from the assemblyman, their relatives or government officials (Table 3). Mothers were a major influence on their decision, as 33.3% of the women indicated that they were involved because of motivation/information received on the project from their mothers.

Table 3. Sources of influence to women's decision to be involved in project

Sources	Percentage
Voluntary/out of will	36.7
Assemblyman	20.0
Sisters	3.3
Mothers	33.3
Grandmothers	3.3
Government officials	3.3

However, a considerable portion (50%) of the women reported that they faced difficulty getting involved in the project even when they have received the information they need and were interested in joining. They added that they did not have the initial capital to buy the raw cassava and frying pan to cook the gari. Some reported that they did not know how to make the gari.

When the women were asked whether or not they made efforts to recruit participants, and what precisely they did to bring them in, over half of them were in agreement that they recruited other participants, especially their relatives. Of this group, 56% of them did so by word-of-mouth and the rest by teaching them how to process the gari. About 81% of the women who recruited others said their recruits were mainly their relatives such as sisters, cousins, sister-in-laws, aunts and children. Non-relatives recruited were friends and neighbors.

Income before and during Project

A significant 60% of the respondents could not tell their incomes before the project. Of the remaining who provided income information, 13% reported a monthly income between GH 10-19, 10% earned between GH □ 20-29, with another 10% who made GH □ 30-39. Thus, none of the women reported monthly income over GH □ 39 before the project (Table 4).

Incomes and reporting on them improved once the women got involved in the project. Only 13.3% reported not knowing their monthly income during their involvement in the project, compared to the 60% before the project. Women who said they earned between GH 30-39 during the project were twice the number before the project. Unlike before the project when none of the women reported a monthly income over GH □ 39, approximately one third earned over GH 39 after being involved (Table 4).

Table 4. Monthly incomes before and during the project

	Before	During
Income	Percentage	Percentage
Did not know	60.0	13.3
Below GH □ 10	6.7	13.3
Between GH □ 10- 19	13.3	5.0
Between GH □ 20-29	10.0	15.0
Between GH □ 30-39	10.0	20.0
Between GH □ 40-49	-	6.7
GH □ 50 and above	-	26.7

Meeting Social Needs before the Project

To determine the project's impact on their social conditions, indicators such as ability to afford day-to-day needs and social obligations were measured. When the women were asked the extent to which they were able to provide food, meet health costs and contributions for religious activities and funerals before the project, none of them was positive (Table 5), except on the later. Thus, majority of the women felt they could not meet them in the pre-project period (comprising those who disagreed and strongly disagreed). Only 3.3% of them were in agreement that they could afford contributions for funerals during this period (Table 5).

Table 5. Extent to which respondents agreed that they met their social needs before the project

	Provided food	Met health needs	Met religious responsibilities	Contributed to funerals
	Percentages			
Strongly Disagreed	26.7	13.3	6.7	6.7
Disagreed	40.0	43.3	56.7	30.0
Neither agreed or disagreed	33.3	43.3	36.7	60.0
Agreed	-	-	-	3.3

The results of statistical test - Kolmogorov-Smirnov – supports the findings in Table 5 as the mean values for meeting health needs, meeting religious contributions and provision of food are 2.3, 2.3 and 2.07, respectively while for funeral contribution is 2.63 (Table 6) (1= strongly disagree, 2 = disagree, 3 = neither agree nor disagree, 4 = agree, 5 = strongly agree).

Table 6. Statistical test of the extent to which respondents agreed that they met their social needs before the project

Items	Mean	Order of rank	Significance Level
1. Contribution to funerals	2.63	1	0.02
2. Meeting of health needs/costs	2.30	2	0.00
3. Meeting religious contributions	2.30	3	0.00
4. Provision of food	2.07	4	0.01

(2 tailed) $P \leq 0.01$ and $P < 0.05$.

Meeting Social Needs While Participating in the Project

Unlike before the project (Table 5), most of the women now were in agreement that they met their needs and honored social obligations after their involvement (Table 7). For example, on the matter of funeral contributions, the majority (83.4%) were positive that they were able to afford it, compared to the 3.3% before the project (Table 7).

The Kolmogorov-Smirnov statistical test shows that on the average they agreed on being capable of meeting their social needs since they were involved in the project, as mean mark ranges from 4.1 to 4.3 (Table 8). Meeting of health costs has the highest mean value, followed by meeting of religious needs, and the provision of food and funerals had the same mean value (Table 8). The findings are also statistically significant as p = 0. 00 for all the social needs.

Table 7. Extent to which respondents agreed that they met their social needs while involved in the project

	Provided food	Met health needs	Met religious responsibilities	Contributed to funerals
	Percentages			
Strongly agree	33.3	43.3	40.0	36.7
Agree	46.7	53.3	50.0	46.7
Neither agreed nor disagreed	20.0	3.3	10.0	16.7

Table 8. Statistical test of the extent to which respondents agreed that their social needs were met while involved in project

Items	Mean	Order of rank	Significance Level
1. Meeting of health needs/costs	4.4	1	0.00
2. Meeting religious contributions	4.3	2	0.00
3. Contribution to funerals	4.1	3	0.00
4. Provision of food	4.1	4	0.00

P = 0.00.

Challenges with the Project

About 90% of the respondents said that they faced difficulties which prevented them from getting full benefits the project. They reported a lack of transportation facilities to convey the raw cassava from their farms and credit facilities. They added that they suffered body pains from overwork and excessive exposure to the sun and heat from cooking the gari (Table 9).

Table 9. Challenges with the project

Item	Percentage
Lack of credit facilities	25.9
Lack of transport	11.1
Body pains	7.4
Too much heat	11.1
Lack of credit facilities and transport	29.6
Lack of credit facilities and body pains	14.8

A considerable portion indicated that they lacked credit facilities to purchase raw materials and utensils to cook the gari (Table 9). Over 25% said this is a barrier, while approximately 30% and 15% cited a combination of issues with credit access and transportation, and credit access and body pains, respectively. Thus, in all about 70% of the respondents somewhat cited a lack of credit facilities as a barrier to their work.

DISCUSSION

Participation in the Gari Processing

Men's involvement in women's income generating work is becoming popular in rural communities but at differing magnitudes. Arku and Arku (2009) study of women in microfinance in rural Ghana shows that many husbands helped their wives in diverse ways. They provided accounting support, monitored the business and offered assistance with tasks involved in the day-to-day micro-finance work and house chores, as women often travelled away from home for a day or two to buy their wares leaving children at home. The women alluded to the fact that the men's lineage group (Asona among the Akan tribe) which generally encourages co-operation between a couple and help for women accounted for this. Interestingly, the evidence among the Korkonu people shows little husband involvement in women's work. Those who helped weeded, harvested and carried the cassava and firewood from the farm to home, helped to cook the gari and some supported the women financially. A significant 70% of the women reported that men do not help in their gari processing work, because they were absentee husbands working in the cities or have other jobs. This demonstrates that either their lineage or tribe does not motivate men's involvement in women's work or husbands are economically active elsewhere and comfortable keeping separate jobs.

It seems that opportunities for increased involvement in income generating work communicated by local political advocates, is inadequate to get women involved. In this study, several women (approximately 37%) decided to be part of the *Milenovisi* out of their voluntary will, and for others (20%) this was owing to an understanding of the project that their local political leader provided to them. However, it was evident that the mothers in the women's lives were more influential in women deciding to join this initiative than their sisters, grandmothers and government officials. Approximately 33% of the women joined the project after knowing about it from their mothers. Thus, women's decision to be involved in formal groupings that facilitate their participation in economic activities can be driven not only by political leaders; mothers also play a key role in sharing the information and encouraging women's involvement.

While information on economic opportunities that rural people can benefit from is important, the skill for the job is also essential for actively recruiting participants. This study showed that 56% of the women told others about the project, and some taught those they recruited how to make the gari. The majority said they passed the information and skills mainly on to their relatives. This suggests that information alone is not sufficient for recruiting potential beneficiaries into such initiatives, as giving people the skills is capable of bringing more people in. And community members are capable of disseminating the skills if they have acquired them.

Impact of the Project on Social Conditions

Agro-processing can improve women's incomes. Daka (2008) indicated that although agro-processing sector in Zambia created employment for many, incomes for the participants are still low. Similarly, it was evident from this study that incomes are yet to reach a point where one can describe it as sufficient for a decent living. While 60% of the women reported not knowing their incomes before the project, none of those who provided income information before the project reported a monthly income of over 40 Ghana cedis ($ 29 U.S). The women were better able to provide information on their incomes during the project. Over 33% reported a monthly income of 40 to over 50 Ghana cedis ($ 29 - 36 U.S), which according to international standards is still low.

The new incomes of the women have affected their social conditions in favorable ways. Whereas none of the women before the project agreed that they were able to meet food and health costs, and make money contributions for their religious activities with the exception of funerals, the situation improved during the project. About 80% - 97% of the women were in agreement that they could afford food, health costs and contributions for religious activities and funerals with an income of not more than $ 36 U.S monthly - just approximately a dollar a day! This perhaps is because they have fewer dependants, given their small young population and benefits from the government's recent National Health Insurance scheme which allows for a subsidized cost for services at public hospitals and participating health centres. However, Daka (2008) points to how incomes from agro-processing have not been adequate for meeting basic needs such as health and education among Zambians. On the contrary, Bangladesh women getting small loans from micro-finance schemes indicated that they could afford food, decent homes and social expenditures such as dowries (Kabeer, 1998). Interestingly in her study of the impacts of women's micro-finance on households' well-being, Arku noted that rural people are primarily concerned with survival than creating wealth. She added that well-being for the rural poor can be described as "a condition of having secure sustainable means of survival, accompanied by a sense of peace among household members." (Arku, 2007:106).

Barriers to Agro-Processing

A lack of adequate capital continues to be a barrier to women's income generating work including agro-processing. Their traditional role as reproductive workers, caring for the home and children have meant that women from especially rural patriarchal societies have limited access to productive resources (e.g., cash, land and other assets). Thus, according to Mayoux (2001) women being unable to lend from traditional financial institutions without collateral has rendered micro-finance an important strategy for addressing gender issues and reducing poverty. Thomas (2001) noted that women desire to have equal rights to financial services and to take actions to protect their personal welfare. A considerable portion of the women in this study reported that a lack of capital for buying the raw material and utensil for cooking the gari was a deterrent to getting into the gari making business. Hence, the association incorporated a lending service to members through small mandatory gari donations each time they use the group-owned gari cooking facility. The gari collected is sold and the cash is loaned to members as micro-loans of $ 71 to 143 U.S. Arku and Arku (2009) study of rural residents obtaining private micro-loans from Fiaseman Rural Bank in Ghana showed that the small size of loans ($ 140 - 350 U.S) caused a heavy workload for the women as they could not afford a shop to avoid carrying their wares to the market and back. The situation for the people of Korkonu may be much more difficult since they do not receive micro-loans from a financial outfit capable of providing loan amounts larger than the little amounts they get from their association. Consequently, approximately 70% of the women cited a lack of credit facilities among others, as a major barrier to their work.

Women's workload is worsened because initiatives that seek to create income opportunities for them lack transportation facilities and machinery to make their work easier- which in turn wears on their health. According to Arku (2010) women who did not have access to clean water facilities in their communities had to walk several kilometers to collect unclean water. While the women were concerned about covering long distances to obtain water, they were more concerned about the time they spent to do so which they could use instead on other economic activities. In this study the men and women carried the cassava on their heads from the farm to home because the roads were not accessible. Citing the problems they faced in their work, about 40% reported transportation difficulties. The result of limited technology or machinery along with this transportation dilemma for gari processers has been poor health, as they suffer bodily pains from over exertion in the hot sun and by the cooking fire.

CONCLUSION

Agro-processing is a growing sector in Africa south of the Sahara because of its potential to reduce poverty. Farmers are increasingly processing their farm produce into products of better sale value which is also reducing post harvest loses. NGOs and governments are assisting to lift the face of this industry and the poor. Assistance from the government of Ghana to Associations like *Milenovisi* is creating more economic opportunities for women in gari processing. In this study the women were able to encourage mostly relatives to be involved with the *Milenovisi* by speaking to them about the project and passing on the skill of making gari to them. However, mothers were largely instrumental in recruiting participants, along with their local project advocate or political leader. By being involved in the *Milenovisi*, the women saw an increase in their incomes and were able to meet costs for health, food and religious contributions which were impossible prior to the project. Since they have fewer dependants with them, a modest increase in their incomes up to about a dollar a day income supported these needs. Nonetheless, they lacked institutionalized credit facilities to provide capital for their work. Transportation difficulties meant that they have had to carry heavy loads of raw cassava from the farm to home, and coupled with little mechanization have created excessive workload and health problems for the women. These findings demonstrate that although agro-processing can improve the social conditions of women and their households, it can increase women's workload. Thus, agro-processing projects need to be supported with appropriate machinery, and the particular challenges to rural communities around transportation need to be assessed and addressed to facilitate more benefits. Government funded credit services with minimal interest rate to rural businesses can be a push to start-up and expansion of agro-processing.

ACKNOWLEDGMENT

The authors are grateful to the Research Assistants of Presbyterian University College, Ghana and their lead, Mr. Nana Sam Gurah, for assisting to collect data.

REFERENCES

Amarendra. (1998). *Poverty, rural development and public policy.* New Delhi: Deep and Deep Publications Pvt. Ltd.

Arku, F. S. (2010). Time savings from easy access to clean water: Implications for rural men's and women's well-being. *Progress in Development Studies* 10, 233-246.

Arku, C. (2007). Changing gender roles and their socio-cultural implications for rural households' well-being: A study of micro-finance in Bogoso, Ghana. Unpublished MSc. Thesis, School of Environmental Design and Rural Development. University of Guelph. Guelph, Ontario.

Arku, C. and Arku, F. S. (2009). More money, new household cultural dynamics: Women in micro-finance in Ghana. *Development in Practice* 19, 200-213.

Chant, S. (2006). Contribution of a gender perspective to the analysis of poverty. In Jaquette, J. S. and Summerfield, G. (Eds.), *Women and gender equity in development theory and practice* (pp. 87-106). Durham: Duke University Press.

Daka, Z. J. (2008). Linkages between trade development and poverty reduction. Advocacy workshop report organized by ODCMT and CUTS-ARC, Central Province, Zambia.

Ghana National Development Planning Commission (2005). *Growth and poverty reduction strategy* (GPRS II) (2006-2009): Volume 1 Policy Framework. Accra: Ghana National Development Planning Commission.

Hambly, H. (2002). Men in women's groups: A gender and agency analysis of local institutions. In Cleaver, F. (ed.), *Masculinities matter! Men, gender and development (pp. 138-165).* London: Zed Books.

Hulme, D. and Shepherd, A. (2003). Conceptualizing chronic poverty. *World Development,* 403-423.

International Fund for Agriculture Development (IFAD). (2001). *Rural poverty report 2001: The challenge of ending rural poverty.* New York: Oxford University Press.

International Development Research Centre (IDRC). (2004). Prospectus for the rural poverty and environment program initiative for 2005-2010 (Proposal submitted to the Board of Governors). Ottawa: International Development Research Centre.

Jackson, D. (1972). *Poverty.* Toronto: MacMillan.

Kabeer, N. (1998). Money can't buy me love: Re-evaluating gender, credit and empowerment in rural Bangladesh. IDS Discussion Paper 363. Brighton: University of Sussex.

Otero, M., and Rhyne, E. (Eds.). (1994). T*he new world of microenterprise finance: Building healthy financial institutions for the poor.* Bloomfield: Kumarian Press.

Riddell, R. C., and Robinson, M. (1995). N*on-governmental organizations and rural poverty alleviation.* Oxford: Oxford University Press.

Rijsberman, F. (2003). Can development of water resource reduce poverty? *Water Policy,* 399-412.

Sautier, D., Vermeulen, H., Fok, M. and Biénabe, E. (2006). Case studies of agri-processing and contract agriculture in Africa. *A report by Rimisp-Latin American Center for Rural Development* (www.rimisp.org).

Segal, H. (2006). T*he challenge of rural poverty: Canada's perpetual frontier.* A paper presented at the Third Annual SIPP Luncheon, Regina, Canada.

Smith, M. S. (2005). Global inequality and poverty. In Brodie, J. and Rein, S. (Eds.), C*ritical concepts: An introduction to politics* (pp. 317-344). Toronto: Princeton Hall.

Thomas, M. L. (2001). Women's empowerment in savings and credit cooperatives in rural Nepal: A study of organizational change. Unpublished MSc. Thesis, School of Environmental Design and Rural Development. University of Guelph. Guelph, Ontario.

Townsend, P. (1984). W*hy are the Many Poor?* London: Fabian Society.

Wilson, F. (1996). Drawing together some regional perspectives on poverty. In Oyen, S. M. Miller and Samad, S. A. (Eds.), P*overty: A global review: Handbook of International Poverty Research* (pp. 19-32). Oslo: Scandinavian University Press.

In: Social Indicators: Statistics, Trends…
Editor: Candace M. Baird
ISBN 978-1-61122-841-0

Chapter 7

EXPLAINING SOCIAL DETERMINANTS AND HEALTH RISK: THE CASE OF FEMALE SEX WORKERS IN HONG KONG AND CHINA

***Eleanor Holroyd*[1,1] *and William WC Wong*[2]**
[1]RMIT University, Melbourne, Australia
[2]Department of General Practice, Melbourne University

INTRODUCTION

The modern study of the social determinants of health were said to have begun with Rudolph Virchow and Friedrich Engels whom not only made the explicit link between living conditions and health but also explored the political and economic structures that create inequalities in the living conditions which lead to health inequalities. (Rather 1985; Engels 1987). Recently, international interest in the social determinants of health has led to the World Health Organization's creating a Commission on the Social Determinants of Health. (WHO 2008) In its final report *Closing the Gap in a Generation: Health Equity through Action on the Social Determinants of Health* the commission succinctly summarises the current state of knowledge:

> "Social justice is a matter of life and death…These inequities in health, avoidable health inequalities, arise because of the circumstances in which people grow, live, work, and age, and the systems put in place to deal with illness. The conditions in which people live and die are, in turn, shaped by political, social, and economic forces."

Sex work provides, perhaps, the most vivid example of which the forces of social and economic inequality and marginalisation, could create power imbalances which contribute to social and health disintegration. This is particularly magnified for migrant female sex workers in rapidly developing countries (Wilkinson, 1996). Limitations of the research to date is the insufficiency of careful empirical address of the complexity of gender, socio economic equity

---

1 Corresponding author.

and migrant health and the skewed view of such under the influences of HIV agenda in the last two decades. Furthermore there is a documented absence of data on migration and sexual health studies that explores issues of vulnerability. This, in turn, has contributed further to the lack of comprehensive responses directed at lower socio-economic migrant women.

ECONOMIC REFORM IN CHINA AND VULNERABILITY AMONG MIGRANT WOMEN

Since the reforms of the 1980s, China has witnessed rapid economic growth and social progress market economies (UNDP 1999). Fast economic growth over the past 30 years lifted China's GDP ranking in the world from 11th in 1978 to second in 2009 only after the United States (IMF 2009) with per capita income surged from US$190 in 1978 to US$3,677 in 2009 (National Bureau of Statistics 2009).

In 1984, Beijing changed its policy to allow migrants to find jobs in cities to help ease the growing shortage of cheap labour, but the large scale mass internal migration did not start until the early 1990s when foreign direct investment began to pour into the country (Hong Kong Immigration Department, 2004). In the ten year period of 1992 to 2003, the number of rural migrant workers doubled from 60 to 120 million (Brooks, and Tao, 2003) and tripled to 210 million in 2008. The International Human Rights Watch (2007) reported that the numbers of women migrants had increased significantly over the last three decades, comprising approximately half of the estimated 200 million migrants worldwide. Rubes Ricupero, Secretary-General of UN Conference on Trade and Development has called migration "the missing link between globalization and development" (IOM, 2001).

In China, the vast disparities of wealth between regional and urban areas as well as in the nearby Hong Kong, combined with neo-capitalistic market reforms, accelerate the rate of impoverished women looking for employment opportunities in China's expanding eastern and southern coastal cities or in Hong Kong. In the period between 1983 and 2001, a total of over 720,000 Mainland Chinese new arrivals were admitted under the scheme, which was equivalent to about 11% of the population of 6.72 million in 2001 with new arrivals admitted under the One Way Permit Scheme from 1997 to 2001 accounted for 93% of the total population growth, mostly male, young (20-59 years of age) and well educated, aimed to provide a steady supply of the labour force to the city (Hong Kong census, 2004).

When China joined the World Trade Organization in 2005, further reforms resulted in greater internal and cross-border shifts in population. Many young Chinese women are increasingly migrating for employment, often not having the skills needed in formal work sectors, and frequently coerced to sex work for income and the associated health and socio-economic vulnerabilities related to being away from traditional support structures. A recent study by the UN Inter-Agency Project on Human Trafficking has found that 58% of female sex workers (FSW) entered into sex work in the wake of the financial crisis, and that 19% of these women were former garment sector workers (US State Department Trafficking Report, 2003).

Migrant FSW Entangled in the Socio-Legal Labyrinths

The previous Bush administration made trafficking an important dimension of foreign policy with the US 'Trafficking in Persons Report' claiming Hong Kong to be a transit and destination of human trafficking (US State Department Trafficking Report, 2006). Escalating anecdotal reports in the popular press depict Hong Kong as being used both as a destination and transit for sex workers; for example, a case recently reported two women who were found huddled in a phone booth claiming that they had escaped a trafficking racket (South China Morning Post, March 15, 2006).

Althoughb fiercely denied by both Chinese and Hong Kong government, there nonetheless have been documented increases in the number of women coming from Mainland China to work as FSW. The vast majority of Hong Kong's current female sex workers come from China with the number arrested by the police in violation of immigration law increasing from 3,055 in 2000 to 10,773 in 2003 (written communication from the Hong Kong Police 2004). It is suggested that about 40% of inmates in female prisons who have been charged with breach of condition of stay/ soliciting for immoral purposes are sex workers (Tourism Commission 2006) but a much larger number was detained in detention centres for repatriation without being charged or admitted to prisons.

In recent years the Hong Kong police have adopted a more explicit and visible border policing by operating a three-tiered approach to include stringent control by way of the Mainland Two Way Permit Issuing Authority; screening at immigration control points and enhancing local enforcement action. For example, Mainland Chinese women convicted for sex work would be deprived of re-entry. Furthermore "name and shame" strategies are often used, an example is provided in a newspaper report on an incidence in which the police arrested 40 Mainland FSW interning them in an open air "cage" like shelter in a public car park under depraved conditions and in public view (Wong, Fong, Yeung and Holroyd 2010). Also in Hong Kong situations of public harassment, in the form of neighbourhood protests against the presence of sex workers have been described.

Migrant FSW and Health Risks

Female lower socio-economic migrant workers occupy what Lyttleton and Amarapibal (2002) call marginal or border zones that shape the 'economies of desire' and have specific and unique health vulnerabilities. There is clearly a pattern in many cases of migrant FSW being more likely to engage in high risk health behaviours than the rest of the population. The relationship between mobile groups, commercial sex industry, gender equity and poverty is complex. Migration disrupts family life, and while for men it can create a demand for prostitution supplied, in turn, by migrant women, and from public health's point of view it can potentially contribute to the spread of sexually transmitted infections (STI)/ HIV.

With rapid increase of STI/ HIV in the region, it is natural to assume FSW entered elsewhere as illegal workers as a vector, if not a reservoir, for the transmission of these infections. A common model on the bridging effects of HIV transmission in the community often depict the FSW as the central source of infection spreading to other groups such as their clients and their families. Indeed statistics from Hong Kong Social Hygiene Clinic showed that 51% of FSW attending these government clinics had STI's, (Abdullah, Fielding, Hedley, and Luk, 2002) and it was believed the "true number" of the infections be much higher, with evidence suggesting that those found in Social Hygiene Clinic might have represented only 20% of the total STI treated in the community (Department of Health, 2005).

Sadly our understanding of the health of this group of women is often patchy and one-sided- it tends to focus on sexual health and often fails to take into account the perspective of FSWs themselves, and the complex issues and problems they face. One of the authors (WW) conducted a literature review on FSW in Hong Kong: all 12 articles identified were focused on STI rates and HIV/ STI prevention reinforcing sex workers as vectors for the transmission of STI with little social agency such as self-determination, autonomy and control (Wong and Wun, 2003). (Table 1) This is despite the fact that international research has convincingly shown that sex work *per se* is not a major risk in the spread of HIV in developed regions (Vanwesenbeeck, 2001).

Table 1. Studies on commercial sex from Hong Kong between 1996 and December 2004 (Wong and Wun, HKMJ 2003)

Study	Population	Study measures
Wong et al, 1994	FSWs* and male clients attending the Social Hygiene Clinic	Condom use
Abdullah et al, 2000	Male clients	Epidemiology of HIV infection
Lau and Siah, 2001	Male clients	Sexual behaviours
Lau and Thomas, 2001	Male clients	Commercial sex activities
Lau and Wong, 2001	Male clients	HIV prevalence
Lee and Shi, 2001	Filipino FSWs	Likelihood approach on latent quantities in AIDS prevention
Chan et al, 2002	FSWs attending the Social Hygiene Clinic	Condom use and point prevalence of STDs +
Lau and Wong, 2002	Male sex workers, men who have with men and male clients	HIV prevalence
Lau et al, 2002	Male clients	Condom use and STD incidence
Lau et al, 2003	Male clients	Condom use in China, Hong Kong, and elsewhere

* FSWs - female sex workers.
+ STDs - sexually transmitted diseases.

On the surface, the findings of high STI incidence amongst Hong Kong's FSW compared to the general population appear to be a cause for public health concern. However, when an outreach approach was adopted to screen asymptomatic FSW working in Hong Kong, we found that the STI rates were quite comparable to the other population presented to Social Hygiene Clinic. When the data were further broken down into different migration status, significant higher rates of syphilis and gonorrhoea are found in the illegal migrant group only (Wong Ziteng and Lynn 2010). (Table 3) Apart from having ≥2 sexual partners which is the only relationship factor (OR 10.01 95% CI 1.59-63.80), the other two significant factors after age, education levels adjusted were: the residence status (new migrants: OR0.30 95%CI 0.15-0.99; visitor FSW: OR2.4 95%CI 1.76-7.62) and frequency of douching (OR2.76 95%CI 1.03-7.31) reflecting more of the social context in which these women operated and exercising the means to protect their own bodies.

Table 2. Comparison of the WHOQOL-BREF (HK) scores between street FSW (N=89) and non-sex workers (N'=89) in Hong Kong (Wong et *al.* Journal of Women's Health 2006)

	Sex workers (N=89)		Non-sex workers (N'=89)		95% C.I. for Adjusted mean difference		
	Adjusted Mean#	Non-adjusted mean	Adjusted Mean#	Non-adjusted mean	Nominal P-values (to 3 decimal places)	Lower Bound	Upper Bound
Q1 Quality of life	2.66	2.63	3.58	3.59	0.000 *	-1.25	-0.58
Q2 Overall health	3.59	3.49	3.56	3.62	0.856	-0.32	0.38
Domain I: Physical Health	12.48	12.34	15.46	15.60	0.000 *	-3.79	-2.17
Q3 Pain and Discomfort	1.88	1.79	3.46	3.56	0.000 *	-2.00	-1.16
Q4 Dependence on Medicine	1.55	1.57	4.86	4.87	0.000 *	-3.61	-3.00
Q10 Energy and Fatigue	3.54	3.52	3.59	3.62	0.814	-0.54	0.42
Q15 Mobility	4.27	4.24	4.51	4.54	0.183	-0.59	0.11
Q16 Sleep and Rest	3.61	3.55	3.37	3.42	0.233	-0.16	0.64
Q17 Activities of Daily Living	3.47	3.43	3.56	3.61	0.594	-0.43	0.24
Q18 Working Capacity	3.53	3.51	3.70	3.70	0.329	-0.53	0.18
Domain II: Psychological	12.12	12.07	14.34	14.42	0.000 *	-3.12	-1.31
Q5 Enjoyment of life	1.98	1.97	3.41	3.44	0.000 *	-1.85	-1.00
Q6 Meaningful life	2.30	2.24	3.78	3.85	0.000 *	-1.91	-1.04
Q7 Thinking, Learning, Memory, and Concentration	3.57	3.53	3.45	3.51	0.601	-0.35	0.60
Q11 Bodily Image and Appearance	3.69	3.71	3.87	3.87	0.404	-0.62	0.25
Q19 Self-esteem	3.38	3.37	3.56	3.57	0.286	-0.53	0.16
Q26 Negative Feelings	2.74	2.79	3.36	3.32	0.001 *	-0.99	-0.26
Q27 Eating	3.12	3.08	3.39	3.44	0.140	-0.62	-0.29
Q28 Being respected and accepted	3.48	3.47	3.85	3.85	0.090	-0.82	0.06
Domain III: Social Relationship (Culturally Adjusted)	13.91	13.66	13.84	14.08	0.882	-0.93	1.08
Q20 Personal Relationships	3.73	3.69	3.49	3.54	0.140	-0.08	0.57
Q21 Sexual Activity	2.93	2.90	3.30	3.31	0.030	-0.71	-0.04
Q22 Social Support	3.78	3.66	3.58	3.71	0.202	-0.11	0.51
Domain IV: Environment	12.05	11.86	13.33	13.49	0.008	-2.22	-0.35
Q8 Physical Safety and Security	2.35	2.37	3.59	3.57	0.000 *	-1.72	-0.77
Q9 Physical Environment	3.19	2.98	2.78	2.98	0.056	-0.11	0.84
Q12 Financial Resources	1.84	1.83	3.31	3.33	0.000 *	-1.95	-1.00
Q13 Opportunities for Acquiring Skills	3.32	3.30	3.54	3.53	0.398	-0.73	0.29
Q14 Opportunities for Leisure Activity	2.27	2.26	3.42	3.43	0.000 *	-1.65	-0.65
Q23 Home Environment	3.29	3.23	3.48	3.53	0.300	-0.55	0.17
Q24 Access to Health and Social Care	3.85	3.79	3.12	3.17	0.000 *	0.43	1.02
Q25 Transport	4.00	3.97	3.41	3.44	0.000 *	0.31	0.86

*Statistically significant at p<0.05 after Bonferroni correction i.e. when nominal p< 0.0017.
#Adjusted for Educational Level, Marital Status and Age.

At the same time, two recent studies examined condom use in FSW in Mainland China and found a relatively high percentage of usage (61% and 71% respectively) (Rogers, Ying, Xin, Fung, and Kaufman,.2002; Zhang et al. 2000). Respondents in both studies, 82% and 87.1% respectively claimed condoms were used to prevent disease but 37% and 13% respectively stated it was difficult to access a condom when needed or at work.

On the other hand, in a series of sex worker studies by the authors, we found that, with the exception in the social relationship domain, FSW on the street scored significantly lower in physical, psychological and environmental health of a quality of life instrument, WHOQOL-BREF (HK) when compared to non-sex workers of the same age groups and sex in Hong Kong (Wong, Gray, Ling and Holroyd, 2006). (Table 2) These women were found to be poorly educated and had crossed the Chinese border to work in Hong Kong for economic reasons. Many women surveyed worked long hours with most of their income going back to China to support their dependents and relatively little money spared for themselves (Holroyd, Wong, Gray, and Ling, 2007). (Table4)

Table 3. Associations between STI and Sexual health/ demographic characteristics among (n=503) FSW (Wong et al. Journal of Travel medicine 2010)

	aOR*	P value	95% CI	
Any previous STI				
No	1.00			
Yes	0.73	0.55	0.21	1.92
Number of abortions				
None	1.00			
1	1.79	0.24	0.68	5.08
2	0.71	0.52	0.24	2.10
3+	1.01	0.98	0.39	2.81
Age at first sex				
<= 17 year old	1.00			
18-20 year old	0.56	0.12	0.27	1.16
>= 21 year old	0.50	0.21	0.15	1.46
Frequency of douching				
occasionally or none	1.00			
daily	*3.02*	*0.02*	*1.23*	*7.35*
weekly	0.90	0.86	0.24	2.72
monthly	*2.18*	*0.06*	*0.95*	*5.06*
Place of work				
sauna/karaoke/massage/call or hotel	1.00			
street/single woman brothel	0.95	0. 91	0.42	2.45
Residence status				
HK resident	1.00			
new immigrant (in HK < 7 yrs)	*0.38*	*0.03*	*0.17*	*0.89*
Visitor	1.85	0.23	0.67	5.04
Duration as FSW				
<= 3 months	1.00			
>3 months, <= 1 year	0.95	0.91	0.42	2.31
>1 year, <= 2 years	0.70	0.47	0.20	2.19
>2 years	0.69	0.54	0.25	1.90
Mean no. of clients per day				
0-2	1.00			
3-5	0.65	0.37	0.26	1.75
6-7	0.67	0.46	0.23	2.00
8-12	0.69	0.52	0.22	2.17
Number of sexual partners				
0	1.00			
1	1.79	0.22	0.73	5.40
2+	*8.33*	*0.002*	*2.17*	*33.46*
Always use condom or NA				
No	1.00			
Yes	0.55	0.10	0.26	1.12

aOR = adjusted odds ratio in multiple logistic regression model controlling for age, education level, smoking and alcohol drinking.

Table 4. Working conditions of street (n=89) FSW in Hong Kong (Holroyd et al. 2008)

	Total N	Subgroup n	% of N
Decision of how long to work by FSWs			
Self	89	64	72%
Decided by clients		6	7%
Employer's decision		1	1%
Flexible(no fixed pattern)		11	12%
Health		2	2%
Maximising the income		1	1%
Others		4	5%
Experience of dangerous working conditions by FSWs*			
Beaten by clients	89	7	8%
Not paid by clients		18	20%
Raped by client		3	3.4%
Robbed by clients		14	16%
Verbally abused by clients		10	11%
ID check		47	53%
Pressured to sign		3	3%
Refused bail		1	1%
Photographed by police		1	1%
Insulted by a passer-by		11	12%
Chatted with a passer-by		21	24%
Number of dangerous working experiences			
0	89	28	31%
1		29	33%
2		13	15%
>2		19	21%
Avoidance of being arrested by FSWs			
Stop working temporary	89	74	83%
Assign someone as a watch dog		1	1%
No method		12	14%
Old clients		1	1%
Be careful		1	1%

* Respondents could check more than one option.

Furthermore, migrant FSW often had a negative image about themselves and felt life to be un-meaningful. A large number of our respondents had experienced violence, robbery, and verbal insults. At the same time, they felt that there was not any protection from the police nor the ability to report crimes occurring within the workplace or in the streets without the risk of criminal charges or deportation due to their illegal working status. More than a quarter of the respondents reported to have considered or attempted suicide. In addition another study found by using predictive probability, that the dangers that were inherent to the sex industry such as having been beaten by clients (incidence rate ratio (IRR) -1.53; $p<0.05$); having identity cards checked frequently (IRR 1.61; $p<0.05$); and, the fear of being arrested by police (IRR 0.13; $p<0.05$) rather than health concerns such as HIV infection ($p<0.10$) were strongly associated with poor psychological health and suicidality (Ling, Wong, Holroyd, and Gray. 2007). (Table 5) Naturally, psychological health and stress factors involve the moral dilemmas posed by migration when leaving behind one's family. When women migrate, they are commonly profoundly insecure because of leaving their family of origin, and the resultant complexity of issues of acceptability and access to services within their host county. In many cases, upon return, they must assume the burden of broken family, both materially and morally, especially with regard to their children. Holroyd,E., Taylor-Pillae,R. and Twinn,, 2003.

Table 5. Reported and predicted probabilities of suicidality and environmental threats among (n=89) FSW in Hong Kong

	N (%) of Suicide Ideation/Attempts		Predicted Probabilities of Suicide Ideation/Attempts	
	Yes, only considered	Yes, attempted suicide	Yes, only considered	Yes, attempted suicide
Afraid of infected with HIV (N=89)				
Yes (n=62)	13 (21.0%)	4 (6.5%)	19.2%	7.3%
No (n=27)	4 (14.8%)	2 (7.4%)	16.3%	6.4%
Have your ID card checked frequently (N=89)				
Yes(n=47)	15 (31.9%)	5 (10.6%)	27.8%	12.3%
No (n=42)	2 (4.8%)	1 (2.4%)	7.8%	1.1%
Beaten by client (N=89)				
Yes(n=7)	2 (28.6%)	1 (14.3%)	25.6%	14.7%
No (n=82)	15 (18.3%)	5 (6.1%)	17.7%	6.4%
Insulted by passer-by (N=89)				
Yes (n=11)	4 (36.4%)	3 (27.3%)	36.3%	26.7%
No (n=78)	13 (16.7%)	3 (3.8%)	15.8%	4.2%
Afraid of being arrested (N=89)				
Yes (n=76)	16 (21.1%)	4 (5.3%)	19.0%	6.2%
No (n=13)	1 (7.7%)	2 (15.4%)	14.3%	11.7%

A considerable proportion of the FSW we surveyed suffered from a number of non-sexual health related illnesses but the consultation rate was only a third of the mean rate of the general population in Hong Kong. (Wong, Gray, Ling and Holroyd, 2006) In the same series of studies many migrant street sex workers experienced difficulty in utilizing health services in Hong Kong but even when they did, it was mainly for acute problems. Affordable access to health public services was excluded and many found private services unaffordable due to the high prices charged by the doctors. It was common therefore for these women to self-medicate, delay in seeking medical help, or travel back to China for treatment.

Our data also found that those most vulnerable of sexual health risk such as migrant FSW where the least likely to receive care as postulated by the Inverse Care Law (Seema, Brennan, and Boffetta, 2003). WW screened 245 FSW at the outreach clinic between 2004 and 2005 (Wong, Wun, Chan and Liu 2008), and found only 35.5% reported that they had had a cervical smear. 9.8% (23/235) FSW had pre-invasive lesions (CIN I-CIN III) in contrast to 5.5% (395/3601) of the Hong Kong general population - one of the highest ever reported in the literature. Again, regression analysis showed that the place of origin (local or non-local FSW) was the single most important risk factor for CIN II-III. (Table 6)

Both in Hong Kong and in China, as in elsewhere, migrant lower socio-economic women are generally regarded as a social category of women who do not adhere to behavioural norms; and frequently, excluded from mainstream society, occupying marginal positions analogous to that of a minority ethnic group. They receive limited access to health care as evidenced by delayed uptake of screening services of late presentation of symptoms, have heightened vulnerability as evidenced from denial of police protection, and repeated beatings and occupational danger.

Table 6. Risk factors of abnormal PAP smear among (n=245) FSW using multi-nominal logistic regression model

Independent variables	p-value	OR (95% CI)
CIN I		
Age	0.46	0.66 (0.22 to 2.00)
Pregnancy	.	.
Gravidity	0.64	1.76 (0.16 to 19.22)
Abortion	0.14	2.51 '(0.75 to 8.44)
Smoking	0.46	0.59 (0.15 to 2.41)
Drinking	0.85	0.85 (0.14 to 4.97)
Exercise	0.65	0.74 (0.21 to 2.66)
Previous STI	0.12	0.40 (0.12 to 1.27)
Previous PAP smear	0.20	2.37 (0.63 to 8.84)
Place of origin	.	.
Non-HK resident	0.53	1.44 (0.46 to 4.48)
HK resident	.	.
CIN II-CIN III	.	
Age	0.57	0.61 (0.11 to 3.35)
Pregnancy		.
Gravidity	---	9.79E-008 (9.79E-008 to 9.79E-008)
Abortion	0.25	0.25 (0.02 to 2.60)
Smoking	0.93	1.11 (.109 to 11.16)
Drinking	1.00	4662213.26 (0.00 to ---.)
Exercise	0.71	0.71 (0.12 to 4.28)
Previous STI	0.08	0.18 (0.03 to 1.19)
Previous PAP smear	0.24	4.30 (0.38 to 48.80)
Place of origin	.	.
Non-HK resident vs. HK resident	0.02	17.132 (1.71 to 171.68)

* The reference category is "first category".

Of note is that since April 2003, non-Hong Kong residents have been subject to a fee seven times higher than what locals are paying when availing of medical services in Hong Kong. It is possible here that power was not a coherent or coercive force merely exercised through class or status position; instead power originated from an external force (Foucault, 1977), such as through the government, realized and passed to individuals as a means that systematically deny women their fundamental human rights to health care.

Many migrant women are exposed to abuse while at work with stressful life events, related to a number of disorders, both psychological and physical (Hogue, 2000; Williams, and Umberson, 2000). In particular mood, personality disorders, depression and anxiety were mediators of other health outcomes and mental health endpoints in themselves; their incidence varying by age, class and ethnicity. Depression and other adverse psychological states placed these women at risk of violence, including sexual assault, and, could possibly be attributable to an increased incidence of chronic and infectious disease. At the same time psychological problems were highly prevalent among FSW: substance use (40.4%), probable depression (53.9%), self-harm tendencies (34-38%), poor self-esteem (48-52%), and pessimistic future outlook (46-47%) and multivariate analyses indicated that they were significantly associated with inconsistent condom use and non-use of prevention services. (Lau et al. 2010)

Many Hong Kong studies have found migrant FSW to have poor or substandard housing, poor occupational and residential safety and prone to street violence. Highlighted in many recommendations put forward was the importance of promoting close working relationship between sex workers, sex industry owner/operators, health agencies and local authorities. Risk awareness programs developed and conducted were recommended to embrace the complexity of occupational health issues given that such programs would also have the benefit of affirming the health rights of sex workers and public health (Holroyd et al. 2007).

Increasingly the nature of the health problems first and third world countries have to provide complex inverventiosn for are converging. The development of a society, affluent or poor, can be judged by the quality of its population's health, how fairly health is distributed across the social spectrum, and the degree of protection provided from disadvantage as a result of ill-health. Clearly sexual and reproductive health needs to be brought together and integrated into a development agenda. Enabling migrant women to break out of poverty traps when combined with the world financial crisis and, STI/ HIV epidemics and climate change all contribute to increasingly fragmented health care systems.

Recommendations

Based on the research outlined above, the authors propose a number of policy and research recommendations for addressing gender and health inequity for migrant Chinese women. We would recommend the adaptation of socio-ecological (Bauer, 2003) approach that allows indicators of health, health promotion and public health theory to be accounted for in a theory driven way stemming form a systems approach. This model has been based on the Ottawa Charter (WHO Ottawa Charter for Health promotion, WHO 1986) as well as a conceptual framework of quality theory in health intervention developed by Donabedian (1988). In respect to health and gender inequity in migrant women this would allow the socio-cultural process to be at the forefront of health promotion interventions while applyinga a theoretical underpinning to the approach. This would consider jointly gender equity and socioeconomic inequality, political and socio circumstances that situate health in specific historical, political, legal and social contexts. Such an approach allows the personal any country specific planned health public intervention to feed into pathways that implicate collective or personal action

The socio-ecological model integrates social, economic, and epidemiological constructs and enables a focus on vulnerable populations. This would further allow complementation of the biological health care delivery public health model that commonly exits in countries such as China. The application of these models would further encourage detailed and sophisticated examination of social, cultural determinates of migrant women's health from a multi-disciplinary perspective, taking account of contextual and individual situations.

Specifically:

1. Advocating for new social norms through engaging family and friends in order to promote changes of societal attitudes towards sex work- an example the idea that

idea that sex work is a form of adultery and that threatens the marital relationship is unfound (Gurkison and Ferguson, 2009). This can be achieved by cross-border collaboration with campaigns, NGO- advocacy and leaders from the industry who are willing to speak out. The added advantage of such an approach is that it also provides an alternative for social motility;
2. Engaging settings that address gender inequity in education, poverty and employment; work place- safety; police and legal systems
3. Public health policies: provide free/ affordable health access; that not only focus on sexual health (Well-women clinics); stigma free service; choices e.g. government and NGO-run clinics.

A multi-level approach that encourages the sharing of techniques, and solutions across disciplinary and international national boundaries, will deepen an understanding of socio and economic structures and so improve policy and programmatic strategies. Included in the adaptation of such model would be more field based, ecological and ethnographic work that provides new insights that enable the generation of theory about marginalized populations.

A further recommendation is to create and maintain appropriate data systems for monitoring, mapping and reporting on socioeconomic inequalities and gender equity. Within this approach appropriate socioeconomic and equity measures must be included as well as migrant women's own stories and understandings.

REFERENCES

Abdullah, AS., Fielding, R., Hedley, AJ, and Luk, YK. (2002) Risk factors for sexually transmitted diseases and casual sex among Chinese patients attending sexually transmitted disease clinics in Hong Kong. *Sex Transm Dis,*. 29, 360-5.

Bauer, G, and Davis, JK. (2003). Advancing a theoretical model for public health and health promotion indicator development. *European Journal of Public health*, 107-113.

Brooks, R, and Tao, R. (2003) China. *IMF Working Paper*. No.03/210.

Depatment of Health; Health Topics, Communicable Disease, Sexually Transmitted Infections 2005. Available from www.chp.gov.hk.

Donabedian, A. (1988) The Quality of Care; Can it be assessed?, *JAMA*, 260:12, 1743-1748.

Engels, F. (1987). The Condition of the Working Class in England. New York: Penguin Classics. *The Condition of the Working Class in England.*

Foucault, M. (1977) *Discipline and Punish: The Birth of the Prison,* trans. Alan Sheridan. London: Penguin Books.

Gurkison S and Ferguson, L 2009 *Reproductive Health Matters* Volume 17. Issue 34 November 2009, Pages 108-118

Hogue, CJR. (2000). Gender, race and class: From epidemiologic association to etiologic hypotheses. In: Goldman, M.B. and Hatch, M.C., Editors. *Women and health*, (pp. 15–23) Academic Press, San Diego.

Holroyd, E., Wong, W., Gray, A., Sr Ling, D. (2007) Environmental health and safety of Chinese sex workers: A cross-sectional study. *International Journal of Nursing Studies* 45:6, 932-941.

Holroyd, E., Taylor-Pillae, R. and Twinn, S. (2003). Investigating Hong Kong's Filippino domestic workers' healthcare behavior, knowledge, beliefs and attitudes towards cervical cancer and cervical screening. *Women and Health,* 38, 169–183.

Hong Kong Immigration Department; Hong Kong Census and Statistics Department (2004), Special Report No.25, *'Persons from the Mainland China having resided in Hong Kong for less than 7 years'*, 2000.

International Human Rights Watch. World Report 2007. Available from: http://www.hrw.org/

International Organization for Migration. *The Link Between Migration and Development in the Least Developed Countries.* Geneva: IOM, 2001.

International Monetary Fund, World Economic Outlook Database. Data for 2009.

Kept in the dark on industry facts. South China Morning Post 2006 Mar 15; Features A14.

Lau JT, Tsui HY, Ho SP, Wong E, Yang X. Prevalence of psychological problems and relationships with condom use and HIV prevention behaviors among Chinese female sex workers in Hong Kong. AIDS Care. 2010; 22(6): 659-68.

Ling, DC., Wong, WCW., Holroyd, EA, and Gray, A. (2007) An Exploration of Psychological Health and Suicidality among Female Street Sex Workers. *Journal of Sex and Marital Therapy,* 33, 281-299.

Link, BG, and Phelan, J. (1995) Social conditions as fundamental causes of disease. *Journal of Health and Social Behavior*, extra issue, 80–94.

Lyttleton, C, and Amarapibal, A. (2002) Sister cities and easy passage: HIV, mobility and economies of desire in a Thai/Lao border zone. *Social Science and Medicine*, 54:4, 505-518.

National Bureau of Statistics of China [information on the web page]. China Statistical Yearbook 2008. Available from http://www.stats.gov.cn/english/

Rogers, SJ., Ying, L., Xin, YT., Fung, K, and Kaufman J. (2002) Reaching and identifying the STD/HIV risk of sex workers in Beijing. *AIDS Education and Prevention*, 14:3, 217-227.

Seema, P., Brennan, P, and Boffetta, P. (2003) Meta-analysis of social inequality and the risk of cervical cancer. *Int J Cancer*, 105, 687-691.

Tourism Commission [information on the webpage]. C2006 [updated 2006 Sep 18]. Available from: http://www.tourism. United), (1999). *Human development report 1999.* New York: United Nations.

U.S. State Department Trafficking Report Undercut by Lack of Analysis [website on the Internet]. c2006 [cited 2003 Jun 22] Available from: http:// www.hrw.org/press/ 2003/06/ traffickingreport.htm.

U.S. Department of State. Trafficking in Persons Report. United States of America; 2006. Available from: http://www.state.gov/documents/organization/ 66086.pdf

Vanwesenbeeck, I. (2001). Another Decade of Social Scientific Work on Sex Work: A Review of Research 1990-2000', *Annual Review of* Sex *Research, 12, 242-89.*

Virchow, R. (1985). The Epidemics of 1848. In L. J. Rather (Ed.), Collected Essays by Rudolph Virchow on Public Health and Epidemiology. Volume 1. (pp. 113-119). Canton MA. *Virchow's Report on the Typhus Epidemic in Upper Silesia.*

Wilkinson, RG. (1996). *Unhealthy societies: The afflictions of inequality*, Routledge, London.

Williams, K, and Umberson, D. (2000) Women stress, and health. In: Goldman, M.B. and Hatch, M.C., Editors. *Women and health*, (pp. 553–562) Academic Press, San Diego.

Wong, WCW, Fong, T, Yeung, CSY, Holroyd, EA. (2009) Hong Kong's female sex workers: Media construction of health and social stigma. *Submitted to Asian Journal of Women's Health.*

Wong, WCW, Gray, A., Ling, DC, and Holroyd, E. (2006) Female Street Sex workers in Hong Kong: Moving beyond sexual health. *Journal of Women's Health*, 15:4, 390-7.

Wong WCW, Leung PWS, Lynn, HSY. (2010) Sexually Transmitted Infections among Female Sex Workers in Hong Kong: The role of migration status. *Journal of Travel Medicine*. (In press).

Wong WCW, Wun YT. (2003) The Health of female sex workers in Hong Kong: Do we care? *Hong Kong Medical Journal*, 9, 471-473.

Wong, WCW, Wun, YT, Chan, L and Liu, Y. (2008) Silent killer of the night: A feasibility study of an outreach well women clinic for cervical cancer screening in sex workers in Hong Kong. *International journal of gynecological Cancer*, 18, 110- 115.

Wong, WCW, Ziteng and Lynn, H. (2009). Sexually Transmitted Infections among Female Sex Workers in Hong Kong: A Displaced Emphasis. Submitted to Sexually Transmitted Infections.

World Bank. (1998). *Engendering development: Enhancing development through attention to gender.* Draft report and commentary.

World Health Organisation. Ottawa Charter for Health promotion: 1986. Available from http://www.who.int.

World Health Organization. (2008). Commission on the Social Determinants of Health. Retrieved March 15, 2008, from http://www.who.int/social_determinants/en/.

In: Social Indicators: Statistics, Trends...
Editor: Candace M. Baird

ISBN 978-1-61122-841-0

Chapter 8

EVALUATING ENVIRONMENTAL AND REGIONAL POLICIES IN THE EUROPEAN UNION THROUGH THE USE OF ENVIRONMENTAL QUALITY INDICES

Panagiotis Evangelopoulos[1], Dimitrios Giannias[2], Panagiotis Liargovas[1] and Loukas Tsironis[3]

[1]Department of Economics, University of Peloponnese, Greece
[2]Department of Economics, University of Thessaly
[3]Department of Production Engineering and Management, Technological University of Crete

ABSTRACT

This chapter uses an amenity-productivity theoretical framework to classify European Union sub-group of countries (EU-27, Eurozone-16, EU-15) according to the extent to which they are influenced by supply-side (producer) and demand-side (consumer) responses to their specific bundle of economic and environmental attributes. The assessment of the environmental quality in each state is based on the development of environmental indices. This kind of classification is useful because it provides information about the relative attractiveness to producers and consumers of the combination of economic and environmental attributes indigenous to each region. It therefore has implications for the design and focus of the regional and environmental policies of the European Union and the Eurozone.

INTRODUCTION

Various studies have investigated the existence of consumer income differentials among regions or countries. The irrefutable conclusion is that they exist and that they can persist for long periods of time (see for example Bellante, 1979, Johnson, 1983 and Eberts and Stone,

1986). Researchers dealing with regional policy in the EU generally assume that income disparities are caused by geographical and economic variables.

The concepts of core and periphery have been the most influential geographical explanation of EU regional disparities. The idea is that regions distant from the core of activity in a country fail to develop equally with areas closer to the core. The EU has a core containing a high concentration of economic development[1], modern infrastructure and advanced social indicators. All of the attributes of post-industrial life are concentrated in the core. By contrast, the periphery contains many regions that would be traditionally designated as underdeveloped. Many of these regions have been outside the main processes of economic development experienced in the core regions.

It is also recognized that some regions are chronically poor not because of their location, but because of economic factors. Many such regions had depended on one major economic activity, such as steel making or textiles. When the economic viability of the activity declined, the region lacked the resources necessary to diversify and fell into chronic recession.

Within a theoretical framework in which regions and factors are identical and all economic agents are free to move, neo-classical analysis supports the view that the output (and income) of different regions should tend to converge over time.[2] This view, however, has been challenged by a number of new growth models.[3] These new growth models suggest, amongst other things, that there are positive externalities arising from the concentration of human capital in core regions so that regional incomes and outputs can actually diverge.[4] Counter to the assumptions of neo-classical economics, regional economic disparities can therefore be exacerbated by the free movement of capital, goods and people. As well as these challenges to the predictions of neo-classical economics, it is also possible that differences in consumer incomes can persist because some factors, such as the infra-structural or environmental characteristics that are unique to a region, are inherently immobile. Economic agents would be willing to pay or accept different levels of income depending on the value they place on these characteristics.

The purpose of this paper is to identify European Union countries according to the extent to which they are influenced by the response of both industry and people to their net bundle of country-specific attributes. Following the development of a theoretical model and an index of environmental quality for each member state, the various member states are classified into four groups based on the relative values of a country's per capita income and environmental quality. Countries are then classified as high amenity (low consumer income, high environmental quality), low amenity (high consumer income, low environmental quality), high productivity (high consumer income, high environmental quality), and low productivity (low consumer income, low environmental quality).

The usefulness of this classification is twofold: First, it provides information about the relative attractiveness to industry and people of the total bundle of environmental and other attributes indigenous to each country of the European Union. Second, it assists European policy makers to formulate the best-suited regional and environmental policies that reflect the

[1] See Krugman (1991) and Krugman and Venables (1990).
[2] See for example Solow (1956).
[3] See Romer (1986), Uzawa (1965) and Conslik (1969).
[4] See Van der Ploeg and Tang (1992), for more details.

specific circumstances of each member state. High amenity countries or regions, for example, require regional policy measures to increase their income. Similarly, low amenity countries or regions require environmental policy measures to increase their quality of life. Finally, in low productivity and low amenity areas both policies, regional and environmental, are important for increasing the per capita incomes and environmental quality.

The following section of the paper reviews regional and environmental policies of the EU, while the subsequent discussion provides a theoretical framework to determine the importance of amenity and productivity differences as sources of income differentials across countries in the EU. The empirical results are then presented and some possible explanations behind observed patterns are put forward. Finally, some conclusions and policy implications are proposed.

1.Regional and Environmental Policies in the EU

Regional and environmental policies are two of the EU's most important policy areas. Regional policy aims at reducing variations in the economic performance of the different member states. The preamble of the Treaty of Rome calls for a reduction "of the differences existing between the various regions and the backwardness of the less favoured regions", while Article 2 refers to the goal of "harmonious development of economic activities, a continuous and balanced expansion".

In 1975, the European Community established the European Regional Development Fund (ERDF) as a response to this issue. The European Regional Development Fund (ERDF) is one of the key Structural Funds. Its commitments for 1996 were more than ECU 11.8 billion. Although the ERDF was created in 1975, in the wake of the accession of Britain, Ireland and Denmark, the development of the single market was the catalyst for strengthening Union solidarity with poorer regions at risk of being left further behind. That is why the Single European Act of 1986 introduced a new Title into the Treaty of Rome called "Economic and Social Cohesion." When the Maastricht Treaty on European Union laid the basis for establishing an Economic and Monetary Union (EMU) by 1999, it was also decided to address the risk that EMU could worsen regional disparities. The treaty's requirement that budget deficits be limited to a maximum of 3% of Gross Domestic Product (GDP) also limits the possibilities of poorer states increasing investments to catch up with their richer partners. In response, therefore, the treaty established a new Cohesion Fund to channel financial assistance to the four poorest states with a per capita GDP of less than 90% of the EU average.

Unlike regional policy, environmental policy is a more recent policy of the EU. When the Treaty of Rome was written in 1956-57, its authors saw no need to provide a common policy on the environment because they did not perceive any common threat. It was not until October 1972 that a conference of Heads of State or Government insisted that a common policy was needed, and since then more than 200 items of Union legislation on the environment have been enacted. These are the products of action programs which the Council of Ministers has been endorsing since 1973.

From a growth-oriented view, environmental protection measures are perceived as constraints to economic development. Growth is also seen by environmentalists as creating adverse ecological consequences that originate from expansions of industrial activity. It is true that in the long run, the economic potential of future production factors will increasingly depend on the state of environmental conditions. This can be clearly depicted by effects that accumulated pollution levels are known to have on human health and land productivity. Due to these interrelationships, development and environment should be brought together into the same conceptual framework from which mutual beneficial objectives may be achieved.[5] Sustainable development is the notion which entails this conceptual framework. Sustainability is defined as maintaining continuity of economic and social developments while respecting the environment and without jeopardizing future use of natural resources. The ideas and theories of sustainable development have been examined and discussed by a number of important Commission policy documents. [6] Sustainable development was made the centerpiece of the EU's Fifth Environmental Action Programme in alignment with the commitments made at the 1992 UNCED at Rio. In the last chapter of the GCE White paper (CEC 1993) the basis for a new development model was explored which focused on the objectives of sustainability. Integrating environmental policy into regional policy field is essential if sustainable development is to succeed. In recognition of the more holistic approach that this intimates, Article 139r of the Maastricht Treaty states the need for all areas of EU policy to make environmental objectives an integral part of any future strategies. Finally, in a recent paper it is argued that environmental protection is easier to achieve with economic growth than without it.[7]

2. The Theoretical Framework for Regional Economic and Environmental Classifications

In this section a theoretical framework is presented which can be used to determine the relative importance of amenity and productivity differences as sources of income differentials across the European Union. This framework assumes that regions or countries are fully described by a bundle of environmental and other attributes. These specify the environmental quality index of a country or region (EQ) which includes all aspects of natural and non-natural environment of a consumer's life. EQ affects the utility of consumers and the production[8] cost of firms. The framework is illustrated in Figure 1.

The downward sloping curves in Figure 1, labeled V(R), show combinations of income[9] (I) and environmental quality (EQ) for consumers that are associated with an equal level of utility in equilibrium. This curve takes an implicit measure of the cost of real estate (R)[10] into account. The slope of these curves is the trade-off that households are willing to make between income and environmental quality for the given level of utility at any given implicit

[5] See WCED (1987) p. 43.

[6] See CEC (1992), (1993), (1994).

[7] See World Bank (1992).

[8] Where the production technologies are assumed to exhibit constant returns to scale.

[9] The income of a consumer is assumed to be determined by a hedonic wage equation which depends among others (e.g., personal characteristics, education, experience, etc.) on environmental quality.

[10] For example, R = (R1, R2, R3) is the vector of implicit prices for the vector of housing characteristics h = (h1, h2, h3), so that the rental price, P, of a house that is described by the vector of characteristics (h1, h2, h3) is P = R h', where h' is the transpose of h.

cost of housing. Along each curve, the implicit cost of housing is fixed and the curves shift up (down) as the implicit costs of housing increase (decrease).

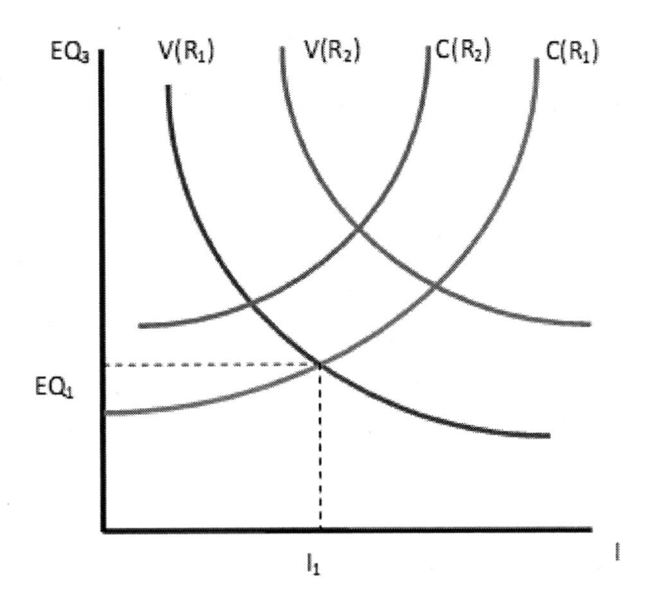

Figure 1. The proposed framework. This framework depicts that Income differentials is a function of amenity and productivity characteristics across EU countries.

The upward sloping curves in Figure 1, labeled C(R), show combinations of income (I) and environmental quality (EQ) which are associated with an equal level of cost for industry in equilibrium.[11] This curve takes an implicit measure of the cost of real estate (R) into account. The slope of these curves is the trade-off that firms are willing to make between productivity and environmental quality for the given level of cost at any given implicit cost of renting industrial property. The value that a firm places on the environmental characteristics of a region is fixed along each curve and the curves shift up (down) as the environmental characteristics of a region increase (decrease) the productivity of firms and the implicit cost of housing.

Thus, within the model, each region is characterized by an environmental quality index and by an implicit measure of the price of real estate associated with a specific pair of iso-cost and iso-utility curves. These iso-cost and iso-utility curves are important because where there are equal costs for industry and utility for consumers there are no incentives to relocate. The intersection of any two curves for each region at the level of its environmental quality then determines the relative income and the implicit prices of the real estate market in equilibrium. In Figure 1, in region 1, where environmental quality equals EQ_1, the equilibrium income will be I_1 and the equilibrium implicit rental prices R_1.

By using this framework, we can hold every other variable constant for any region to examine the implications of differences in environmental quality and income. By examining the patterns of environmental quality and incomes across regions, we can determine whether environmental quality and income differences reflect inter-regional differences in amenities or productivity. If environmental quality and income differences primarily reflect amenity

[11] Under the assumption that production technologies exhibit constant returns to scale.

differences across regions, we would see a negative relationship between environmental quality and incomes. If they reflect productivity differences, the relationship would be positive.

Within the same framework, we can also classify individual regions on the basis of whether their incomes and environmental quality differ from the average. Thus we can distinguish between regions with above average or below average levels of amenities and between regions with above or below average levels of productivity. These classifications are summarized in Figure 2. Environmental quality is higher than the average in the high amenity and high productivity regions and lower than the average in the low amenity and low productivity ones. On the other hand, incomes are relatively higher in the high productivity and low amenity regions

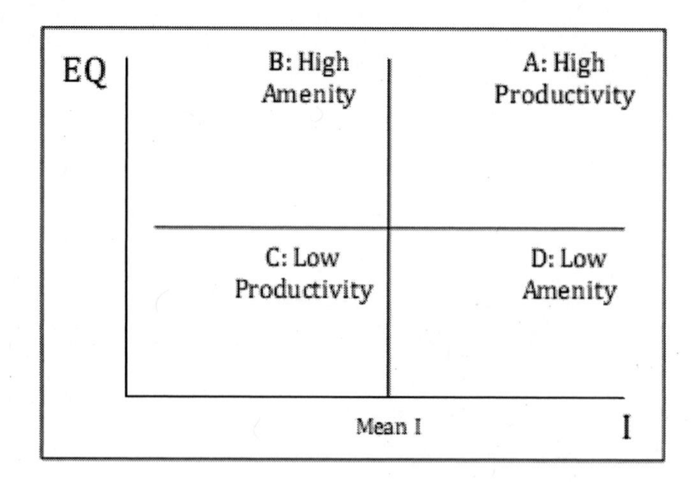

Figure 2. Classification of EU regions based on their incomes and environmental quality index.

Each region within this analysis is characterized by an environmental quality index (EQ) whose effect on household utility and production costs differs from region to region. The problem of classifying regions by the relative magnitude of these two effects becomes one of identifying the environmental quality and income differences that are experienced in equilibrium when each curve shifts. This can be done by identifying the combinations of EQ and I in equilibrium that are associated with equal shifts of both curves and determining how incomes and environmental quality change relative to these shifts. For any region with above average incomes and environmental quality, the shift of the C(R) (productivity) curve must be less than the shift of the V(R) (amenity) curve. The less the direct effect of environmental quality on utility, the greater the increase in consumer income needed to offset the increase in rents and, consequently, the greater the shift of the V(R) curve needed to keep the maximum utility level unchanged in equilibrium.

Any region with environmental quality and income combinations in quadrant A in Figure 2 is classified as a "high productivity" region. This is because the primary reason that this region's incomes, environmental quality, and rents differ from those of the average region is the above-average productivity effects of environmental quality. This above-average productivity effect is reflected in the ability of producers in these regions to pay above average incomes and rents for having at their disposal a greater than average level of environmental quality. Similarly regions with below average incomes and environmental quality as in quadrant C in Figure 2 are classified as "low productivity" regions. This below-average productivity effect is reflected in the ability of producers in these regions to pay below average incomes and rents for having at their disposal a lower than average level of environmental quality. Finally, an above average amenity effect for a region is associated with increases in rents and decreases in incomes reflecting consumers' willingness to pay relatively more for a region's high environmental quality. Quadrant D then identifies regions where the environmental quality is greater than the average and that this high amenity effect has a dominant influence on incomes and rents. For regions in quadrant B, the dominant influence is their below-average amenity value.

3. Empirical Results: An Amenity-Productivity Classification for the EU Member States

The theoretical framework introduced above can be used to classify the European Union member states. To calculate the environmental quality (EQ) for each country, the data presented by World Resources Report (1992-1993) and by the United Nations Human Development Index (1993) was used for the natural and non-natural environmental indicators set out in Appendix 1. These indicators were used to develop an overall index of environmental quality for each member state. The methodology for this approach is also presented in Appendix 1.

Table 1a, b and c, contains the deviations of environmental quality (EQ) from its mean, m(EQ), and the deviation of per capita income (I^*) from its mean, m(I^*). Table 1a presents the combinations for the initially 15 EU member states[12], while table 1b those of the 16 EU countries in the EURO zone and table 1c the complete list of 27 EU members. Data presenting on table 1 was used to classify countries according to figure's 2 framework. Each country classified according to the pair of values taken from the appropriate table.

The EQ columns values concern the Indicators mean values for each member state, while the I columns values is the quotient of the difference between GDP per capita minus the minimum index value in the sample of countries ($I_{ij}^{\min}$) divided by the range of the index value in the sample of countries.

That is: $$I = \text{GDP per capita} - I_{ij}^{\max} \Big/ R_I$$

where: $R_I = I_{ij}^{\max} - I_{ij}^{\min}$

From this and from our theoretical analysis we can position the various member states according to our distinction between high and low amenity and high and low productivity regions. The results of this are set out in Figures 3, 4 and 5.

[12] Missing values for a Yij variable have been replaced by the mean of the existing ones. These missing values were for Luxembourg: Y1, Y11, Y12, Y14, Y16, Y17, Y18, Y30, Denmark: Y12, Greece: Y15, Y17, Germany: Y32, Belgium: Y33, Ireland:Y1, Y16.

Table 1. Derivations of Environmental Quality and Income per capita from their mean values

Table 1a: The 15 initial EU members states

	EQ	I*
Austria	67.297	34.303
Belgium	51.726	30.732
Denmark	65.899	49.528
Finland	72.438	38.304
France	54.845	29.719
Germany	59.173	30.894
Greece	58.287	12.773
Ireland	71.877	45.461
Italy	46.010	19.699
Luxembourg	50.408	100.000
Netherlands	47.588	33.693
Portugal	51.770	0.000
Spain	47.013	11.235
Sweden	77.741	46.489
UK	59.338	38.239

Table 1b: The 16 EU members in the EURO zone

	EQ	I*
Austria	71.207	42.438
Belgium	56.115	39.309
Cyprus	53.999	19.589
Finland	77.208	45.945
France	59.037	38.423
Germany	62.996	39.452
Greece	62.130	23.575
Ireland	74.363	52.215
Italy	51.137	29.643
Luxembourg	55.417	100.000
Malta	57.173	10.606
Netherlands	53.655	41.904
Portugal	57.965	12.384
Slovakia	60.654	0.000
Slovenia	63.704	14.002
Spain	50.265	22.227

Table 1c: The complete 27 EU member states

	EQ	I*
Austria	68.339	45.622
Belgium	56.210	42.666
Bulgaria	54.515	0.000
Cyprus	55.024	24.037
Czech Rep	58.031	9.257
Denmark	69.195	58.224
Estonia	66.679	9.030
Finland	75.537	48.934
France	57.485	41.828
Germany	60.353	42.801
Greece	60.406	27.801
Hungary	54.960	7.437
Ireland	73.171	54.858
Italy	49.716	33.534
Latvia	71.419	6.609
Lithuania	63.007	5.831
Luxembourg	56.343	100.000
Malta	55.645	15.550
Netherlands	52.233	45.117
Poland	57.418	6.359
Portugal	58.986	17.229
Romania	49.317	0.364
Slovakia	60.178	5.531
Slovenia	64.000	18.758
Spain	48.111	26.529
Sweden	76.656	55.709
UK	62.772	48.880

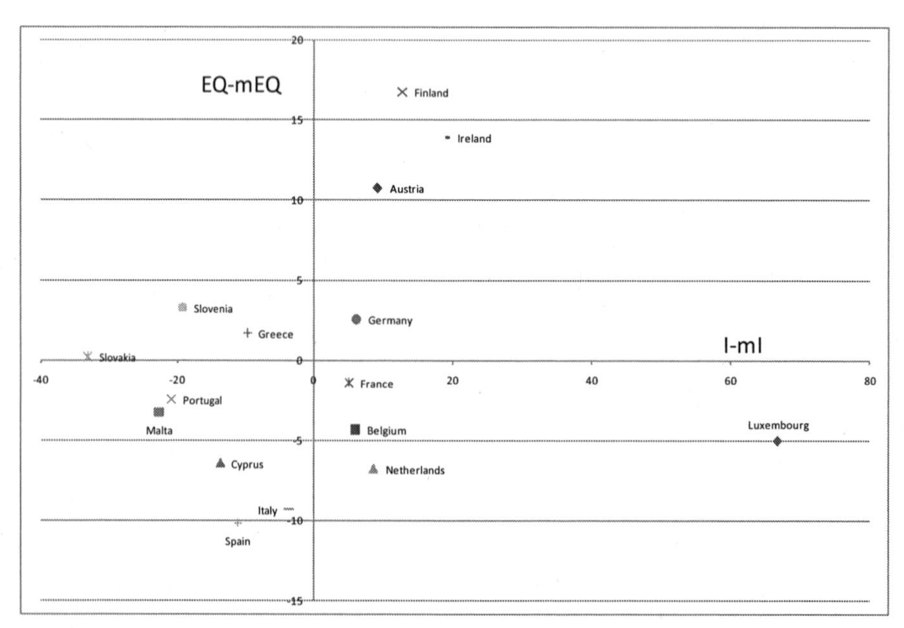

Figure 3. The 16 EU members in the EURO zone.

Figure 3 presents results for the 16 EU members in the EURO zone. The analysis identifies four groups of countries within the EU: the high-productivity countries (Finland, Austria, Ireland and Germany), the low-productivity countries (Portugal, Malta, Cyprus, Italy and Spain), the low-amenity countries (France, Belgium, Netherlands and Luxemburg) and the high amenity countries (Slovenia, Greece and Slovakia).

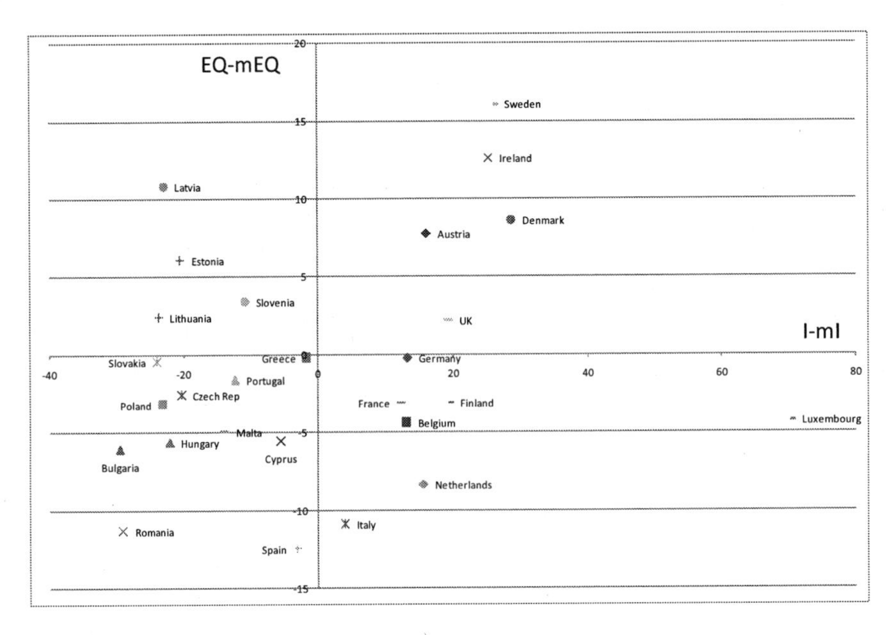

Figure 4. The complete 27 EU member states.

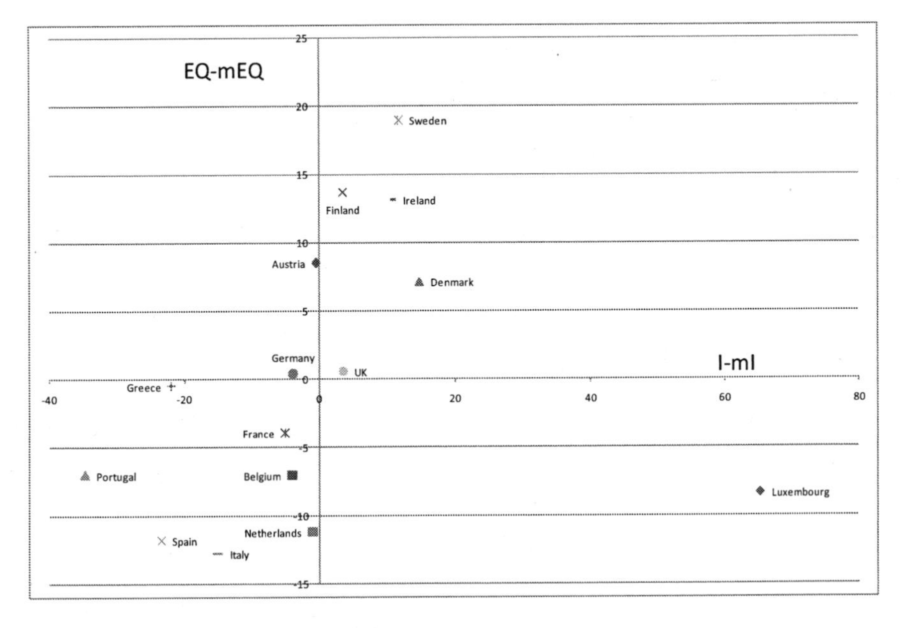

Figure 5. The 15 initial EU member countries.

Figure 4 presents results for the complete 27 EU members states. The analysis identifies four groups of countries within the EU: the high-productivity countries (Sweden, Ireland, Austria, Denmark and UK), the low-productivity countries (Greece, Slovakia, Czech

Republic, Poland, Portugal, Malta, Hungary, Bulgaria, Cyprus, Spain and Romania), the low-amenity countries (Germany, France, Belgium, Finland, Netherlands and Italy) and the high amenity countries (Latvia, Estonia, Lithuania and Slovenia).

Figure 5 presents results for the 15 initial EU member states. The analysis identifies four groups of countries within the EU: the high-productivity countries (Sweden, Finland, Ireland, Denmark and UK), the low-productivity countries (Greece, France, Belgium, Portugal, Netherlands, Italy and Spain), the low-amenity countries (Luxembourg) and the high amenity countries (Austria and Germany).

In the high productivity countries, measures of both amenity and productivity are above average. Consequently, if the goal of policy is to reduce regional disparities, it may be appropriate to focus the attentions of both economic and environmental policies elsewhere. In the low productivity group of countries, amenity and productivity appear to be mutually compatible policy objectives. This would appear to suggest that policies can be brought forward to enhance both economic and environmental conditions simultaneously. In the low amenity group emphasis should be given to environmental measures since this group is characterized by its high income and low environmental quality. Finally, in the case of the high amenity countries, emphasis should be given to regional policy, since the country is characterized by low income and high environmental quality.

Conclusions and Policy Proposals

This paper put forward a theoretical framework based on the development of environmental indices that can be used to classify European Union countries according to the extent they are influenced by supply-side (producer) and demand-side (consumer) responses to their net bundle of country-specific attributes. As Giannias and Liargovas (1998) proved, this kind of classification is useful because it provides information about the relative attractiveness to producers and consumers of the combination of economic and environmental attributes indigenous to each region. It therefore has implications for the design and focus of the regional and environmental policies of the European Union.

The applied analysis showed that Slovenia, Greece (which are Eurozone members) and Slovakia, Latvia, Estonia, Lithuania and Slovenia (which are among the 27 member countries) can be characterized as high amenity countries. This fact can be justified because high amenity countries are characterized by a combination of relatively low levels of income and high environmental quality.

Among the other member states, Finland, Austria, Ireland, Germany (Eurozone members) Sweden, Ireland, Austria, Denmark, UK (which are among the 27 member countries) and are high productivity countries characterized by a combination of relatively high levels of income and environmental quality. From the initial 15 members Sweden, Finland, Ireland, Denmark, UK are the high productivity countries. Giannias and Liargovas (1998) found that Sweden, Germany, Finland, Austria, Denmark and Netherlands classified at the time as high productivity.

Luxemburg (Eurozone member) is the only one low amenity country which is characterized by a combination of relatively high incomes and low levels of environmental quality. However France, Belgium, Netherlands, Luxemburg (which are among the 27 member countries) stated classified as low amenity countries. Giannias and Liargovas (1998) classified France, Belgium and Luxemburg as low amenity countries.

Finally, Portugal, Malta, Cyprus, Italy, Spain (Eurozone members) are low productivity countries characterized by a combination of relatively low levels of income and environmental quality. While, Greece, Slovakia, Czech Republic, Poland, Portugal, Malta, Hungary, Bulgaria, Cyprus, Spain, Romania (which are among the 27 member countries) are also characterized as low productivity countries. Comparing with Giannias and Liargovas (1998) results, our analysis showed that among the initial 15 members, Greece, France, Belgium, Portugal, Netherlands, Italy, Spain are classified as low productivity members while Giannias and Liargovas showed that Ireland, Portugal, Spain, Italy and Greece are the low productivity members. These differences are important given the goal of EU regional policy to reduce the levels of disparity between regions. They are also important given the stated aim of the EU that has been reinforced in various Treaties to integrate environmental considerations into economic decision making. However, the relative differences in environmental quality suggested by the analysis should not be taken as a call for a convergence of environmental conditions toward the average. It is apparent in many instances that environmental policies need to promote the transfer of best practice to secure a general increase in the level of environmental quality.

APPENDIX 1. DEVELOPING AN ENVIRONMENTAL QUALITY INDEX

The indicators used to develop the environmental quality index were as follows:

Y1,j	Internal Renewable Water Resources (IRWR): Per capita / Units: Cubic meters (m^3) per person per year (2007)
Y2,j	Protected Areas: IUCN categories I-VI and Other, percent of total land area / Unit: Percent (2006)
Y3,j	Mammal species, number threatened / Units: Number of species threatened (2007)
Y4,j	Bird species, number threatened / Units: Number of species threatened (2007)
Y5,j	Reptile species, number threatened / Units: Number of species threatened (2007)
Y6,j	Amphibian species, number threatened / Units: Number of species threatened (2007)
Y7,j	Forest area (original) as a percent of total land area / Units: Percent (1996)
Y8,j	Waste paper recycled as % of paper consumption / Units: Percent (2006)
Y9,j	Fertilizer use intensity / Units: Kilograms per hectare (kg/Ha) (2007)
Y10,j	Pesticide use intensity / Units: Kilograms per Hectare (2001)
Y11,j	CO2 emissions per capita / Units: Metric tons of carbon dioxide per person (2005)
Y12,j	Urban population as a percent of total population / Units: percent (2005)
Y13,j	Population density / Units: People per square kilometer (2005)
Y14,j	Life expectancy at birth / Units: Years (2005-2010)
Y15,j	Average length of schooling (primary to tertiary) / Units: Years (2006)
Y16,j	Maternal mortality ratio / Units: Maternal deaths per 100,000 live births (2005)
Y17,j	Television sets per 1000 people / Units: Per 1000 people (2000)
Y18,j	Main telephone lines per 1000 people / Units: Per 1000 people (2007)
Y19,j	Passenger cars per 1000 people / Units: Per 1000 people (1998)
Y20,j	Deaths due to road accidents / Units: Number of deaths (2004)

An index of environmental quality could be taken to be equal to the mean of each of a range of environmental variables. However, a mean cannot be computed directly because of differences in the units of measurement of the range of variables. Therefore, these variables need to be scaled before a mean is computed. Consequently, the above variables are scaled from 0 to 100 for each country using the following transformations:

$$y_{ij}^{*} = 100\ (Y_{ij} - Y_{ijmin})/(Y_{ijmax} - Y_{ijmin}) \quad (1)$$

where, y_{ij}^{*} is the transformed variable, Y_{ijmin} is the minimum value of Y_{ij}, and Y_{ijmax} is the maximum value for all variables having a positive relationship with environmental quality (that is for i = 2, 3, 4, 10, 11, 12, 16, 22, 23, 25, 28, 29, 30, 31and for all j), and

$$y_{ij}^{*} = 100 - [100\ (Y_{ij} - Y_{ijmin})/(Y_{ijmax} - Y_{ijmin})] \quad (2)$$

where, y_{ij}^{*} is the transformed variable, Y_{ijmin} is the minimum value of Y_{ij} in the sample of countries and Y_{ijmax} is the maximum value for all variables having a negative relationship with environmental quality (that is for i = 1, 5, 6, 7, 8, 9, 13, 14, 15, 17, 18, 19, 20, 21, 24, 26, 27, 32, 33 and for all j).

Finally, to compute the environmental quality for each country we have (i) used data from the World Resources 1992-1993 and the Human Development Index 1993, and (ii) taken the mean of the scaled variables y_{ij}^{*}.

The per capita income, I, of each country is also scaled from 0 to 100 using the following transformation:

$$I_j^{*} = 100\ (I_j - I_{min})/(I_{max} - I_{min})$$

where, I^{*}_{j} is the transformed index, I_{min} is the minimum index value in the sample of countries and I_{max} is the maximum value, and j = 1, 2, 3, ..., m.

REFERENCES

Bellante, D. (March 1979) The North-South Differential and the Migration of Heterogeneous Labor, *American Economic Review*, vol. 69, no 1.

CEC (Commission of the European Communities) (1992) *A Community Programme of Policy and Action in Relation to the Environment and Sustainable Development* (the Fifth Action Programme), COM(92) 23 final, Brussels.

CEC (Commission of the European Communities) (1993) Growth, *Competitiveness and Employment: The Challenges and Ways Forward into the 21st Century*, White Paper, Office of Official Publications for the EC, Luxembourg.

CEC (Commission of the European Communities). (1994) *Economic Growth and the Environment: Some Implications for Economic Policy Making*, COM (94) 465 final, Brussels.

Conlisk, J. (1969) *A Neoclassical Growth Model with Endogenously Positioned Technical Change Frontier*, Economic Journal, 348-62.

Eberts, R and Stone, J, (1986) *Metropolitan Wage Differentials: can Cleveland Still Compete*?, Federal Reserve Bank of Cleveland, Quarter 2.

Giannias D. and Liargovas P., (1998) Focusing Regional and Environmental policies in the EU through the Development of Environmental Quality Indices", 1998, European Environment, Vol. 8, Number 3, pp. 86-93

Johnson, G. (1983) *Intermetropolitan Wage Differentials in the United States*, in Jack E. Triplett, ed., *The Measurement of Labor Cost*, Chicago: University of Chicago Press.

Krugman P. and Venables A. (1990) *Integration and the Competitiveness of Peripheral Industry*, in Bliss, C. and Braga de Macedo, J. (eds), *Unity with Diversity in the European Economy: The community's Southern Frontier, pp.56-75*, Cambridge University Press, Cambridge.

Krugman, P. (1991) Increasing Returns and Economic Geography, *Journal of Political Economy*, 99, 3.

Romer, P.M. (1986) Increasing Returns and Long-Run Growth, *Journal of Political Economy*, 98, S71-S102.

Solow, R. M. (1956) A contribution to the Theory of Growth, *Quarterly Journal of Economics*, 70, 65-94.

United Nations Development Programme (1993) Human Development Report, United Nations, New York.

Uzawa, H. (1965) Optimum Technical Change in an Aggregative Model of Economic Growth, *International Economic Review*, 6, 18-31.

Van der Ploeg and Tang (1992) The Macroeconomics of Growth: An International Perspective, *Oxford Review of Economic Policy*, 8, 4, 15-28.

World Bank (1992) *Development and the Environment*, World Bank, Washington DC.

World Commission on Environment and Development (WCED) (1987) *Our Common Future*, Oxford University Press, Oxford.

World Resources 1992-93, (1992) *A Guide to the Global Environment, Towards Sustainable Development*, Oxford University Press.

In: Social Indicators: Statistics, Trends...
Editor: Candace M. Baird

ISBN 978-1-61122-841-0

Chapter 9

IS GENERALIZED TRUST USEFUL AS THE INDICATOR OF SOCIAL CAPITAL FOR SMALL AREA ANALYSIS IN JAPAN?

Yoshikazu Fujisawa[1] [1]**, *Tsuyoshi Hamano***[2] ***and Akio Koyabu***[3]

[1]Division of Public Policy, School of Administration and Informatics, University of Shizuoka, Yata, Suruga-Ku, Shizuoka City, Japan
[2]Organization for the Promotion of Project Research, Shimane University
[3]Faculty of Letters, Arts and Sciences, Waseda University

ABSTRACT

Several studies have used generalized trust as an indicator of social capital. However, its validity in Japan due to cultural differences is questioned. Here, we emphasize the need for more sophisticated discussions underlying trust measurement for social capital, specifically generalized and particularized trust. The aim of this study is to investigate which questions are appropriate as a indicator of social capital of small area analysis in Japan.

We conducted a nationally representative survey based on the geodemographic segmentation system, which classifies households by allocating them to one of 212 segments. Each neighborhood was randomly selected from within each segment. A postal questionnaire was sent out in 2008 to household heads and their spouses in these neighborhoods. A total of 8,221 individuals responded to the survey. Generalized and particularized trust was measured by a single item. These questions were rated on a 10-point scale. We finally conducted a multilevel analysis on 6,863 individuals nested within 202 neighborhoods.

The null model with no predictors revealed a significant variation in the generalized trust between neighborhoods. However, this variation was insignificant after adjusting for potential confounders. The second multilevel analysis showed variance in the neighborhood trust between neighborhoods. The null model revealed a significant variation in this trust. This variation remained after adjusting for potential confounders.

---

[1] Corresponding Author: Yoshikazu Fujisawa, Division of Public Policy, School of Administration and Informatics, University of Shizuoka, 52-1, Yata, Suruga-Ku, Shizuoka City 422-8526. E-mail: fujisawa@u-shizuoka-ken.ac.jp.

Neighborhood trust could be seen as a truly contextual factor; generalized trust might be confounded by compositional factors. This indicates that neighborhood differences in generalized trust may arise from differences in personal characteristics. We need more nuanced attentions toward measuring social capital in different cultural contexts.

Several studies have used generalized trust as an indicator of social capital. This idea was derived from a concept of the most influential social capital theorist, Robert D. Putnam. According to him, "generalized trust" was a crucial component of civic life, which was an important aspect of social capital (Putnam 2000). Originally, he developed the concept of social capital based on his research in Italy for approximately 20 years and adapted his understanding of social capital to analyze the American society. According to his definition, social capital is a characteristic of social networks, though he defined social capital in several ways such as ''features of social organization, such as trust, norms, and networks, that can improve the efficiency of society by facilitating coordinated actions'' (Putnam, 1993, p.167) and ''connections among individuals - social networks and the norms of reciprocity and trustworthiness that arise from them'' (Putnam, 2000, p. 19). Further, Putnam has pointed out that trust in other people, which could be generalized trust as well as an important feature of social capital, has fallen dramatically in the United States over the past four decades (Putnam, 2000).

Generalized trust is understood as expectations that most people are reliable, honest, good and kind, and acting fairly (Rosenberg, 1956; Yamagishi and Yamagishi, 1994). Moreover, Fukuyama said that the "radius of trust" is potentially extended to include those individuals about whom we may know very little (Fukuyama, 1995). The most widely employed measure of trust in the social sciences is the survey question, "Generally speaking, do you believe that most people can be trusted or can't you be too careful in dealing with people?" which has been used cross-nationally in the World Values Survey and other national and cross-national surveys including the General Social Survey and the Asian Barometer, among others. Also, many academicians highlighted the variation of generalized trust in each country and its importance in many societal and economic spheres using these survey data (Inglehart, 1999; Knack and Keefer, 1997; Rothstein and Uslaner, 2005; Alesina and La Ferrara, 2002).

However, some opinions question the validity of generalized trust in Japan due to its difference in the context of generalized trust. For example, Yamagishi and his colleagues pointed out that Japanese were generally less trusting than Americans and low trusters are more likely to stick to the same partner despite losing out on the potential advantages of interacting with a new partner (Yamagishi et al., 1998). In other words, Japanese relatively prefer long-term relations between particular partners or within particular groups, which means that particularized trust might work in Japanese society rather than generalized trust, which could be popular in western society. It could be said that the Japanese have developed collectivistic cultural norms of preserving the status quo of the group or social structure. This situation in which the Japanese people have been placed could be very different from that of western society, which has been based on civil societies and closely connected with the concept of social capital.

If this assumption had some implications for considering the concept of social capital in terms of the cross cultural context and "generalized trust" as the important indicator of social capital, it should be useful to examine whether generalized trust could be validated as an indicator of social capital of small area analysis in Japan. We attempt to examine this issue using our original data in the following sections.

METHODS

Data

We conducted a nationally representative survey based on the geodemographic segmentation system, which covers almost all households across Japan. The geodemographic segmentation system classifies Japanese households by allocating them to one of 212 segments at the small-area unit level (a *cho-cho* or *aza* unit level). In the present study, we define a cho-cho or aza unit, which has approximately 250 households in each unit, as a neighborhood; 212 neighborhoods were randomly selected from within each segment (1 neighborhood was selected from within each 212 segment). A postal questionnaire was sent out in 2008 to all the heads of households and their spouses living in the 212 neighborhoods. A total of 3937 males (47.9%) and 4148 females (50.5%) responded to the survey, while 136 (1.7%) responses were incomplete.

Measures

Generalized trust was measured by a single item. The respondents were required to respond to the following items based on previous studies (Cabinet Office of the Government of Japan, 2003): "Would you say that people can be trusted or that you need to be very careful in dealing with them?" In addition, particularized trust (neighborhood trust) was also measured by a single item, "Would you say that people in your neighborhood can be trusted or that you need to be very careful in dealing with them?" These questions were rated on a 10-point scale (1 being excellent, 9 being very poor, do not know), and the "do not know" responses were excluded from our study.

In addition, our survey data had individual characteristics, which could be useful in accounting for the neighborhood differences in trust. Specifically, these variables included age, sex, educational attainment, annual household income, residence year, number of household members, and housing condition.

Analyses

Multilevel linear regressions are used to provide an understanding of the measurement issues of social capital (Subramanian et al., 2003). After excluding the missing responses on all the variables, we conducted a multilevel analysis on 6,863 individuals nested within 202 neighborhoods (random intercept models). The following are detailed descriptions of the multilevel models: The first model is a two-level null (empty) model of individuals nested within neighborhoods (level 2) with only the constant term in the fixed and random parts. Variation in the variable, "trust," was partitioned across individuals (within neighborhoods) and between neighborhoods. After that, we included all individual characteristics (age, sex, income, educational attainment, residence year, number of household members, and housing condition) in the fixed part.

Statistical analyses were performed using the MLwiN software package (version 2.10).

RESULTS

Table 1 provides a summary of the data for the multilevel analysis. Close to half of the sample was female (50.3%), 23.1% were 70 years of age or older, and the single-person households were 15.6%. With regard to socioeconomic characteristics, 81.8% were more than high school graduates, and 10.6% had household incomes of over 10 million yen. Moreover, about 50% had 21 years of residence, and 62.4% owned their single-family house.

Table 1. Descriptive statistics for multilevel models

	N	Mean/%	SD	Range
Generalized Trust	6,863	4.49	±2.08	1.00-9.00
Particularized Trust	6,863	3.97	±2.03	1.00-9.00
Sex				
Male	3,414	49.7		
Female	3,449	50.3		
Age				
-20	15	0.2		
20-29	376	5.5		
30-39	802	11.7		
40-49	888	12.9		
50-59	1,287	18.8		
60-69	1,910	27.8		
70-79	1,258	18.3		
80-89	307	4.5		
90-	20	0.3		
Household income				
No income	176	2.6		
Under 1 million yen	303	4.4		
From 1 to 2 million yen	545	7.9		
From 2 to 3 million yen	1,014	14.8		
From 3 to 4 million yen	1,043	15.2		
From 4 to 5 million yen	800	11.7		
From 5 to 6 million yen	634	9.2		
From 6 to 7 million yen	426	6.2		
From 7 to 8 million yen	476	6.9		
From 8 to 9 million yen	279	4.1		
From 9 to 10 million yen	272	4.0		
From 10 to 11 million yen	170	2.5		
From 11 to 12 million yen	114	1.7		
Over 12 million yen	440	6.4		
I cannot answer	171	2.5		
Educatioalattainment				
Secondary school	845	12.3		

	N	Mean/%	SD	Range
High school	2,773	40.4		
Two-years college	952	13.9		
University	1,693	24.7		
Graduate school	196	2.9		
Other	404	5.9		
Residence year				
-1	252	3.7		
1-2	394	5.7		
3-5	716	10.4		
6-10	755	11.0		
11-15	657	9.6		
16-20	640	9.3		
21-	3,449	50.3		
Number of household members				
1	1,072	15.6		
2	2,608	38.0		
3	1,431	20.9		
4	922	13.4		
5	434	6.3		
6	273	4.0		
7	92	1.3		
8	25	0.4		
9	3	0.04		
10-	3	0.04		
Housing condition				
Home owenership (single-family house)	4,285	62.4		
Home owenership (cluster housing)	766	11.2		
Hired house	974	14.2		
Company housing	132	1.9		
Public housing	541	7.9		
Boarding	106	1.5		
Dormitory	8	0.1		
Others	51	0.7		

As the first step, we focused on generalized trust. Model 1 showed that the null model with no predictors revealed a significant variation in the generalized trust between neighborhoods (σ^2_{u0} = 0.055, p = 0.001). However, this variation was insignificant after adjusting for individual characteristics (σ^2_{u0} = 0.021, p = 0.082) such as age, sex, educational attainment, annual household income, residence year, number of household members, and housing condition (Model 2).

Model 3 showed the variance in the particularized trust (neighborhood trust) between neighborhoods. The null model with no predictors revealed a significant variation in particularized trust (neighborhood trust) between neighborhoods (σ^2_{u0} = 0.176, $p < 0.001$). Furthermore, Model 4 showed that this variation remained even after adjusting for individual characteristics such as age, sex, educational attainment, annual household income, residence year, number of household members, and housing condition (σ^2_{u0} = 0.056, p = 0.001).

Table 2. Multilevel model used in generalized trust[a]

	Model 1	Model 2	
Constant	4.481	5.291	
Sex		0.061	(0.051)
Age			
20-29		-0.137	(0.532)
30-39		-0.004	(0.530)
40-49		-0.192	(0.530)
50-59		-0.388	(0.530)
60-69		-0.685	(0.530)
70-79		-0.658	(0.531)
80-89		-0.936	(0.541)
90-		-0.973	(0.693)
Household income			
Under 1 million yen		-0.323	(0.190)
From 1 to 2 million yen		0.023	(0.175)
From 2 to 3 million yen		-0.213	(0.165)
From 3 to 4 million yen		-0.300	(0.165)
From 4 to 5 million yen		-0.224	(0.169)
From 5 to 6 million yen		-0.353	(0.174)
From 6 to 7 million yen		-0.485	(0.183)
From 7 to 8 million yen		-0.533	(0.182)
From 8 to 9 million yen		-0.335	(0.198)
From 9 to 10 million yen		0.329	(0.200)
From 10 to 11 million yen		-0.387	(0.221)
From 11 to 12 million yen		-0.413	(0.246)
Over 12 million yen		-0.362	(0.185)
I cannot answer		0.067	(0.218)
Educatioalattainment			
High school		-0.076	(0.081)
Two-years college		-0.413	(0.101)
University		-0.308	(0.093)
Graduate school		-0.376	(0.169)
Other		-0.029	(0.124)
Residence year			
1-2		0.187	(0.163)
3-5		0.307	(0.150)
6-10		0.261	(0.155)
11-15		0.070	(0.162)
16-20		0.131	(0.166)
21-		0.003	(0.153)
Number of household members			
2		-0.089	(0.080)
3		0.011	(0.089)
4		-0.181	(0.102)
5		-0.096	(0.126)
6		-0.091	(0.147)
7		-0.038	(0.227)
8		-0.186	(0.410)
9		-1.331	(1.165)
10-		-3.866	(1.180)
Housing condition			

	Model 1	Model 2	
Home owenership (cluster housing)		0.049	(0.086)
Hired house		0.130	(0.091)
Company housing		-0.383	(0.190)
Public housing		0.471	(0.105)
Boarding		0.013	(0.218)
Dormitory		-1.143	(0.716)
Others		0.872	(0.290)
Random parameters			
Between neighbourhoods[b]	0.055 (0.001)	0.021 (0.082)	

[a] SE in parentheses. [b] A p-value in parentheses.

Table 3. Multilevel model used in particularized trust (neighborhood)[a]

	Model 3	Model42	
Constant	3.959	5.415	
Sex		-0.004	(0.050)
Age			
20-29		-0.648	(0.515)
30-39		-0.669	(0.513)
40-49		-0.815	(0.514)
50-59		-1.012	(0.514)
60-69		-1.246	(0.513)
70-79		-1.352	(0.515)
80-89		-1.607	(0.524)
90-		-2.045	(0.671)
Household income			
Under 1 million yen		-0.009	(0.184)
From 1 to 2 million yen		0.114	(0.169)
From 2 to 3 million yen		-0.094	(0.160)
From 3 to 4 million yen		-0.226	(0.160)
From 4 to 5 million yen		-0.123	(0.164)
From 5 to 6 million yen		-0.268	(0.169)
From 6 to 7 million yen		-0.259	(0.178)
From 7 to 8 million yen		-0.338	(0.176)
From 8 to 9 million yen		-0.266	(0.192)
From 9 to 10 million yen		-0.257	(0.194)
From 10 to 11 million yen		-0.327	(0.214)
From 11 to 12 million yen		-0.517	(0.239)
Over 12 million yen		-0.308	(0.180)
I cannot answer		0.016	(0.211)
Educatioalattainment			
High school		-0.005	(0.079)
Two-years college		-0.238	(0.098)
University		-0.231	(0.091)
Graduate school		-0.392	(0.165)
Other		0.047	(0.120)
Residence year			
1-2		0.108	(0.158)
3-5		0.159	(0.146)
6-10		0.009	(0.150)
11-15		0.001	(0.157)

Table 3. (Continued)

	Model 3	Model42	
16-20		-0.101	(0.161)
21-		-0.228	(0.148)
Number of household members			
2		-0.195	(0.078)
3		-0.104	(0.087)
4		-0.339	(0.099)
5		-0.332	(0.122)
6		-0.355	(0.143)
7		-0.124	(0.220)
8		-0.590	(0.398)
9		-0.634	(1.132)
10-		-3.337	(1.145)
Housing condition			
Home owenership (cluster housing)		0.254	(0.086)
Hired house		0.577	(0.089)
Company housing		-0.102	(0.185)
Public housing		0.772	(0.110)
Boarding		0.611	(0.212)
Dormitory		-0.195	(0.694)
Others		0.860	(0.281)
Random parameters			
Between neighbourhoods[b]	0.176 (< 0.001)	0.056 (0.001)	

[a] SE in parentheses. [b] A p-value in parentheses.

CONCLUSION

We were able to show the reaming variance of neighborhood trust after adjusting for individual characteristics, while that of generalized trust disappeared. To be precise, we found that neighborhood trust might be a truly contextual factor; on the other hand, generalized trust was confounded by compositional factors. These results implied that generalized trust could not have contextual characteristics in Japanese society. Therefore, it may be difficult to conceive of generalized trust as an adequate indicator of social capital in Japan, especially for small area analysis in Japan.

Our results highlight the need for more nuanced attention toward measurement issues of social capital within a geographic locality. In other words, making comparisons between regions, especially small areas such as a neighborhood in Japan, with generalized trust is not as adequate as in the US or European countries. As we pointed out, one reason is that Japanese society might not possess the mechanisms to make generalized trust function efficiently.

Japanese society has been said to be relatively homogeneous, and its characteristic of homogeneity still remains in Japanese society. The concept of social capital, which has mainly been developed by Putnam, is rooted in the concept of civil society and individualism, which might be ideal in western society. Therefore, it is not easy to adapt the social capital concept automatically to other cultural contexts such as Asian ones and specifically Japanese society. We should try to consider the concept of social capital again to explore its adaptability and possibility for future researches of social capital.

This paper was reviewed by the reviewer, Professor. Masaki Sakata, Faculty of Letters, Arts and Sciences, Waseda University. We appreciate his considerable coments for this article. And this article was part of a research outcome that was funded by the Grant-in-Aid for Young Scientists (A) (18683004) by JSPS-MEXT (Principle Investigator: Yoshikazu Fujisawa) and the Grant-in-Aid for Challenging Exploratory Research (22653056) by JSPE (Principle Investigator: Yoshikazu Fujisawa).

References

Alesina, A., and La Ferrara, E. (2002). Who Trusts Others? *Journal of Public Economics, 85* (2), 207–234.

Cabinet Office of the Government of Japan. (2003). Social Capital: Looking for A Good Circle of Rich Human Relationships and Civic Activities. Tokyo: Government Printing Office.

Fukuyama (1995): F. Fukuyama: Trust; the social virtues and the creation of prosperity, Free Press.

Inglehart, R. (1999). Trust, Well-being and Democracy. In M. E. Warren (Ed.), Democracy and Trust (pp. 88–120). UK: Cambridge University Press.

Knack, S., and Keefer, P. (1997) Does Social Capital Have and Economic Payoff? A cross-country investigation. *The Quarterly Journal of Economics, 112* (4), 1251–1288.

Putnam, R. D. (1993). Making democracy work: Civic tradition in modern Italy. Princeton: Princeton University Press.

Putnam, R. D. (2000). Bowling Alone: The Collapse and Revival of American Community. New York: Simon and Schuster.

Rosenberg, M. (1956). Misanthropy and Political Ideology. *American Journal of Sociology, 21*, 690–695.

Rothstein, B., and Uslaner, E. M. (2005). All for All: Equality, Corruption, and Social Trust. *World Politics, 58* (1), 41–72.

Subramanian, S. V., Lochner, K. A., and Kawachi, I. (2003). Neighborhood differences in social capital: a compositional artifact or a contextual construct? *Health and Place, 9* (1), 33–44.

Yamagishi, T., Cook, K. S., and Watabe, M. (1998). Uncertainty, Trust, and Commitment Formation in the United States and Japan. *American Journal of Sociology, 104* (1), 165–94.

Yamagishi, T., and Yamagishi, M. (1994). Trust and commitment in the United States and Japan. *Motivation and Emotion, 18*, 129–166.

INDEX

D

E

F

G

H

P

Q

R

S

T

U